FORGING THE SWORD:
DEFENSE PRODUCTION
DURING
THE COLD WAR

Dr. Philip Shiman

USACERL Special Report 97/77
July 1997

A Study Jointly Sponsored by:

United States Air Force
Air Combat Command

Department of Defense Legacy
Program, Cold War Project

FOREWORD

The Department of Defense (DoD) Legacy Resource Management Program was established in 1991 to "determine how to better integrate the conservation of irreplaceable biological, cultural, and geophysical resources with the dynamic requirements of military missions." One of Legacy's nine task areas is the Cold War Project, which seeks to "inventory, protect, and conserve [DoD's] physical and literary property and relics" associated with the Cold War.

In early 1993, Dr. Rebecca Hancock Cameron, the Cold War Project Manager, assisted by a team of DoD cultural resource managers, formulated a plan for identifying and documenting the military's Cold War era resources. They adopted a two-pronged approach. The first phase was to conduct a series of studies documenting some of the nation's most significant Cold War era sites. The second step had a much broader focus. Recognizing the need to provide cultural resource managers and historians with a national framework for future Cold War studies, the Cold War Project recommended conducting a series of theme and context studies that would examine the impact of prominent military weapon systems and missions on the American landscape.

The Cold War Project's first studies documented the nation's missile systems. Dr. Cameron directed a team from the U.S. Army Construction Engineering Research Laboratories (USACERL), headed by Virge Jenkins Temme, which produced *To Defend and Deter*, a report on the Army and Air Force facilities and systems; and contracted with R. Christopher Goodwin and Associates for the *Navy Cold War Guide Missile Context*. In the spring and fall of 1995, Ms. Temme met with Dr. Paul Green of the Air Force Air Combat Command (ACC) to discuss ACC involvement and scope of funding for follow-on Cold War studies. With ACC to provide the majority of the funding, Dr. Green, Dr. Cameron, and Ms. Temme authorized Dr. John Lonnquest, the lead historian on CERL's Cold War missile study, to determine which mission areas warranted further study.

Dr. Lonnquest recommended a three-part study containing separate volumes on the areas of defense research, development, test, and evaluation; defense production; and military training. Each of the studies was written by a different historian. In addition to serving as the series coordinator, Dr. Lonnquest also wrote the first volume, *Developing the Weapons of War: Military Research and Development, Test and Evaluation (RDT&E) During the Cold War*. The study explores the changes in RDT&E wrought by the rapid evolution of science and technology during the period. The second volume in the series, *Forging the Sword: Defense Production During the Cold War*, was written by Dr. Philip Shiman. Drawing on a wealth of diverse source material, Dr. Shiman has written an engaging and informative account of the challenges the military and industry faced to produce the myriad of weapons and products DoD needed during the Cold War. The last

Forging the Sword: Defense Production During the Cold War

volume in the Cold War series is an overview of military training and education written by David Winkler. A PhD candidate at the American University, Mr. Winkler has written extensively on the Cold War. In his current study, *Training to Fight: Training and Education During the Cold War,* Mr. Winkler addressed the challenges of military training and education in an era of rapid technological advances, geopolitical instability, and social change.

Julie L. Webster
USACERL Principal Investigator

PREFACE

This was a particularly difficult project because there were few precedents or models to go by, and little of a historical nature has ever been published on the subject of production during the Cold War. However, many people provided the advice and support that ultimately made this study possible. Dr. Paul Green of the U.S. Air Force Air Combat Command at Langley AFB, VA, co-sponsor with the Legacy Cold War Project, provided helpful comments on the manuscript draft. Dr. John Lonnquest patiently guided this study and played a key role in shaping the final product. David Winkler introduced me to the various history repositories in the Washington, DC, area. Virge Jenkins Temme, the first principal investigator of the project at the U.S. Army Construction Engineering Laboratories in Champaign, IL, gave support and encouragement. Her successor, Julie Webster, took on the onerous task of providing the encouragement, support, prodding, and cajoling necessary to shepherd this project to completion.

No history can be performed without the assistance of librarians and archivists, and this one is no exception. Those deserving special thanks include Yvonne Kinkaid and Rian Arthur of the Air Force History Office Library at Bolling AFB, Washington, DC; Catherine Turner and the staff at the National Defense University Library at Fort Leslie J. McNair, Washington, DC; Geraldine Harcarik and the staff of the Historical Resources Branch, U.S. Army Center of Military History, Washington, DC; the staff of the Naval Historical Center in Washington, DC; Louis Arnold-Friend and the staff at the Historical Reference Branch of the U.S. Army Military History Institute, Carlisle Barracks, PA; Richard Sommers and the staff of the Special Collections Branch, U.S. Army Military History Institute, Carlisle Barracks, PA; the staff at the National Archives, College Park, MD; and Dotti Sappington and the staff at the U.S. Naval Institute, Annapolis, MD.

I also received invaluable assistance from public historians and civil servants throughout the country, who gave freely of their time. Dr. Rebecca Cameron of the Air Force History Office, the Director of the Legacy Cold War Project, helped focus my research. Appreciation is due to Lynn Engelman, Cultural Resource Manager for Headquarters Air Force Materiel Command (HQ AFMC), Wright-Patterson AFB, OH. Ms. Engelman provided Air Force points of contact and a critical review of the study. John D. Weber and Bill Suit of the HQ AFMC History Office also offered helpful information on the Air Force plants. Dr. Richard Hayes of the Naval Facilities Engineering Command, Alexandria, VA, spent hours showing me the files at the Legacy/Harp Program Office, Code 150. Dr. Robert Darius and Mike Bellafaire of the Army Materiel Command, Alexandria, VA, also provided time and assistance. E. Lowell Martin of the Naval Facilities Engineering Command and Chris Haskette of the Naval Command, Control, and Ocean Surveillance Center, both in San Diego, provided documentation and information concerning Air Force Plant 19 in San Diego; Sanda Trousdale and Michael E. Baker of

Forging the Sword: Defense Production During the Cold War

the U.S. Army Missile Command provided information regarding that organization's facilities; and Steve Diamond of the Sacramento Air Logistics Center, McClellan AFB, CA, provided suggestions and information regarding the Air Force's Air Logistics Centers. Richard Altieri of the Industrial College of the Armed Forces, National Defense University, also gave suggestions as to sources and points of contact. Gary Weir of the Naval Historical Center supplied me with a copy of his book. Joseph Murphey of the U.S. Army Corps of Engineers, Fort Worth District, Fort Worth, TX, provided information as well as copies of the historical studies he has been directing on the Army's ammunition plants during World War II. Frank Tokarsky, Fred Beck, and Bill Suit all read the manuscript and provided helpful comments. Linda Wheatley of USACERL carefully and patiently edited the manuscript and caught many errors that I had missed.

Special thanks go to Timothy Tuttle of Scranton Army Ammunition Plant; Mike Mills of Holston Army Ammunition Plant; Elaine Robinson of the Mississippi Army Ammunition Plant; Wayne Gouget of Mason Technologies, Inc.; and Deborah Franz-Anderson of Puget Sound Naval Shipyard, all of whom provided documents and photographs. Ann M. Bos of the History Office, U.S. Army Tank-automotive and Armaments Command (TACOM), Warren, MI, receives my sincerest gratitude for her generous donation of time, photographs, histories, and documents relating to the Detroit Army Tank Plant, and Art Volpe of the Public Affairs Office at TACOM spent hours providing information by telephone.

Above all, my love and gratitude goes to my wife, Vicki Arnold, who accompanied me on the research outings; patiently performed searches, took notes, and attended meetings; uncomplainingly endured the trauma of the writing of the study; and read the manuscript with a critical eye. Whenever I say "I" in this preface, I mean "we." She deserves far more credit for the result than I can ever give her here.

Philip Shiman
Springfield, VA
April 1997

CONTENTS

Foreword	iii
Preface	v

Chapter 1: Introduction — 1

Chapter 2: The Legacy of Total War — 3
- The Arsenal System — 3
- Mobilization for Total War — 5
- The Expansion of the Aircraft Industry — 8
- The Production Record — 10

Chapter 3: The Production Base in 1945 — 15
- The Industrial Base — 15
- Aircraft Plants — 15
- Ammunition Plants — 16
- Gun Plants — 25
- Tank Plants — 30
- Shipyards — 31

Chapter 4: From World War to Cold War, 1945–1953 — 39
- Demobilization — 39
- Preparedness Planning — 43
- The Korean Emergency — 45

Chapter 5: The Missile Era, 1953–1961 — 53
- The New Look — 53
- Air Force Production and Facilities — 54

Navy Production and Facilities	61
Army Production and Facilities	64

Chapter 6: The Vietnam Era, 1961–1973 — 69
McNamara	69
Vietnam	73

Chapter 7: The End of the Cold War, 1973–1987 — 77
Modernization	77
Decline of the Industrial Base	80
The Reagan Buildup	83
Conclusion	84

Bibliography — 87
Miscellaneous References	87
Records Repositories	87
Congressional Hearings and Reports	91
Miscellaneous Reports and Documents	93
Command Histories	99
Books	100
Articles	105

Appendix: Industrial Facilities Owned by the Department of Defense, 1996 — 109

Alabama	109
Redstone Arsenal	109
Arizona	110
Air Force Plant 44	110
Arkansas	111
Pine Bluff Arsenal	111
California	112
Air Force Plant 42	112
Air Force Plant 19	113
Air Force Plant 70	114

Barstow Marine Logistics Center	114
Long Beach Naval Shipyard	115
Mare Island Naval Activities	116
Riverbank Army Ammunition Plant	117
Sacramento Air Logistics Center	118
Colorado	**118**
Air Force Plant PJKS	118
Rocky Mountain Arsenal	119
Connecticut	**120**
New London Naval Submarine Base	120
Stratford Army Engine Plant	120
District of Columbia	**121**
Washington Navy Yard	121
Florida	**123**
Pensacola Naval Complex	123
Georgia	**124**
Air Force Plant 6	124
Warner-Robins Air Logistics Center	124
Hawaii	**125**
Pearl Harbor Naval Complex	125
Illinois	**126**
Rock Island Arsenal	126
Indiana	**128**
Crane Army Ammunition Activity	128
Indiana Army Ammunition Plant, Facility One	129
Iowa	**130**
Iowa Army Ammunition Plant	130
Kansas	**131**
Kansas Army Ammunition Plant	131
Sunflower Army Ammunition Plant	133
Kentucky	**133**
Louisville Naval Ordnance Depot	133
Louisiana	**134**
Louisiana Army Ammunition Plant	134
Maryland	**135**
Edgewood Arsenal	135
Naval Surface Warfare Center	136
Massachusetts	**137**
Boston Navy Yard	137

Michigan	138
Detroit Arsenal	138
Minnesota	139
Twin Cities Army Ammunition Plant	139
Mississippi	141
Mississippi Army Ammunition Plant	141
Missouri	142
Lake City Army Ammunition Plant	142
Nevada	143
Hawthorne Ammunition Depot	143
New Hampshire	144
Portsmouth Naval Shipyard	144
New Jersey	145
Picatinny Arsenal	145
New York	146
Air Force Plant 38	146
Air Force Plant 59	146
Watervliet Arsenal	147
Ohio	148
Air Force Plant 36	148
Air Force Plant 85	149
Lima Army Tank Plant	150
Ravenna Army Ammunition Plant	151
Oklahoma	152
Air Force Plant 3	152
McAlester Army Ammunition Plant	153
Oklahoma City Air Logistics Center	154
Pennsylvania	154
Philadelphia Naval Base and Shipyard	154
Scranton Army Ammunition Plant	155
South Carolina	156
Charleston Naval Shipyard	156
Tennessee	157
Holston Army Ammunition Plant	157
Milan Army Ammunition Plant	159
Volunteer Army Ammunition Plant	160
Texas	161
Air Force Plant 4	161
Lone Star Army Ammunition Plant	161
Longhorn Army Ammunition Plant	162

Utah	163
Air Force Plant 78	163
Ogden Air Logistics Center	164
Virginia	165
Norfolk Naval Shipyard	165
Radford Army Ammunition Plant	165
Yorktown Naval Weapons Station	167
Washington	167
Puget Sound Naval Shipyard	167
Wisconsin	168
Badger Army Ammunition Plant	168
Index	171

List of Figures

Chapter 3

Chance-Vought Plant at Stratford, CT	17
Propellant and Explosives Plants	18
Metal Parts Plants	18
Small Arms Ammunition Plants	19
Load, Assemble, and Pack Plants	19
Cannon Powder Blender, Picatinny Arsenal	21
Nitroglycerin Nitrating House, Sunflower AAP	22
Vertical Press House, Sunflower AAP	22
Plant B, Holston AAP	23
Watervliet Arsenal in 1945	26
Seacoast Gun Shop (Exterior), Watervliet Aresenal	27
Seacoast Gun Shop (Interior), Watervliet Aresenal	28
Seacoast Gun Shop, 16-inch Gun on Lathe, Watervliet Aresenal	28
Naval Gun Factory, Washington Navy Yard	29
Detroit Army Tank Plant	30
Puget Sound Naval Shipyard	32
Mare Island Naval Shipyard	33
Machine Shop, Puget Sound	34
Melting Pots, Puget Sound	34
Forge, Puget Sound	35
Shipfitters Shop, Puget Sound	35
Puget Sound Layout	36

Chapter 4

Extrusion Press, Indian Head, MD	42
Shell Bodies at Scranton AAP	46
Air Force Plant 43, Stratford, CT	48
Aircraft Sales Chart	49
Machining the Race Ring, Detroit Army Tank Plant	50

Chapter 5

Tomahawk Missiles	58
Atlas Missile Stainless Steel Sheets	59
Atlas Missile Stainless Steel Bands	59
Atlas Missile Tank	60

Tomahawk Cruise Missile Assembly   63
Tarheel Army Missile Plant   65

Chapter 6

Anchor Chain Link   71
Boston Naval Shipyard   72
Small Arms Ammunition Production   74

Chapter 7

Mississippi AAP, Picayune, MS   79
Load, Assemble, and Pack Plant, Mississippi AAP   80
Metal Parts Manufacturing, Mississippi AAP   81
Navy Shipbuilding, 1962-1977   83
Defense Spending   84
Major Weapons Procurement   85

Chapter 1

Introduction

This study is a contextual overview to assist anyone researching Cold War industrial facilities in the United States. It gives a broad overview of the structure of the government-owned portion of the defense industrial base and discusses the various trends that affected that structure from the 1940s to the 1980s. This report is not a general history of defense production, but focuses on production by government-owned facilities. For the purposes of this study, a defense production facility is defined as one that manufactures any article or product for military use and in which the Department of Defense has a significant investment in all or some of the land and/or equipment. This definition includes facilities with a main purpose other than production. For example, the Air Force's air logistics centers have, as their primary mission, the repair, maintenance, and overhaul of aircraft, but they also perform modification work, installing new equipment or changing the airframe of the craft. Many Navy depots load, assemble, and pack ammunition as well as store, maintain, and ship it. On the other hand, industrial facilities that perform only repair and maintenance work, such as the Army's depots, are not considered in this study. Other categories are excluded, as much for practicality as for any abstract definition of "production." For example, electronics manufacturing facilities are not discussed because so many installations perform electronics work that it would be nearly impossible to determine just what is and is not a "production facility." Furthermore, facilities that produce nuclear warheads (which is done under the supervision of the Department of Energy and, before that, the Atomic Energy Commission) are also excluded, even when performed in defense plants. However, facilities that work on missile bodies and nuclear ships are included.

A major theme of this study is the role of government in production and the various factors—technological, political, economic, and military—that influenced that role. The Federal government had always played a significant role in producing its own munitions, and it owned its own plants for that purpose from the very beginning. The Army's arsenals and the Navy's shipyards are excellent examples of this. During World War II, the government's role in promoting and even managing defense-related industries rose to unprecedented levels, with the government financing, building, and operating plants on an unheard-of scale. New administrative forms, such as the government-owned, contractor-operated (GOCO) plants, were created. The pressures of the Cold War and the growing complexity and expense of defense technology helped ensure that government involvement in industry would remain high. Traditional public antipathy towards government involvement in the marketplace—especially when the government was perceived to be in competition with private producers, as in the case of the shipbuilding industry—led to significant tensions and to repeated (and occasionally sincere) expressions of the government's intention to get out of the manufacturing business. The government's share of the military-industrial base, and the number of facilities it owns, has been gradually but steadily shrinking since the Korean War.

Another major theme of this study will be the nature of the production facilities themselves. One reason for the government's high level of direct involvement in industry is the need for specialized facilities that are suitable for only one purpose: military production. Such is the case, for example, with ammunition plants and gun factories. These facilities depend entirely on the military situation and the state of the defense procurement budget. They experience great booms in wartime, but in peacetime, as demand slackens, they rarely can be made profitable. Thus, while the great majority of government-financed defense plants were converted to civilian production after World War II, a core of plants remained that, for a variety of reasons, could not be sold. The government has to maintain its specialized plants in the event of an emergency, often operating them at a low level of production or shutting them down altogether. In the case of arsenals and shipyards, the government maintained expensive, all-purpose facilities and a skilled labor force which would be needed in war but which made the facilities uneconomical in peace. This practice seemed to many observers to be an expensive and wasteful way to meet the needs of a war that might never come. Thus, continuous pressure was placed on the military services to recycle their plants and to find some use for vacant and unused facilities.

Just as politics and economics made an impact on the industrial base and on individual facilities, new technology brought new military requirements and industrial needs. For example, the innovation of sophisticated weapon systems such as missiles and high-speed jet aircraft placed a premium on electronics and expensive new materials such as titanium, which required new manufacturing equipment and processes. The Navy's increasing reliance on accurate and lethal missiles and aircraft meant that it needed far fewer big-gun ships. For this reason, the Navy's requirements for guns and ammunition declined so much after the Korean War that its main source of guns, the Naval Gun Factory at the Washington Navy Yard, was closed in the early 1960s. Meanwhile, the huge missiles and jet aircraft of the 1950s and 1960s increased the demand for plants with large assembly buildings, test cells for rocket motors and jet engines, and clean environments for electronic components. Some plants adapted to the new technology, such as the Naval Ordnance Plant at Louisville, which made the transition from gun production to electronics and missiles; others did not and were closed, such as the Naval Gun Factory and some of the arsenals.

This overview is necessarily brief, selective, and general. It is intended primarily as a guide for those who wish to pursue further research on specific installations or the subject as a whole. Many other issues could be addressed and should be for any study of the industry to be considered complete. These topics include social issues, such as the make-up of the workforce (including the role of women and minorities and the impact of technology on that workforce) and the impact of defense industrial establishments on local politics and economies. One could explore, for example, the role of politics in deciding which facilities are closed and which are not. However, such questions are beyond the scope of this study.

Chapter 2

The Legacy of Total War

The Arsenal System

When studying defense production during the Cold War, one must necessarily begin with World War II, which was the model for a total war mobilization. Whereas the chaotic industrial effort for World War I was a lesson in what not to do, the effort of the second war was a demonstration of how industry, government, and society could successfully mobilize its resources in an all-out, life-or-death struggle. Throughout the Cold War, planning for another such struggle was based on that experience, both in terms of what to do and, because of changing circumstances, what not to do. The lessons of that war are with us still.

Also still with us are the facilities erected for the prosecution of World War II. The industrial effort for that war involved a massive building program to create the physical plant and equipment needed to manufacture the tanks, airplanes, ships, submarines, guns, and munitions required by the armed forces. Although much of this physical plant was absorbed back into civilian society and applied to commercial uses, much was not, either because it was not needed or because the military wanted it. Recycled and adapted to Cold War purposes, these facilities remained the core of the government-owned portion of the production base, and many have remained in service well beyond the fall of the Berlin Wall. The World War II production effort is an amazing story and, although it has been well told elsewhere, it is worthwhile to examine its most salient features.

For peacetime (and, to a lesser extent, wartime) military procurement, the armed forces before World War II traditionally relied on a number of permanent establishments scattered around the country in what was known as the "arsenal system." These government-owned, government-operated (GOGO) installations tended to be flexible, all-purpose facilities capable of supplying all of the varied needs of the Army and Navy. Within the Army, the production of ordnance—guns, ammunition, and tanks—was centered on the half-dozen so-called "old line" arsenals in the eastern part of the country. These arsenals were multipurpose manufacturing establishments, with the facilities and highly skilled workforce capable of producing almost any needed items. During peacetime, they satisfied the relatively small requirements of the Army, but supplying the Army was not their primary function. The arsenals served as research and development centers, designing new equipment for the Army. For example, Massachusetts' Springfield Arsenal, the Army's primary center for small arms production, developed the M-1 Garand rifle, an important infantry weapon of World War II. The arsenals also served as repositories of manufacturing knowledge. These industrial monasteries studied the production processes, preparing plans of all ordnance items and instructions on how to manufacture those items. During wartime, the arsenals served as the nucleus of the production effort, teaching private industry how to manufacture unfamiliar military goods. Thus their impact was entirely out of proportion to their own production capacity.[1]

Forging the Sword: Defense Production During the Cold War

Although multipurpose, the arsenals specialized in various types of ordnance supplies. Springfield Arsenal (or Armory), established in 1777 during the Revolutionary War, had long been the Army's main center for producing small arms. Most of the Army's primary infantry weapons, including the Springfield Rifle used in the Civil War and the '03 Springfield of World War I, were developed there. The Watervliet Arsenal in New York (est. 1813) was the Army's primary producer of finished artillery, including big guns. The Frankford Arsenal in Philadelphia (est. 1815) produced small arms ammunition, fuzes and other metal parts for artillery ammunition, and fire control mechanisms for the artillery. The Watertown Arsenal in Massachusetts (est. 1816) made gun castings, carriages, and recoil mechanisms for artillery. Rock Island Arsenal in Illinois (est. 1863) manufactured small arms, carriages, recoil mechanisms for field guns, and tanks, although not many. The Picatinny Arsenal in Dover, NJ (est. 1880), was the Army's main source of propellant for artillery and small arms ammunition.[2]

The Chemical Warfare Service (CWS) maintained an arsenal of its own at Edgewood, MD. Founded during World War I, Edgewood largely produced gas masks during the 1920s and 1930s. It also had production lines for chemical munitions. Although not particularly old, these lines had been abandoned in 1918 and were already so run down as to be nearly unusable.[3] The Army Air Corps did not operate its own manufacturing facilities; it relied on industry for all of its procurement. However, it did operate its own air depots, which were mostly intended for supply, maintenance, and repair. Like the arsenals of the Ordnance Department, the depots used a small but highly skilled workforce capable of performing any assigned mission on a variety of airplanes. Four such depots existed in 1939.[4]

The Navy's version of the arsenal system was a complex of eight shipyards, including Portsmouth, NH; Boston, MA; Philadelphia, PA; New York, NY; Norfolk, VA; Charleston, SC; Puget Sound, WA; and Pearl Harbor, HI. Like the arsenals of the Army, these shipyards were multipurpose establishments, with facilities for a wide range of production, repair, and maintenance tasks, including ship construction, modification, and overhaul. They also provided extensive non-industrial support for the fleet, such as supply, medical care, recreation, and training. Like the arsenals, they tended to be quite old, some of them dating back almost to the founding of the Republic. Portsmouth, Boston, and New York were designated as navy yards in 1800, although they had been founded even earlier—the shipyard at Portsmouth was established in 1692. Philadelphia and Norfolk dated to 1801. By 1940, these yards suffered from inadequate, obsolescent facilities.[5] Philadelphia, in addition to being a functioning shipyard, was also the site of the Naval Aircraft Factory. Built during World War I to avoid reliance on private manufacturers, the factory produced observation planes, trainers, and drones.[6] Portsmouth was the Navy's primary facility for the design, production, and testing of submarines; its first, the L-8, was built in 1917.[7]

For weapons and munitions other than ships and submarines, the Navy maintained a handful of factories and depots. The Navy's guns were produced by the plant at the Washington Navy Yard (later named the Naval Gun Factory), a large complex on the Anacostia River in Washington, DC. Rebuilt after the War of 1812, the factory produced the armament used by the fleet in the Civil War and the Spanish-American War. The factory was expanded after the turn of the century to manufacture large caliber barrels, and it was the Navy's only facility for producing the huge, 16-inch guns used by U.S. battleships.[8]

The Navy's supply of powder and explosives came largely from the Naval Powder Factory at Indian Head, MD. The facility was established in the late 1890s, at a time when the Navy wholly depended on commercial sources for these materials. By 1900, the factory produced its first powder and shortly before World War I became the Navy's sole supplier of powder in peacetime after some well-publicized price-fixing scandals by the commercial explosives manufacturers. During the war, the factory produced over 10 million pounds of new powder and reworked some 800,000 pounds of old powder. By the time the Armistice was signed in 1918, the Powder Factory was one of only three sources of propellant in the country, the others being the Picatinny Arsenal and the duPont plant at Carney's Point, NJ. The Indian Head facility produced enough powder and explosives to meet the Navy's postwar needs, but the Navy placed small orders with duPont to keep its plant operational.[9]

The explosives and powder were loaded into the ammunition at the Naval Ammunition Depots. All but one of the nine ammunition depots were on the Atlantic or Pacific coasts. The exception was the depot at Hawthorne, NV. Hawthorne was a relatively new facility built to replace the ill-fated depot at Lake Denmark, NJ, which had exploded during an electrical storm in 1926 while crammed full of surplus munitions left from World War I. Hawthorne was built according to principles derived from a careful study of the Lake Denmark disaster, with small, widely spaced buildings erected on a remote site far from populated areas.[10]

There had, of course, been a major buildup of defense industries during the Great War, but, after the Armistice in 1918, the country quickly dismantled this industrial base in its haste to return to what President Warren G. Harding described as "normalcy." Defense production was negligible in the succeeding years. For example, naval ship construction, severely limited by the Washington Naval Treaty of 1922, slowed dramatically. This downturn coincided with a severe depression in the commercial shipping industry that began after World War I. From 1921 to 1928, contracts for the construction of merchant ships dropped from 178 to 9, and 11 of the 25 private U.S. shipyards closed. During 1935, only nine ships were completed in the entire United States: three for the merchant fleet and six for the Navy.[11] The fledgling aircraft industry produced only $36 million worth of airplanes in 1933. Military procurement represented only a portion of the total—just 437 of 1,209 airplanes—produced in 1934.[12] The only tanks manufactured during the interwar years were a handful of experimental, hand-tooled models assembled by the Army at the Rock Island Arsenal.[13]

Mobilization for Total War

The reduction in the military-industrial base meant the United States found itself all but disarmed as the international situation in Europe and Asia grew increasingly unstable in the 1930s. The administration of President Franklin D. Roosevelt began a very modest program of rearmament, beginning with naval construction in 1934. This program accelerated in the face of Japan's brutal war in China and of Germany's aggressive expansion in Europe during the latter part of the decade, culminating in the outbreak of general war in Europe in September 1939. Although the country did not want to become involved in the European conflict, Roosevelt was concerned that the United States might be drawn in, and he declared a limited state of emergency on 8 September 1939, 7 days after the German invasion of Poland. Roosevelt's concern became outright alarm in the spring of 1940, when the Germans defeated the Anglo-French armies in a blitzkrieg attack, throwing the British off the continent of Europe and knocking France out of the war. In response, Roosevelt called for a stepped-up rearmament program. Impressed by the German use of air power, he emphasized aircraft production in particular, calling for an output of 50,000 airplanes per year, an astonishing figure at the time. Congress readily voted funds for procurement. In December 1940, the President declared that the United States should be the "arsenal of democracy" and encouraged Congress to pass the Lend-Lease Act to allow the government to supply armaments to the anti-German coalition. In June 1941, with a growing German submarine threat in the Atlantic, Roosevelt declared a full state of emergency.[14]

The results were dramatic. Contracts for war supplies were let by the thousands, sometimes with full production orders, sometimes with only small-scale "educational orders" to give a company experience in manufacturing a given item in anticipation of future requirements. The period from June 1940 to December 1941, known as the Emergency Period or Defense Period, also saw a crash building program to achieve the production goals set by the administration. The government expanded existing facilities, such as the arsenals and navy yards, and opened other facilities that had been inactive since World War I, such as the Naval Ordnance Plant at South Charleston, WV. Such facilities could not begin to meet the requirements, however. New facilities for ammunition, ship, and aircraft production were erected around the country, sometimes with extraordinary speed.

The story of the Detroit Tank Arsenal exemplifies this spirit. In 1940, the United States had no plants dedicated to the large-scale production of tanks. Four days after the British evacuation of Dunkirk, the government asked an automobile company, Chrysler, to make tanks and offered to pay for a "self contained, permanent tank arsenal." Chrysler—which knew nothing about tank manufacture—agreed to build the plant at cost and signed a contract on 15 August 1940. The noted industrial architectural firm Albert Kahn Associates designed the building, and construction began on the Warren, MI, plant in November 1940, even as Chrysler's engineers were still planning the layout of the production lines for the manufacture of a tank that had not yet come off the drawing board. Two months later, with only three walls of the plant erected and with a locomotive engine providing heat, workers began to install the machinery. The first tank was ready in April 1941, and the arsenal began rolling tanks off the assembly line in quantity in July—only 13 months after the government had first approached Chrysler.[15]

The government preferred that industry make the necessary investment for this expansion, and many firms did. Aircraft companies alone invested $83 million to expand their capacity between June and December 1940. They preferred to expand their own capacity than to see new plants built which might be used by a competitor after the war.[16] Yet after the long, lean years of the Great Depression, most companies did not have enough money to invest, or they were unwilling to jeopardize their growing earnings by purchasing floor space and equipment for which they might have no use after the war. The experience of the first war, and the severe recession that had followed it, were fresh in their memories. Foreign countries provided some funds; Britain invested $74 million for the expansion of aircraft plants and also built an ammunition plant in Tennessee. Yet it was clear from the beginning that the U.S. Government would have to play a far more active role in the mobilization than ever before.[17]

The government initially offered financing through Emergency Plant Facilities (EPF) contracts. With this vehicle, a company found financing either privately or through a Federal agency, the Reconstruction Finance Corporation. The government then reimbursed the company over 5 years for the cost of construction and would take title of the property after the emergency was over. By 1941, however, the EPF contract had largely been supplanted by direct financing through the Defense Plant Corporation (DPC). On behalf of the Army or Navy, the DPC built and retained the title to the plant, which was then operated by a company that paid a small rent. The government also purchased the machinery for the plant. By the time of the attack at Pearl Harbor, HI, the DPC had invested more than a billion dollars in new construction. All told, 935 DPC facilities or "plancors" were built under War Department sponsorship alone, almost all of which were initiated by mid-1942.[18]

With both the EPF and the DPC financing, the company had the option, upon the cessation of the emergency, of purchasing the facility by paying the construction cost minus depreciation. Indeed, the government hoped that all the facilities would be purchased in this manner and applied to civilian production when no longer needed for military purposes. However, many facilities were too specialized for such reconversion and would be hard to sell. Also, the military services often wanted to retain such plants permanently in the event of a future emergency. These facilities included the new Navy ordnance plants and the Army's huge complex of ammunition plants. The services themselves had built the facilities or supervised their construction. Congress gave the services the option of operating the plants as well, but they preferred not to become too deeply involved in industrial affairs and wanted to make use of the managerial skills available in industry.[19]

Thus was created a new, unprecedented arrangement, the government-owned, contractor-operated (GOCO) plant, in which private companies signed cost-plus-fixed-fee contracts to run the plants. This arrangement differed from the plancors in that the plant itself was designated a military installation. A small military staff remained on the premises to inspect the work and serve as a liaison with the contractor, although the actual management of the plant was left to the contractor. The Army in particular relied heavily on GOCOs. Between 1940 and 1945, the Ordnance Department alone maintained 77 such plants, manufacturing tanks, guns, and ammunition.[20] The Navy's new ordnance plants were also operated as GOCOs. All told, the Army invested $5 billion on plants and machinery during the war, while the Navy invested $3 billion.[21]

The feverish activity of the Emergency Period gave the United States a running start on gearing up for the war that finally came with the Japanese bombing of Pearl Harbor in December 1941. For the first time in its history, the nation was not entirely unprepared for war upon the outbreak of hostilities. Full mobilization of manpower and industrial resources began with the declaration of war. Requirements rose sharply, far beyond what military planners had anticipated. In its effort to meet those requirements, industry was hampered by shortages of machine tools, critical materials such as copper, aluminum, and rubber, and, late in the war, of manpower. These difficulties were all overcome as production of weapons, ships, and vehicles reached its peak in 1943 and 1944. Even before the end of the war in 1945, cutbacks were being made because of an oversupply in production areas such as airplanes and tanks.[22]

The Expansion of the Aircraft Industry

The aircraft industry provides an idea of the scale of the production effort during World War II. At the start of the war, the aircraft industry consisted primarily of 14 companies operating 16 plants. Three of these companies manufactured aircraft engines, while the other 11 assembled airframes. In 1940, these companies delivered 15.9 million horsepower and produced 20.3 million pounds of airframe.[23]

Expansion of the industry occurred in several ways. First, the aircraft companies operated their prewar home plants around the clock at full capacity. They also enlarged their plants by purchasing land and erecting new buildings, largely with government funds. At the Grumman plant in Bethpage, Long Island, NY, the Navy funded an addition to the original facility and then built four completely new plants on adjacent tracts of land during the war. These new facilities, which cost the government $18 million, included assembly buildings, hangars, and warehouses. At the Glenn L. Martin Company site at Baltimore, MD, the Army and Navy together spent $25 million to construct two complete plants on land owned by the company.[24]

Many companies subcontracted the component and subassembly work they could not handle themselves, and they also established their own small, local "feeder" plants for this task. For example, Grumman opened a score of such detached units throughout Long Island. These plants were established in any readily available buildings, including an old Pan Am base, a wheelbarrow factory, and an underground shooting gallery. A few were just garages, large enough to house four or five workers.[25]

During the Emergency Period of 1940 and 1941, many of the airframe companies built government-financed branch plants, which were self-contained manufacturing facilities. Indeed, in many cases, they were larger and more productive than the home plant. At least 16 major airframe plants were built, including large bomber factories in Nebraska, Kansas, Oklahoma, and Texas. The engine manufacturers also built several plants, mostly in the Ohio Valley. As a rule, the new airframe plants were located in the interior of the country. This dispersal was partly for security, to get the plants behind the protective barriers of the Appalachian and Rocky Mountains. It was also to tap into new sources of labor away from the heavily industrialized coasts, and to make it easier to find sites with plenty of land for airstrips.[26]

In the fall of 1940, the government began to bring in non-aircraft companies, especially automobile manufacturers, to produce airplanes under license. Logically enough, these companies, including Studebaker, Dodge, Ford, Chevrolet, and Packard, largely assembled aircraft engines, which were made with the same tools and techniques as automobile engines, albeit with more care and precision. The largest of these plants—indeed, the largest of any sponsored by the government—was a $173 million facility built by the Dodge Division of Chrysler Corporation in Chicago. This plant had a floor area of 6.43 million square feet, more than the combined floorspace of the entire aircraft engine industry at the start of 1941.[27]

However, a few automobile manufacturers and related companies, including General Motors, Ford, and the Goodyear Tire and Rubber Company, were licensed to produce airframe components and subassemblies. This licensing method was used with the crash program to build bombers, especially the B-24 Liberator. The government hoped that the companies could adapt their assembly-line techniques to mass produce aircraft—a particularly difficult challenge, as building an airframe was nothing like manufacturing a car. Hitherto, airframe plants had largely been job shops—flexible, all-purpose factories where components were individually handcrafted and handfitted. This practice suited not only the state of the technology but also the prewar market, which was too small to justify mass production. The introduction of the assembly line, with its steady, controlled flow of products through successive stages, was an ambitious enterprise. It was mostly applied to the production of components, but in one notable experiment at Willow Run, MI, Ford struggled to mass produce finished B-24s in a huge, $59-million plant. The effort proved extremely difficult but was ultimately successful.[28]

The old airframe manufacturers themselves adopted assembly-line techniques to some degree. Not only did this speed production, but it eased the problem of training new, unskilled workers who had only to learn a few repetitive tasks.[29] In addition, the industry adopted new methods to avoid using exotic and expensive tools such as heavy forging hammers, which were in short supply. As a result, the productivity of each plant greatly increased, even above what was initially planned, which contributed to a sizable excess of production capacity by 1944.[30]

The primary obstacle to mass production was the fact that aircraft designs changed continually as requirements changed and as the lessons of combat were absorbed. Such design instability presented no problems to a job shop but was anathema to an assembly line, where interruptions for redesign and retooling brought production to a standstill. The solution was to establish modification centers, plants whose only function was to put the finishing touches on the airplanes before sending them into battle. Twenty-eight such centers were in operation at some point during the war. They were largely operated by the airlines, which could use the maintenance facilities they already possessed for the work. The work these centers performed included the addition of armor, guns, and communications and target-finding equipment. Some airplanes, such as Doolittle's raiders,* were modified for special missions.[31]

The permanent air depots, which were already servicing aircraft for the Army Air Corps (now called the Army Air Forces), were also assigned the task of modification. The number of depots increased from 4 to 11. Like the airframe manufacturers, the depots reorganized their operations to run like automobile assembly lines, allowing the new workers to work at narrow, repetitive tasks as opposed to general or multiple duties requiring extensive training and experience. The depots also began to specialize in particular aircraft. Among bombers, for example, B-17s went to Fairfield (OH), Oklahoma City (OK), and Warner Robins (GA); B-24s went to Middletown (PA), Ogden (UT), and Spokane (WA); and B-25s went to San Antonio (TX) and San Bernardino (CA). Although maintenance and repair was still their primary mission, the depots devoted 30 to 45 percent of their resources to modification work. Fairfield installed torpedo racks on B-25s and photographic equipment on B-24s, for example; Middletown modified the B-24s for antisubmarine missions, while Mobile and Warner Robins added central fire control systems to the same airplane. Between 1943 and 1945, depot maintenance shops serviced 36,000 aircraft and more than 230,000 engines.[32]

The Production Record

Ultimately, thousands of firms contracted or subcontracted to produce war materiel for the Army and the Navy. In some cases, huge industries arose where none had existed before. As much as possible, of course, the government sought out firms with experience in a given product—having aircraft companies manufacture airplanes, for example, and sporting arms companies produce small arms and ammunition. Yet the government often was forced to turn to companies with little or no such experience. Sometimes, these companies had general machine tools and skilled workers for producing needed items; so, for example, locomotive companies produced guns and tanks. Perhaps the company possessed specialized equipment and production experience of particular value in a certain industry. For example, pharmaceutical manufacturers contracted to make powder for the Navy because their pelleting machines, which they had used in peacetime for making medicinal tablets, were easily adapted to making the pellets used in "flashless" powder.[33] Often the firms had nothing more than effective management and experience in quantity production and packaging. Thus, companies such as Coca Cola and Quaker Oats received contracts to load and assemble ammunition.[34]

Production during the war was marked by a high level of cooperation among the services. To avoid the confusion and wasteful duplication of World War I, the War and Navy Departments had established a high-level Army and Navy Munitions Board (ANMB) in

---

*In April 1942, Lieutenant Colonel (later Lieutenant General) James Doolittle led a raid of 16 carrier-launched B-25 bombers against the Japanese homeland. The attack, which struck Tokyo, Yokohama, and other cities, caused little physical damage, but it boosted American morale and shocked the seemingly invincible Japanese.

1922 to coordinate procurement and industrial planning. After 1927, the ANMB did not meet formally for 14 years—what was the point of coordinating production and procurement, when there was hardly any going on?—but its staff did prepare several Industrial Mobilization Plans, and the board itself was revitalized in 1941. The ANMB helped coordinate the distribution of vital raw materials and machine tools as well as allocate production for the armed services, until it was finally supplanted in 1942 by the War Production Board and by the services' own procurement organizations.[35] During the war, one or the other of the services was responsible for the entire production of certain commonly needed items such as guns, ammunition, and bombs, and each shared their output with little rivalry or difficulty.[36]

The wartime production record was remarkable. Between 1937 and 1944, aircraft production increased from a rate of 270 airplanes per month to 9,000 per month; the value of this output increased over a hundred times, from $157 million to $16 billion. Employment in the industry increased from 30,000 to 2.1 million, and the industrial floor space expanded from 10 million square feet (in 1939) to 175 million square feet. By 1944, the aircraft industry was the largest in the United States. In that year it produced 96,000 airplanes—16 times the output of 1940, and nearly double Roosevelt's 50,000 goal, which had so astonished the nation. If any single factor can account for the victory over the German Luftwaffe in the air war over Europe, it was the production represented by these statistics.[37]

The output of guns and ammunition was similarly staggering. From 1940 to 1945, 2.7 million machine guns and 12.7 million rifles were produced, including more than 4 million Garand rifles and 6 million carbines.[38] The Army's Ordnance Department also procured 519,031 pieces of artillery of all types, including more than 156,000 aircraft guns, 116,000 tank guns, 54,000 heavy and light field guns, and 105,000 mortars.[39] Small arms ammunition production totaled almost 42 *billion* rounds, mostly 0.30 and 0.50 caliber. The government also procured more than a billion rounds of artillery ammunition and 145 million bombs, mines, and grenades.[40] During those 5 years, industry produced 88,410 tanks, of which one quarter came from the Detroit Tank Arsenal.[41]

Endnotes

1. Levin H. Campbell, Jr., *The Industry-Ordnance Team* (New York: McGraw-Hill Book Co., 1946), 35–46.
2. Ibid., 37–42; Harry C. Thomson and Lida Mayo, *The Ordnance Department: Procurement and Supply,* in *The United States Army in World War II: The Technical Services* (Washington, DC: Office of the Chief of Military History, Dept. of the Army, 1960), 72–73, 160, 191; R. Christopher Goodwin and Associates, Inc., *Historic Context for the Army Materiel Command's World War II Facilities* (Frederick, MD: Goodwin and Associates, March 1996; prepared for the U.S. Army Corps of Engineers, Baltimore District, under contract DACW31-89-D-0059. Hereafter cited as Goodwin and Associates, *AMC's World War II Facilities*), 57–65.
3. Leo Brophy, Wyndham D. Miles, and Rexmond C. Cochrane, *The Chemical Warfare Service: From Laboratory to Field,* in *The United States Army in World War II: The Technical Services* (Washington, DC: Office of the Chief of Military History, Dept. of the Army, 1959), 229–230, 234.
4. Bernard J. Termena, Layne B. Peiffer, and H. P. Carlin, *Logistics: An Illustrated History of AFLC and Its Antecedents, 1921–1981* (Wright Patterson AFB, OH: Office of History, Headquarters, Air Force Logistics Command, n.d.), 49.

5. John W. Dolan, Jr., "The Naval Shipyard Complex," *Naval Engineers Journal,* 82 (December 1970): 26; U.S. Bureau of Yards and Docks, *Building the Navy's Bases in World War II: History of the Bureau of Yards and Docks and the Civil Engineer Corps, 1940–1946* (2 vols.; Washington, DC: GPO, 1947), 1:169.
6. William F. Trimble, *Wings for the Navy* (Annapolis, MD: Naval Institute Press, 1990).
7. *Portsmouth Naval Shipyard, Portsmouth, New Hampshire: Cradle of American Shipbuilding* (n.p., n.d. [1976?]).
8. *Ordnance Production* (Washington, DC: Public Information Office, Naval Gun Factory, March 1951; copy found in National Defense University Library, Fort Leslie J. McNair, Washington, DC), 1–2; Buford Rowland and William B. Boyd, *U.S. Navy Bureau of Ordnance in World War II* (Washington, DC: Bureau of Ordnance, Department of the Navy, 1953), 252.
9. Rowland and Boyd, *Bureau of Ordnance,* 190–191; Rodney Carlisle, *Powder and Propellants: Energetic Materials at Indian Head, Maryland, 1890–1990* (n.p., n.d. [Indian Head, MD: Naval Ordnance Station, 1990?], 54–61, 81–107.
10. Rowland and Boyd, *Bureau of Ordnance,* 210–11; Bureau of Yards and Docks, *Building the Navy's Bases,* 1:323–325.
11. U.S. Surplus Property Administration, *Shipyards and Facilities: Report of the Surplus Property Administration to the Congress, January 31, 1946* (Washington, DC: GPO, 1946), 8.
12. Surplus Property Administration, *Aircraft Plants and Facilities: Report to the Congress, January 14, 1946* (Washington, DC: GPO, 1946), 10, 12.
13. Kevin Thornton, *Tanks and Industry: The Detroit Arsenal, 1940–1954* (Warren, MI: History Office, U.S. Army Tank-automotive and Armaments Command, 1995), 13.
14. Kimberly L. Kane, *Historic Context for the World War II Ordnance Department's Government-Owned Contractor-Operated (GOCO) Industrial Facilities, 1939–1945,* U.S. Army Materiel Command Historic Context Series, Report of Investigations Number 1 (Plano, TX: Geo-Marine, Inc., under contract no. DACA63-93-D-0014 to the Fort Worth District of the U.S. Army Corps of Engineers; copy found in Historical Library, Headquarters U.S. Army Corps of Engineers, Alexandria, VA), 29–30, 44, 48–49.
15. Thornton, *Tanks and Industry,* 15–25; Thomson and Mayo, *Ordnance Procurement and Supply,* 228–230.
16. Wesley Frank Craven and James Lea Cate, eds., *The Army Air Forces in World War II,* vol. 6: *Men and Planes* (6 vols.; Chicago, IL: The University of Chicago Press, 1948–1958; repr. Washington, DC: GPO, 1983), 6:305; William Glenn Cunningham, *The Aircraft Industry: A Study in Industrial Location* (Los Angeles, CA: Lorrin L. Morrison, 1951), 76–77.
17. Campbell, *Industry-Ordnance Team,* 111–112; Craven and Cate, *Army Air Forces,* 306–308; Cunningham, *Aircraft Industry,* 77; Thomson and Mayo, *Ordnance Procurement and Supply,* 110.
18. R. Elberton Smith, *The Army and Economic Mobilization,* in *The United States Army in World War II: The War Department* (Washington, DC: Office of the Chief of Military History, Department of the Army, 1959), 476–496; Campbell, *Industry-Ordnance Team,* 113–115; Craven and Cate, *Army Air Forces,* 6:308.
19. Joseph J. Mathews, "The New Naval Ordnance Plants," *U.S. Naval Institute Proceedings,* 70 (October 1944): 1220.
20. Kane, *GOCO Industrial Facilities,* 7, 22–32; see also "List of Ordnance Establishments, 1940–1945," U.S. Army Center of Military History, Archives, Washington, DC (hereafter cited as CMH).
21. Harry B. Yoshpe and Charles F. Franke, *National Security Management: Production for Defense* (Washington, DC: Industrial College of the Armed Forces, 1968), 44; Mathews, "The New Naval Ordnance Plants," 1220.
22. Thomson and Mayo, *Ordnance Production and Supply,* 255–257.
23. Tom Lilley et al., *Problems of Accelerating Aircraft Production During World War II* (Boston: Division of Research, Graduate School of Business Administration, Harvard University, 1947), 34–35; Cunningham, *Aircraft Industry,* 47–51.
24. Cunningham, *The Aircraft Industry,* 78–83; Surplus Property Administration, *Aircraft Plants and Facilities,* 45, 46; Richard Thruelsen, *The Grumman Story* (New York: Praeger Publishers, 1976), 122–123, 132–133, 138–139; Bureau of Yards and Docks, *Building the Navy's Bases,* 1:394–398.
25. Cunningham, *Aircraft Industry,* 83–85; Thruelsen, *Grumman Story,* 139.
26. Cunningham, *Aircraft Industry,* 85–88.
27. Craven and Cate, *Army Air Forces,* 6:315, 320.
28. Ibid., 6:329–330, 332–333; Irving Brinton Holley, *Buying Aircraft: Materiel Procurement for the Army Air Forces,* in *The United States Army in World War II: Special Studies series* (Washington, DC: Office of the Chief of Military History, Department of the Army, 1964), 518–529.
29. Craven and Cate, *Army Air Forces,* 333.

30. Ibid., 6: 311–314, 317, 333; Lilley et al., *Accelerating Aircraft Production,* 71–72.
31. Holley, *Buying Aircraft,* 529–538; Craven and Cate, *Army Air Forces,* 6:334–337; Cunningham, *Aircraft Industry,* 94–95.
32. Craven and Cate, *Army Air Forces,* 336–337; Termena et al., *Logistics,* 47–74.
33. Thomson and Mayo, *Ordnance Procurement and Supply,* 241; Rowland and Boyd, *Bureau of Ordnance,* 193.
34. Thomson and Mayo, *Ordnance Procurement and Supply,* 112–113.
35. Robert H. Connery, *The Navy and the Industrial Mobilization in World War II* (Princeton, NJ: Princeton University Press, 1951), 35, 154–178.
36. Ibid., 315; Rowland and Boyd, *Bureau of Ordnance,* 496–504.
37. Surplus Property Administration, *Aircraft Plants,* 12–13; Craven and Cate, *Army Air Forces,* 6:331–332; see also ibid., 350–361.
38. Thomson and Mayo, *Ordnance Procurement and Supply,* 174, 181.
39. Ibid., 101.
40. Ibid., 153, 189.
41. Ibid., 242.

Chapter 3

The Production Base in 1945

The Industrial Base

The U.S. Army and Navy ended the war with an enormous industrial establishment. In May 1945, the Army's Ordnance Department alone possessed 73 government-owned, government-operated (GOGO) and government-owned, contractor-operated (GOCO) facilities, including:[1]

- 7 manufacturing arsenals
- 7 ammonia and ammonium nitrate works
- 8 smokeless powder works
- 12 high explosives works
- 21 loading plants
- 1 gun plant
- 5 tank and armor plants
- 8 miscellaneous plants

The Navy Bureau of Ordnance had more than 100 field establishments, including 20 ammunition depots, 11 Naval Ordnance Plants, and a big-gun factory.[2] Hundreds of other plants, the plancors, were owned by the Defense Plant Corporation (DPC).

These plants were of widely varying types and layouts characteristic of their respective industries. This section will describe some of the key types of specialized facilities, including aircraft plants, ammunition and gun plants, tank plants, and shipyards.

Aircraft Plants

The government financed part or all of 350 aircraft plants during the war, including 290 facility expansions and new construction. Of the latter, 190 plants were in production for the Army Air Forces and 100 for the Navy Bureau of Aeronautics. Of these plants, 84 had been used to produce airframes and their subassemblies and 18 manufactured engines. The government's inventory also included 40 plants for the manufacture of major parts (turrets, propellers, and instruments); 127 for miscellaneous parts, accessories, forgings, service, and training; and 21 modification centers.[3]

The home airframe plants tended to be a mix of prewar and new construction, while the Midwestern branch plants were all new. These plants had large assembly areas with wide bays and high (25–40 feet) ceilings. The newer buildings in particular were generally long and narrow to accommodate progressive assembly lines.[4] Normally, these plants had access either to a private airstrip owned by the government or the manufacturer or to a public airport. A typical facility was the Douglas plant at Long Beach, CA, owned by the Army. It consisted of two final-assembly buildings (approximately 280,000 square feet each), two subfinal-assembly buildings (410,000 and 488,000 square feet), two subassembly buildings (approximately 205,000 square feet), two receiving buildings, a hangar, an office, an engineering building, and 20 additional structures. The buildings used the "blackout design," having no windows or skylights. The plant was adjacent to Long Beach Municipal Airport and had a railroad siding.[5]

Another airframe plant was the old Sikorsky plant at Stratford, CT, owned and operated during the war by Chance-Vought to produce the F4U-1 Corsair for the Navy. The prewar plant consisted of an administration building; an all-purpose service building; and the main factory (Building 2), a steel and glass structure with a large assembly bay 80 feet high with three smaller assembly bays on each side. In addition to having access to Bridgeport Municipal Airport, the plant built its own causeway into the Housatonic River from which it could test seaplanes. To this plant, the Navy and DPC added over a million square feet of floor space, most of it in a large addition to Building 2 that doubled the capacity of the plant. Other additions included two large hangars, a test cell building for testing aircraft engines, and sundry support structures. The total government investment in the plant was about $9.3 million.[6]

The engine plants were of a more generic industrial character. Some were also quite large. The largest of these, and indeed of all aircraft plants, was the Dodge plant in Chicago, which had almost 6.5 million square feet of industrial floor space, including 4.3 million square feet under one roof. In addition to the main manufacturing building, it included aluminum and magnesium foundries, a heat treat and die shop, forges, an oil storage and chip building, test cells, tool shops and boiler houses, and an office building.[7] Manufacturing buildings in the engine plants tended to be more square and nondescript than those of the airframe plants because much of the work involved the fabrication of engine parts as well as their assembly on production lines.[8]

Ammunition Plants

During the war, one of the industries with the greatest governmental involvement was in the production of ammunition for small arms, artillery, and rockets. Not only did such work require very specialized equipment, but considerations of safety dictated the siting and layout of the plants in ways that virtually precluded private investment in them. To minimize the danger from attacks or accidental explosions, most of the facilities established during the war were built in rural areas, far from concentrations of labor. Like the aircraft plants, the ammunition plants were scattered around the interior, mostly between the Appalachians and the Rockies, for protection against bombing attacks. The plants also required a good deal of land, because the production lines were kept widely separated to prevent an explosion on one from spreading to others. The

Chance-Vought Aircraft Plant at Stratford, Connecticut, ca. 1943. The main assembly buildings are at center; note the World War II addition (with the light roofs). Source: HAER No. CT-14, Stratford Army Engine Plant, p. 35, Prints and Photographs Division, Library of Congress.

Illinois Ordnance Plant covered an area of 24,000 acres, one and a half times the size of Manhattan Island. With the exception of certain chemical plants, which could manufacture fertilizer, there was no commercial market for their products, and the plants could not be easily reconverted to civilian production. However, because they were so specialized, the government wanted to preserve its interest in them after the war in the event of a future emergency.[9]

Ammunition production depended on a complex web of interdependent and relatively specialized plants that produced or assembled the components. Chemical plants produced "smokeless powder," the propellant for bullets, shells, and rockets; explosive fillings such as TNT and RDX Composition; or component chemicals, especially nitrates. Other plants manufactured the metal parts, including shell bodies, cartridge cases, and fuzes. Still others, called Load, Assemble, and Pack (LAP) plants, loaded the shells, assembled the complete rounds, and packed the ammunition for shipment. Assembly of small arms ammunition took place where the metal parts were manufactured.

Forging the Sword: Defense Production During the Cold War

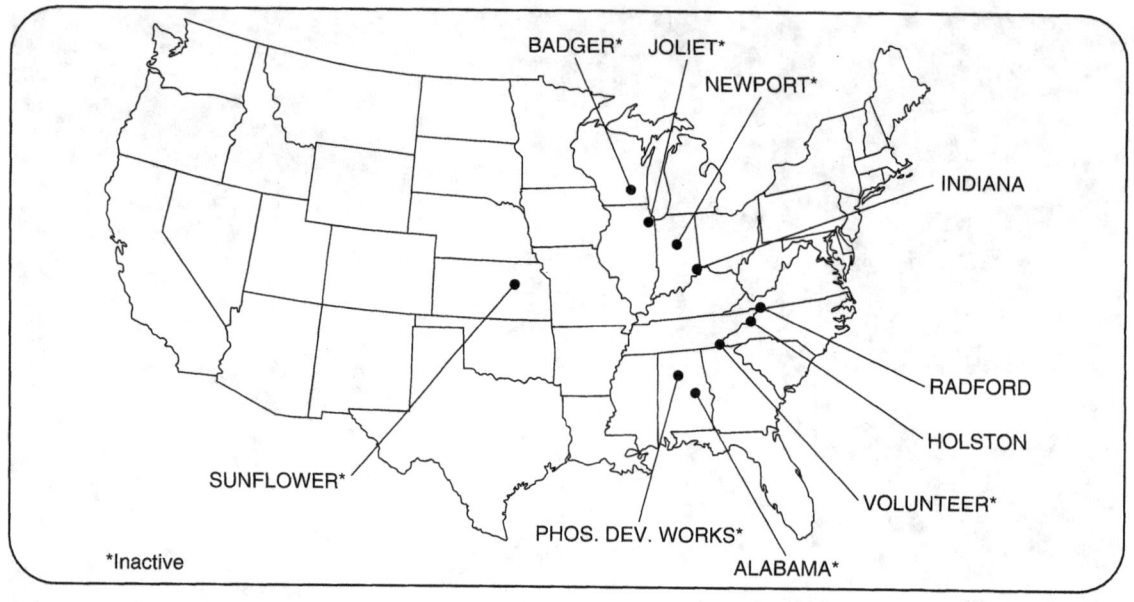

The ammunition production base (1), ca. 1977: propellant and explosives plants. Source: U.S. Army Armament Materiel Readiness Command, *Annual Historical Review, FY 1977,* Vol. I (Rock Island, IL: Historical Office, U.S. Army Armament Materiel Readiness Command, 1977), p. 24; U.S. Army Military History Institute, Carlisle, PA.

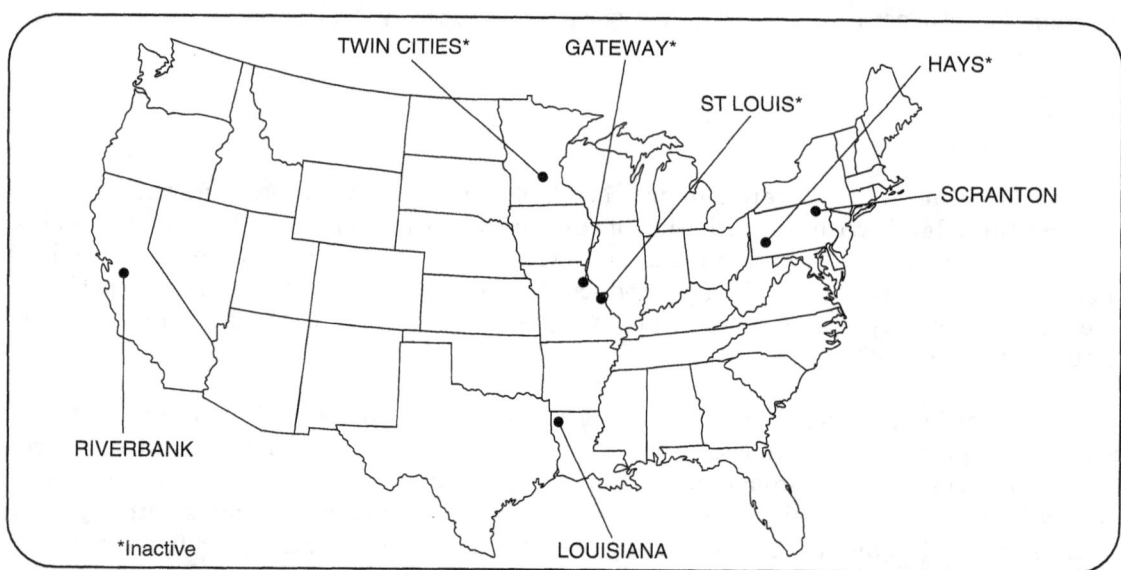

The ammunition production base (2), ca. 1977: metal parts plants. Source: U.S. Army Armament Materiel Readiness Command, *Annual Historical Review, FY 1977,* Vol. I (Rock Island, IL: Historical Office, U.S. Army Armament Materiel Readiness Command, 1977), p. 25; U.S. Army Military History Institute, Carlisle, PA.

The Production Base in 1945

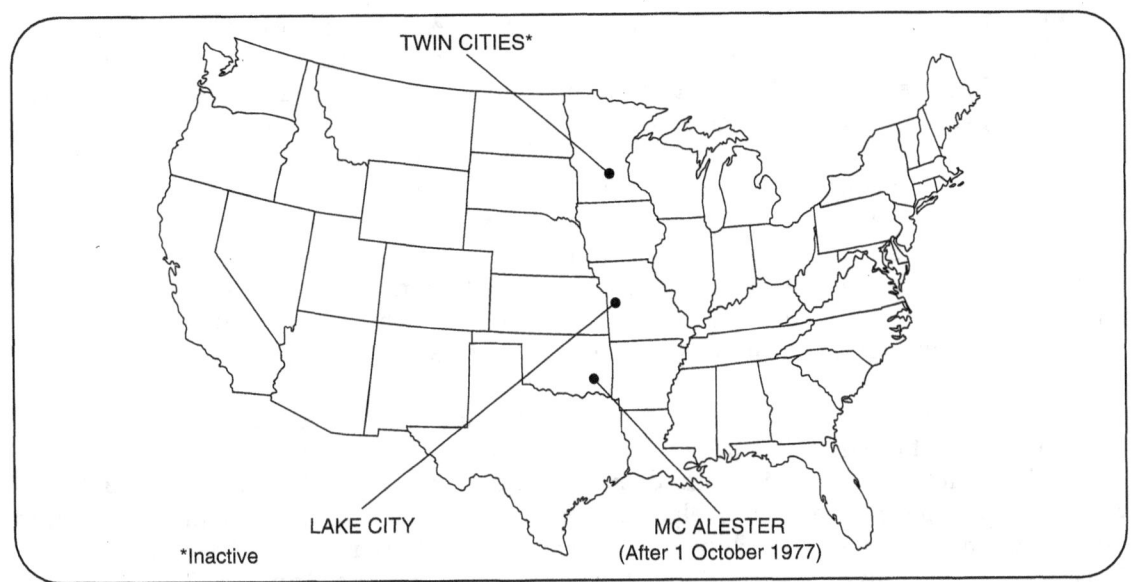

The ammunition production base (3), ca. 1977: small arms ammunition plants. Source: U.S. Army Armament Materiel Readiness Command, *Annual Historical Review, FY 1977,* Vol. I (Rock Island, IL: Historical Office, U.S. Army Armament Materiel Readiness Command, 1977), p. 26; U.S. Army Military History Institute, Carlisle, PA.

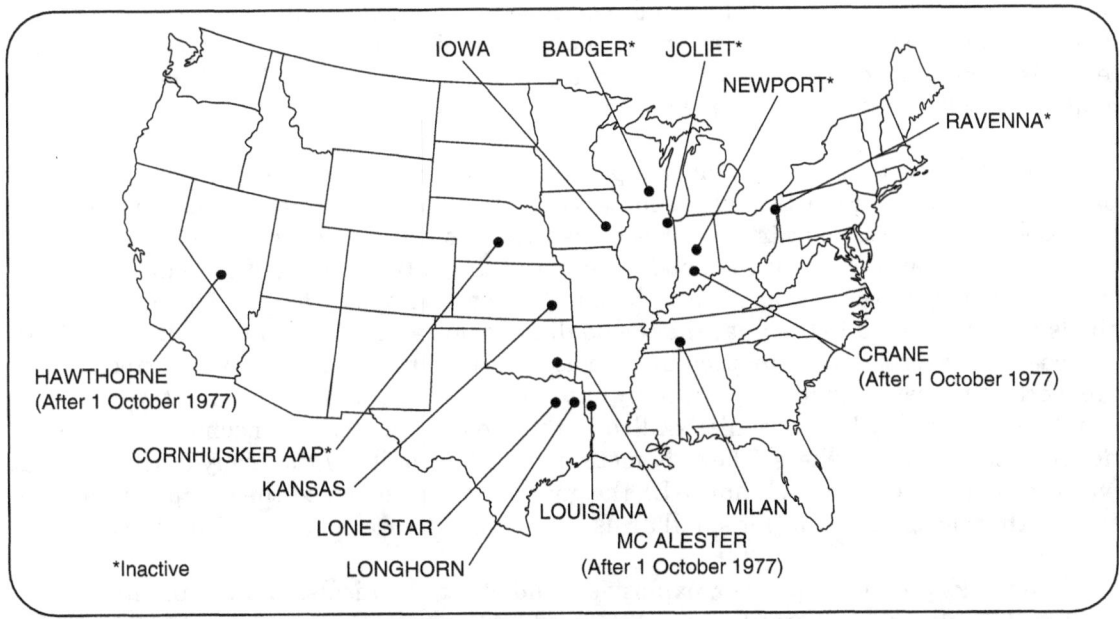

The ammunition production base (4), ca. 1977: load, assemble, and pack plants. Source: U.S. Army Armament Materiel Readiness Command, *Annual Historical Review, FY 1977,* Vol. I (Rock Island, IL: Historical Office, U.S. Army Armament Materiel Readiness Command, 1977), p. 27; U.S. Army Military History Institute, Carlisle, PA.

Often the loading plants were next to a powder or explosives works to facilitate the transfer of the dangerous materials. The plants usually operated with multiple lines, which could be easily opened or shut down to permit the fine-tuning of the output according to the current estimate of requirements.[10]

Typically, the facilities in any given plant were laid out in several widely-spaced areas, consisting of administrative, support, or production facilities grouped by function. Safety was a critical feature of the production layout. The various lines were separated, with 1,800 yards between the assembly lines of a LAP plant, for example.[11] Unlike a civilian industrial plant with facilities housed under one roof whenever possible, the ammunition plants had separate buildings connected by covered walkways.

The new plants producing ammunition for the Army during the war were built under the supervision of the Quartermaster Corps and, after December 1941, the Corps of Engineers. The styles of construction varied greatly. The early plants, those begun in 1940, were built with permanent, relatively solid construction. At Twin Cities Ordnance Plant in Minnesota, for example, the buildings were constructed of brick, steel, and concrete.[12] In 1941, as the scale and urgency of the mobilization increased, the Ordnance Department ordered that the facilities be made as spare and utilitarian as possible, with no useless ornamentation or excess materials. The buildings were to be of temporary construction and were only intended to last 5 years. Wood frame construction replaced brick, for example.[13] Safety considerations were manifested in a number of features. Buildings contained interior blast-resistant walls and construction to direct the force of an explosion upward and away from other rooms. Glass windows and skylights also were designed to explode upward and outward. Some of the buildings were surrounded by large barriers to contain an explosion. Special light fixtures were used to minimize the chance of a spark, and trolley rails were made of wood instead of metal. Two-story buildings included special escape chutes every few feet to allow the workers a quick exit in case of an accident.[14]

Of the various types of ammunition plants, the government owned very few metal parts plants. The manufacture of the metal components of ammunition, including fuzes, shell bodies, primers, and cartridge cases, involved basic metalworking operations. For example, the manufacture of shell bodies required the initial forging of steel disks into "cups," which were then "drawn" into the familiar ogive shape by forges. The finished shells were machined to the final shape and dimensions and then painted.[15] Because the process required relatively unspecialized tools and skills that could be reconverted to civilian work in peacetime, industry willingly entered into production. Similarly, fuze parts could be made easily by companies skilled in the production of small mechanical components, such as watchmakers. The only metal parts plant built by the Army during the war was the Gadsden Ordnance Plant (AL); the government also owned the equipment at one facility that made case cups for small arms cartridges, the Detroit Case Cup Plant.[16]

The works producing powder, explosives, and other chemicals, and the plants that produced small arms ammunition or performed LAP operations, were nearly all owned by the government because of the difficulty and danger of the work and the specialized nature of the facilities. In 1945, the government owned 51 powder, explosives, and chemical facilities, of which all but one were owned by the Army. These included 34 GOCOs of the Ordnance Department, 5 GOCOs of the Chemical Warfare Service (CWS), 4 GOGO

Building 561, Cannon Powder Blender, Picatinny Arsenal. Note the escape chutes to allow the workers to escape the building quickly. Source: HAER No. NJ-36C-83, Picatinny Arsenal, Prints and Photographs Division, Library of Congress.

facilities of the Chemical Warfare Service (CWS), 7 plancors, and Picatinny Arsenal in New Jersey. Only the Naval Powder Factory in Indian Head, MD, belonged to the Navy. Of the GOCOs, 6 produced smokeless powder, 14 produced explosives, and 12 manufactured an assortment of other chemicals, including ammonia, nitrates, and toluene. Two GOCOs produced both explosives and smokeless powder.

A brief description of the process of manufacturing propellant illustrates the nature of these facilities. "Smokeless powder" propellant is actually neither smokeless nor a powder. It is called smokeless to distinguish it from black powder, and it consists of grains of various shapes and sizes, up to an inch long, depending on the weapon for which they are intended. These grains are either of nitrocellulose ("single-based" powder) or a mixture of nitrocellulose and nitroglycerin ("double-based" powder). Nitrocellulose is created by soaking an organic cellulose product such as cotton or wood pulp in nitric acid. The resulting mixture is combined with chemical solvents, forming a doughy, pliable mass. This nitrocellulose is then extruded through a press into long cords, which are cut into grains of the appropriate size. The grains are then dried and the solvents removed for reuse. Propellant for the new rockets then beginning to be used required a new process that did not require solvent, because rocket grains were up to several feet long, and the grains tended to warp during drying. A new, solventless technique was developed, whereby the nitrocellulose was rolled into a sheet, cut into 4-inch-wide strips, and extruded dry. This process was first tried at Radford Ordnance Works in Virginia and was later installed at Badger Ordnance Works in Wisconsin.[17]

Forging the Sword: Defense Production During the Cold War

These large timber-and-earth barricades are shielding the Nitroglycerin Nitrating House (Building 5657-2) at the Sunflower Army Ammunition Plant. The small structure at right is a service building. Source: HAER No. KS-3, Sunflower Army Ammunition Plant, p. 31, Prints and Photographs Division, Library of Congress.

Vertical Press House (Building 4513-3), Sunflower Army Ammunition Plant. Note the interior blast walls projecting from the roof and walls, which compartmentalized an explosion and projected it outward, away from the rest of the building. Also note the escape chutes. Source: HAER No. KS-3, Sunflower Army Ammunition Plant, p. 29, Prints and Photographs Division, Library of Congress.

The Production Base in 1945

The Army owned 34 LAP plants for conventional munitions, including 27 GOCOs and 2 GOGOs (Picatinny and Frankford Arsenals).[18] Loading operations included loading of the propellant into bags, cartridge cases, and rockets; loading explosives into shells and bombs; and loading primers and fuzes. A typical loading plant was the Kansas Ordnance Plant near Parsons, KS, which included 562 buildings, most of them storage facilities, on 13,727 acres. The area was divided into 21 numbered sections, 9 of which related to production. Each section performed a different function: manufacturing boosters or detonators, or loading fuzes, primers, bombs, or shells. Each area was isolated from the others, and the buildings within each area were similarly kept apart, connected only by long covered walkways. The buildings themselves were generally long and narrow, and were made of structural clay tile. Buildings used for loading and assembling the rounds were broken up by concrete partition walls that extended beyond the outer walls to prevent explosions and the spread of fire.[19]

Production lines for the manufacture of the high explosives RDX and Composition B at Plant B, Holston Army Ammunition Plant. Note the covered walkways and the blast barriers that isolate and shield each of the manufacturing buildings on the enormous plant complex. Source: Holston Army Ammunition Plant.

The process of loading, assembling, and packing a shell was relatively simple. The shell body was inspected and painted. The explosive, TNT or Amatol, was screened, melted at 196 °F, then cooled slightly to the pour temperature of 176 °F. The liquid explosive was then poured, at first by hand and later by tubes, into the shell body, a small amount at a time to allow for shrinkage of the cooling material. After the fill had solidified, a hole was drilled in it and the booster (which detonated the charge) inserted. Finally, the fuze was screwed on. For the smaller types of ammunition, such as the 105-mm howitzer, a brass or steel cartridge case containing a primer and propellant was attached to the shell. The finished round was then sealed in a container and packed for shipment.[20] The process was improved during the war by using tubes to load the shell and by using automatic core melt units to permit the shell to be filled and topped off only once, without regard to the shrinkage of the fill.[21]

The small arms ammunition plants were a special kind of loading facility. These plants manufactured the metal parts and loaded them on site. Twin Cities Ordnance Plant was a typical example. Plant Number 1, built in the fall of 1941, consisted of two 0.30-caliber and one 0.50-caliber manufacturing shops, as well as support areas, utilities, storage, maintenance, and administration facilities. Each manufacturing shop contained five production lines, housed under one roof. As noted above, these shops were built using permanent construction; additional 0.30- and 0.50-caliber manufacturing facilities were built later with inexpensive, temporary wooden construction. The shop for manufacture of highly sensitive primers was separated from the rest of the facilities. A typical 0.30-caliber manufacturing shop consisted of a long central section with several smaller wings projecting from the side. The central section housed the metal parts activities, with shops for manufacturing cartridge cases and bullets and shops for weighing, inspecting, and packing the final products. The wings housed the more dangerous activities: shops for inserting tracer compounds in the bullets, for inserting primers in the cases, and for loading the rounds.[22] The Army's official history captured the essence of these plants:

> Each small arms plant was a self-contained unit wherein thousands of workers—including as many women as men—completed the whole process of manufacture amid rows of huge automatic machines, conveyor belts, and annealing furnaces. Raw material in the form of brass strips or cups, lead billets, steel wire, and smokeless powder came in at one end of the plant; millions of bright and shining cartridges came out the other end.[23]

Certain other facilities, run by the CWS, produced chemical munitions: poison gas weapons, phosphorus shells, incendiary bombs, and so on. These facilities included Edgewood Arsenal in Maryland and four new arsenals: Redstone and Huntsville in Alabama; Pine Bluff, AK; and Rocky Mountain in Colorado. Although originally intended to specialize in particular products, the CWS arsenals were expanded into versatile, multi-product production facilities. Their primary task was to load and assemble shells and bombs with mustard gas, incendiary mixtures, and other chemical agents.[24] Nineteen other plants, all but four of them GOCOs, impregnated clothing, manufactured chemicals, and produced charcoal for gas masks.[25]

Redstone Arsenal was a typical CWS plant. It was assigned the production of chemical shells ranging from 77- to 155-mm, 30- and 100-pound chemical bombs, and bursters for these items. The plant initially included four production lines—two for loading and two for the assembly of shells and bursters—as well as warehouses and igloos for storage. The first line in operation, Burster Line 1, included 15 buildings in an octagonal arrangement on approximately 25 acres. Later in the war, four new buildings were added, including a three-story melt-pour building, two screening and storage facilities, and a change house. The line produced 200,000 pounds of tetryl bursters (used to burst open the shells) per month. The plant underwent significant expansion as the workload increased, with two lines being added. Furthermore, this plant and others underwent extensive modernization in 1944 and 1945, with the facilities renovated for increased mechanization through conveyor belts, automatic loading machines, mechanical lifting and handling machines, and special handling equipment.[26]

The Navy owned and operated its own facilities for LAP activities. Most of the work was performed at the Naval Ammunition Depots, which also served as storage facilities. These facilities included the four huge inland depots at Hawthorne, NV; Crane, IN; McAlester, OK; and Hastings, NE. The inland depots loaded and assembled large-caliber shells, powder bags, rocket motors, and mines. The coastal depots and magazines also had production facilities for overhauling gun ammunition and loading mines. In addition, the Cohasset Naval Magazine in Massachusetts loaded rocket motors, the Shumaker Naval Ordnance Plant in Arkansas manufactured and assembled rockets, and the Naval Torpedo Factory at Yorktown, VA, assembled torpedoes. The Navy loaded its own small arms ammunition, especially 20-mm anti-aircraft rounds, at several facilities, including Hingham Naval Ammunition Depot in Massachusetts, Mare Island Naval Ammunition Depot in California, and St. Juliens Creek in Virginia. Plants for loading 20- and 40-mm rounds were at Charlotte, NC; Bristol, VA; Mayfield, KY; Chillicothe, OH; Elkton, MD; Peru, IN; and Hanover, MA.[27]

Like the Army's ordnance plants and works, the Navy's inland depots were located in thinly settled areas, and their facilities were dispersed over a wide area. Hawthorne, for example, covered 140 square miles, of which 80 square miles were used for production and storage. These facilities were serviced by 535 miles of roads, 150 miles of railroads, 57 miles of fencing, 42 miles of telephone lines, and 55 miles of water lines. As the inland depots were all intended to be permanent additions to the Navy's shore establishment, the buildings were of durable construction.[28] The coastal depots, sited as they were to serve the fleet, were generally smaller and less isolated than those inland.

Gun Plants

The government operated nearly all the plants it owned for the manufacture of small and large caliber guns. For small arms, the primary facility was the Springfield Armory, which produced rifles, pistols, machine guns, and submachine guns. Private contractors performed the bulk of the production.[29] For artillery, the Army's main facilities were Watervliet (NY), Watertown (PA), Frankford (PA), and Rock Island (IL) Arsenals and the Dickson Gun Plant in Houston, TX. The arsenals were old-line, government-operated plants that specialized in various gun components. Watervliet produced large and small caliber guns and mortars, including the tubes. Watertown and Rock Island manufactured carriages and recoil mechanisms, while Frankford focused on fire control instruments

Forging the Sword: Defense Production During the Cold War

such as telescopes, sights, and plotting boards. The Dickson Gun Plant was a GOCO facility that produced 8-inch howitzers and centrifugally cast gun tubes. It was the most modern plant in the country for casting gun tubes.[30]

Watervliet Arsenal is a good example of a gunmaking facility. Established in 1813 to make cannons for the war against Great Britain, it occupies approximately 140 acres along the Hudson River. At least 20 of its buildings date to the 19th century. The gun factory was established in the 1880s for the manufacture of the new large-caliber guns just becoming available for use in coastal defense. The Seacoast Gun Shop was a large brick structure consisting of a central section flanked by two wings. The north wing was divided into three aisles and housed machine tools such as lathes and bores. The south wing, considerably larger, was also divided into three aisles. It was intended for the machining of the largest guns, up to 16-inch caliber. This wing held the gun tubes for boring and turning them on the lathe. The central section included a boiler house and

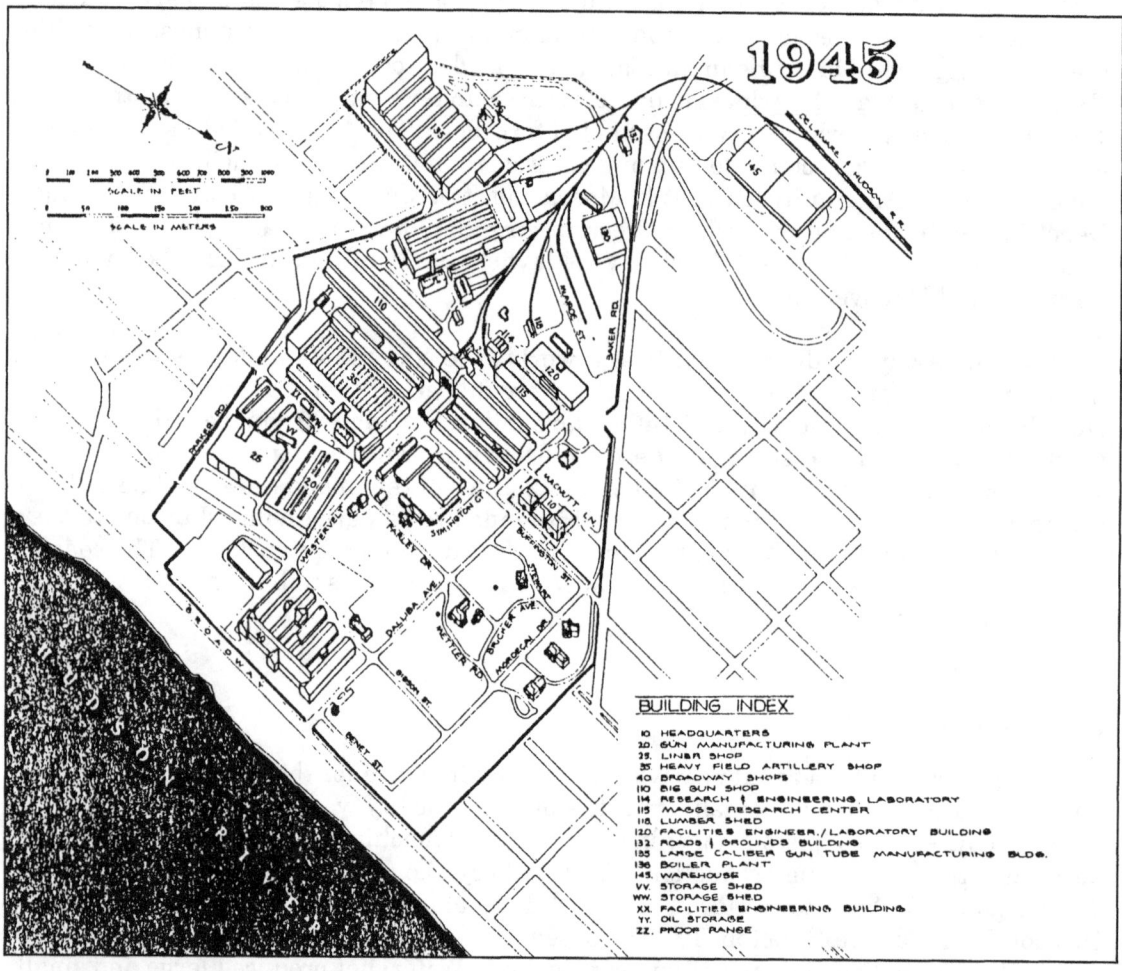

Plan of Watervliet Arsenal in 1945. Source: HAER NY-1A, Watervliet Arsenal, Prints and Photographs Division, Library of Congress.

engine room to supply power for the equipment, and a 50-foot shrinkage pit. The gun tube was lowered muzzle down into this pit, and the hoops and jacket were heated in a furnace and lowered over the tube. When cooled by water, they shrank onto the tube, adding tremendous strength to the gun to resist the stresses of firing. Railroad spurs entered the shop in the central section to allow railroad cars to carry the guns away.[31]

During World War I, facilities had been added to the gun factory at Watervliet, including another gun shop, a mobile artillery shop, carpenter and tool shops, a forge, a foundry, and a blacksmith shop. During World War II, the facilities were again expanded, with the addition of another large-caliber gunshop, a smaller artillery shop, and shops for tank repair and reconditioning. The new gunshop, which produced 155-mm "Long Tom" gun tubes during the war, occupied 186,645 square feet. It consisted of a long high bay with a 50-foot clearance and a smaller bay parallel to it. Huge cranes mounted on rollers carried the tubes back and forth and lowered them into the shrinkage pit at the south end. The facility was equipped with modern machinery for turning and boring the large tubes.[32]

The primary gunmaking plant for the Navy was the Gun Factory at the Washington Navy Yard. Located on 125 acres along the Anacostia River, the Navy Yard and its annex, like Watervliet Arsenal, incorporated a number of buildings to provide for the ordnance needs of the fleet. The Production Department of the yard included three divisions: the

Big Gun Shop (Building 110), Seacoast Gun Shop, Watervliet Arsenal, 1984. Source: HAER NY-1B-2, Watervliet Arsenal, NY, Prints and Photographs Division, Library of Congress.

Forging the Sword: Defense Production During the Cold War

Interior view of the Big Gun Shop (Building 110), Seacoast Gun Shop, Watervliet Arsenal, 1985. Shown is the main bay with overhead cranes used for maneuvering the heavy gun tubes. Source: HAER NY-1B-50, Watervliet Arsenal, NY, Prints and Photographs Division, Library of Congress.

Sixteen-inch gun tube mounted on machining lathe, Big Gun Shop (Building 110), Seacoast Gun Shop, Watervliet Arsenal. The gun extends beyond the main bay of the shop and into the West Aisle. Source: HAER NY-1B-62, Watervliet Arsenal, NY, Prints and Photographs Division, Library of Congress.

The Naval Gun Factory at the Washington Navy Yard. Source: HABS No. DC-442-C-35, Washington Navy Yard, DC, Prints and Photographs Division, Library of Congress.

Metal Processing Division, with foundries, forges, and sheetmetal shops; the Light Machining and Assembly Division, with shops for precision machine work, fire control and fuze assembly shops, and other metalworking facilities; and the Heavy Machining and Assembly Division, with shops for the manufacture, assembly, and repair of guns and carriages.[33]

In addition to the Naval Gun Factory, the Navy owned nine smaller Naval Ordnance Plants (NOPs). All but one of these, Pocatello NOP in Idaho, were GOCO facilities. Three of the GOCOs, at Canton, OH, Center Line, MI, and Louisville, KY, were also known as "extension gun plants," because they supported and extended the work performed at the Gun Factory by manufacturing and assembling medium-caliber guns and carriages. Macon (GA) NOP assembled fuze parts, Indianapolis (IN) NOP manufactured bomb sights and torpedo directors, and St. Louis (MO) and Forest Park (IL) NOPs produced torpedoes. South Charleston (WV) NOP, an old World War I plant, produced armor and gun barrels, while Pocatello (ID) NOP relined worn gun barrels sent in from the Pacific Fleet.[34]

Forging the Sword: Defense Production During the Cold War

Tank Plants

The government's primary tank-producing facility was the Detroit Tank Arsenal, operated by Chrysler. The construction of this arsenal has already been described. It consisted of a main plant building, personnel office, office building, boiler house, and garage. The main plant building was a single-story, steel frame structure measuring 520 feet by 1,382 feet. The building had two main bays, an 80-foot wide assembly bay at the south end and a 60-foot high receiving bay at the north end, through which railroad tracks passed. Between the main bays were 23 manufacturing bays, each 60-feet wide. Materials were brought by rail to the receiving bay and then moved to one of the manufacturing bays for processing. Final assembly took place in the assembly bay, and the completed tanks were then hauled away by rail.[35]

The government also owned four tank depots, at Chester, PA, Lima, OH, Toledo, OH, and Richmond, CA. These depots served a similar purpose as the Army Air Force's modification centers: They added accessory equipment to tanks—300 items in all—that were not installed at the factory. The Lima Depot was originally constructed as a gun plant,

Detroit Army Tank Plant, Warren, MI, ca. early 1980s. Source: Historical Office, U.S. Army Tank-automotive and Armaments Command, Warren, MI.

but it was never put into production because of the decline in orders for guns late in the war. The plant was converted to a tank depot and, from 1943 until 1945, processed some 100,000 vehicles.[36]

Shipyards

The United States ended World War II with a vast complex of shipyards to support its wartime program of naval and merchant construction. This complex included 9 government-owned and -operated shipyards and approximately 132 privately owned shipyards.[37] The government invested over a billion dollars in this complex; half of the funds were provided by the Navy for 80 yards, the other half by the Maritime Commission for 43 yards. Ninety percent of the funding went into the 60 private yards in which the government had invested more than $5 million each for land and facilities. At its peak, the shipbuilding industry employed 1.7 million workers, up from 102,000 in 1940.[38]

The Navy shipyards, like the arsenals of the Army, tended to be all-purpose production facilities, able to handle any of the fleet's needs, including new ship construction, the fabrication of components and equipment, repair, overhaul, and regular maintenance. Puget Sound Naval Shipyard at Bremerton, WA, was typical. At the start of World War II, Puget Sound had been the premier navy yard in the Pacific and the only one with the facilities to handle large capital ships such as battleships. After the attack at Pearl Harbor, five of the six surviving battleships returned to Bremerton for repair and modernization. As with the other navy yards, shipbuilding was only a small part of Puget Sound's mission. The report of the Greenslade Board in January 1941 had recommended that no more than 20 percent of the capacity of the navy yards be used for new construction; the rest of the facilities should be reserved for repair activities in the event of war. Construction activity at Puget Sound appears to have been limited to smaller vessels such as destroyer escorts; however, the yard performed extensive work modifying and upgrading the ships of the Pacific Fleet.[39]

On its waterfront, Puget Sound had five large drydocks (a sixth was added later). These docks ranged in size from Drydock No. 1 (completed 1896), 639 feet long by 120 feet wide by 39 feet deep, to Drydock No. 5 (completed 1942), 1,030 feet long by 147 feet wide by 54 feet deep. One of them, Shipbuilding Dock No. 3, was, as its name suggests, used for ship construction. Instead of sliding down the traditional inclined ways, a new vessel was launched simply by flooding the dock. This was an innovation that Puget Sound introduced at the end of World War I. Shipbuilding Dock No. 3 was made of concrete and was divided into two compartments by a large, steel-clad bulkhead to allow greater control of flooding. It was adjacent to the primary industrial shops and, like all the docks, was served by heavy-gauge crane rail and railroad tracks that were used for moving and distributing components and materials.[40] The yard also had four new shipbuilding ways for the construction of escort vessels. These ways were built in pairs, each pair being 400 feet long and 109 feet wide.[41]

Forging the Sword: Defense Production During the Cold War

Puget Sound also had at least 22 specialized industrial shops, including:

- Shop 11, shipfitter shop
- Shop 17, sheet metal shop
- Shop 23, forge shop
- Shop 25, gas manufacturing shop
- Shop 26, welding shop
- Shop 27, galvanizing shop
- Shop 28, plating and polishing shop
- Shop 31, machine shop, inside
- Shop 38, machine shop, outside
- Shop 41, boiler shop
- Shop 51, electric shop

Two ships under construction at Puget Sound Naval Shipyard, April 1964. Source: Naval Institute Photographic Library, "Puget Sound Naval Shipyard," Annapolis, MD.

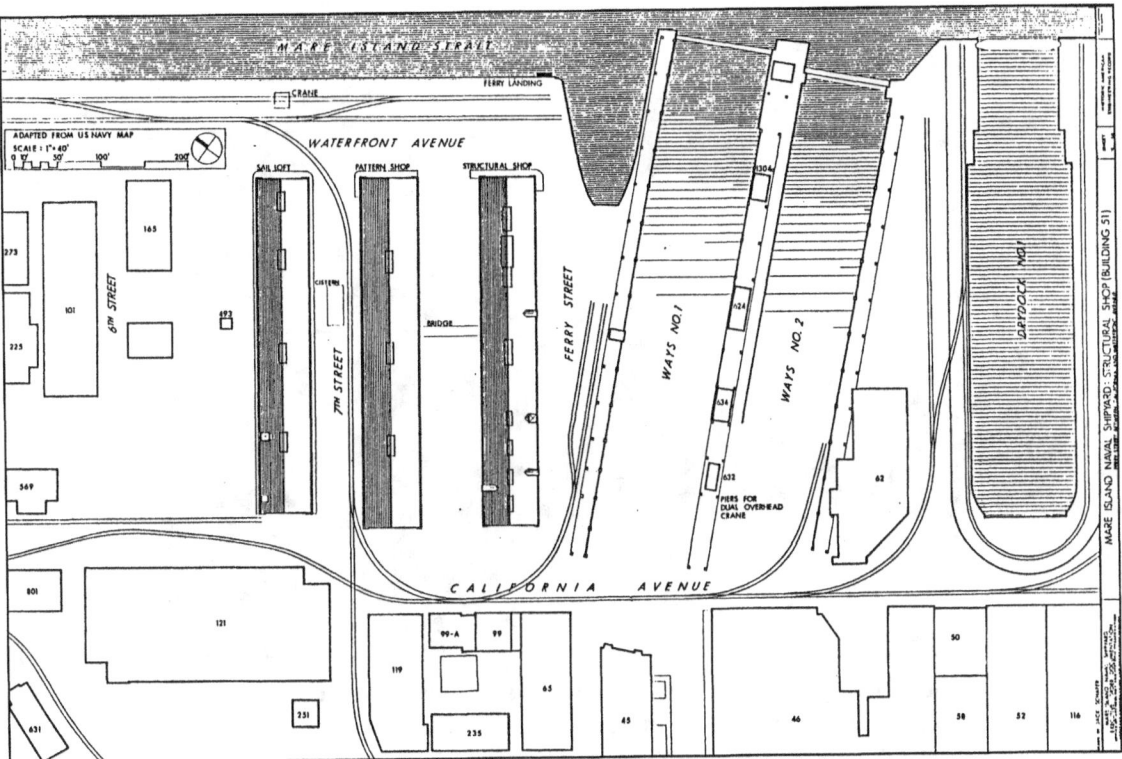

Portion of waterfront at Mare Island Naval Shipyard, showing Drydock No. 1, two building ways, and three industrial shops (Sail Loft, Pattern Shop, and Structural Shop). Source: HAER CAL, 48-MARI, 1-20.

- Shop 56, pipe and copper shop
- Shop 61, shipwright shop
- Shop 68, boat and joiner shop
- Shop 71, paint shop
- Shop 72, riggers and laborers
- Shop 74, sail loft
- Shop 81, foundry
- Shop 93, consolidated printing facility
- Shop 94, pattern shop.

Other shops built during the war included shops for chains, carpentry, asbestos, range finders, battery repair, and a radio, instrument, and gyroscope shop. In addition, a number of central tool facilities (Shop 06) were scattered about the yard, probably to supply tools to shipboard personnel.[42]

Forging the Sword: Defense Production During the Cold War

The Machine Shop at Puget Sound Naval Shipyard, where sundry metal-working tasks were performed, August 1951. Source: Puget Sound NSY, Photo No. YV-533.

Melting pots at the Foundry, Puget Sound Naval Shipyard, January 1946. Source: Puget Sound NSY, Photo YV-1643.

A forge at the Forge Shop, Puget Sound Naval Shipyard, January 1963. Source: Puget Sound NSY, Photo YV-1265.

The Shipfitters Shop at Puget Sound Naval Shipyard, January 1963. This shop is where the parts of the ship's hull were laid out and assembled during construction. Source: Puget Sound NSY, Photo No. YV-832.

Forging the Sword: Defense Production During the Cold War

The shipfitters shop was the primary facility for the production of ship hulls. There, using wooden templates prepared by loftsmen, the highly skilled shipfitters shaped the hull plates using cranes, presses, hoists, and forges, making all the pieces fit together. The boiler shop prepared the ship's boilers. The forge shop, divided into light and heavy forge areas, hammered out many of the large metal components such as propeller shafts, and the foundry produced large castings such as anchors, using molds produced in the pattern shop. The output from these shops were then finished in the machine shops. The sheet metal, electric, carpenter, pipe and coppersmith, and chain shops manufactured additional components for the ship. The gas manufacturing shop provided natural gas for the others.[43]

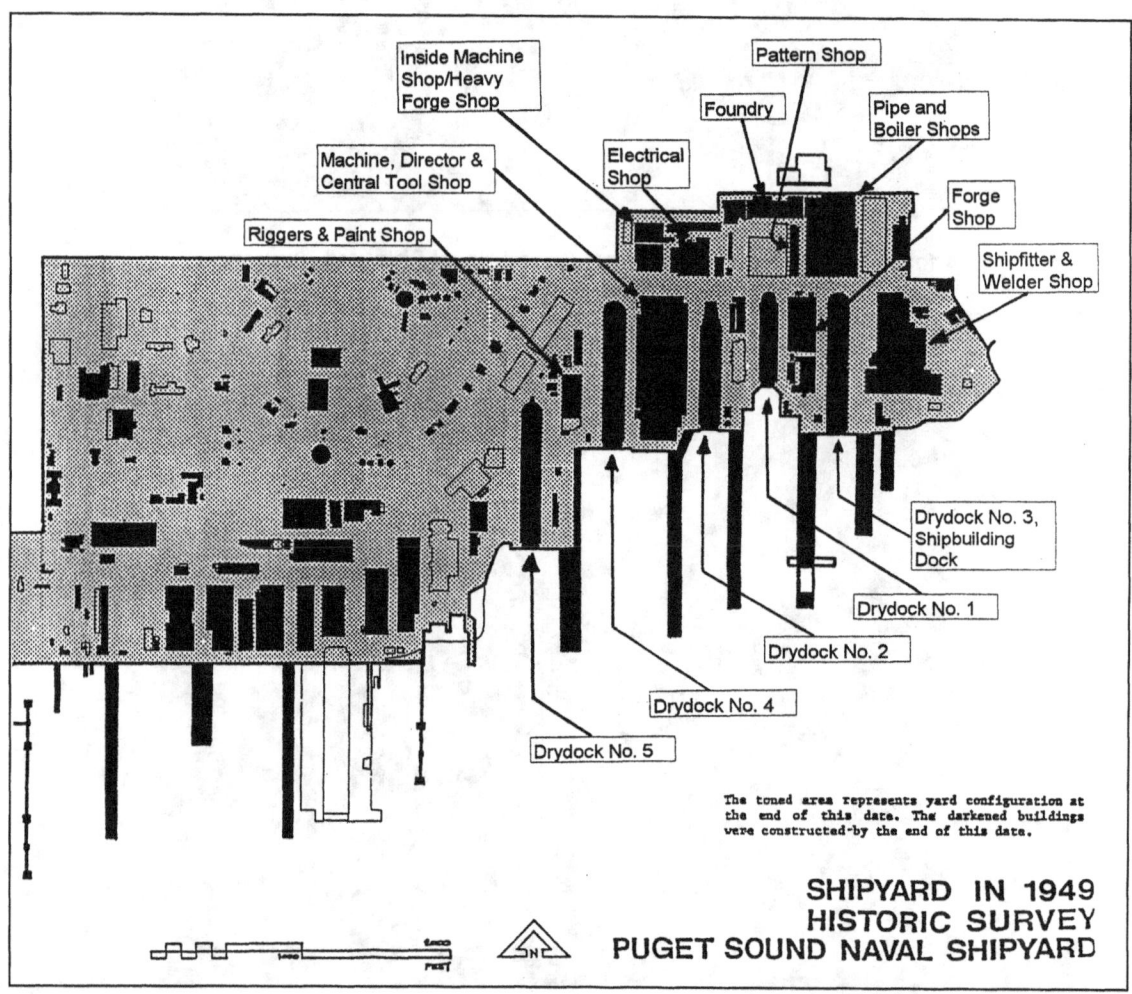

Puget Sound Naval Shipyard in 1949, showing layout of docks and shops. Source: Based on plan in Grulich Architecture and Planning Services, "Historic Survey: Puget Sound Naval Shipyard, Bremerton, Washington," Tacoma, WA: Grulich Architecture and Planning Services, April 1986); on file at Naval Facilities Engineering Command, Code 150, Legacy and HARP Program Office, Alexandria, VA.

At Puget Sound, as at the other yards, the various shops were laid out so components and materials flowed smoothly from one process to another. The shops were largely clustered around Shipbuilding Dock No. 3, so work from the other docks, such as hull plates needing repair in the shipfitters shop, were carried the length of the yard by huge cranes. Along with the cranes, railways serviced the docks and shops, and these were the primary distribution system for the yard.[44]

Endnotes

1. Ordnance Dept. Order No. 11–45, Office of the Chief of Ordnance, Army Service Forces, Washington, DC, 14 May 1945, in U.S. Army Center of Military History Archives (hereafter cited as CMH Archives), "Directory of Ordnance Establishments," file HRC 331, Ordnance Installations.
2. Rowland and Boyd, *Bureau of Ordnance*, 505.
3. Surplus Property Administration, *Aircraft Plants*, 8–9, 25–27.
4. Surplus Property Administration, *Aircraft Plants*, 8–9, 23–24; Lilley et al., *Accelerating Aircraft Production*, 41.
5. Surplus Property Administration, *Aircraft Plants*, 44; Cunningham, *The Aircraft Industry*, 82.
6. Surplus Property Administration, *Aircraft Plants*, 42; [David G. Buchanan and John P. Johnson, Historic American Engineering Record, *Stratford Army Engine Plant*, HAER No. CT-14 (National Park Service, 1984), 13–15, 30–33.]
7. Surplus Property Administration, *Aircraft Plants*, 24–25, 47.
8. Lilley et al., *Accelerating Aircraft Production*, 41.
9. Thomson and Mayo, *Ordnance Procurement and Supply*, 108–110.
10. Ibid., 107–108.
11. Kane, *GOCO Industrial Facilities*, 82, 87–89.
12. Robert C. Vogel and Deborah L. Crown, *The World War II Ordnance Department's Government-Owned Contractor Operated (GOCO) Industrial Facilities: Twin Cities Ordnance Plant*, Historic Investigation, U.S. Army Materiel Command Historic Context Series, Report of Investigations Number 8A (Plano, TX: Geo-Marine, Inc., December 1995; under contract to U.S. Army Corps of Engineers, Fort Worth District, Contract No. DACA63-93-D-0014), 18–24.
13. Lenore Fine and Jesse A. Remington, *The Corps of Engineers: Construction in the United States*, in *The United States Army in World War II: The Technical Services* (Washington, DC: Office of the Chief of Military History, U.S. Army, 1972), 317–327; Kane, *GOCO Industrial Facilities*, 84–85.
14. Thomson and Mayo, *Ordnance Production Facilities*, 130–133; Kane, *GOCO Facilities*, 87–89; Goodwin and Associates, *World War II Facilities*, 74, 75.
15. Thomson and Mayo, *Ordnance Production and Supply*, 114.
16. Thomson and Mayo, *Ordnance Procurement and Supply*, 115–124.
17. Kane, *GOCO Industrial Facilities*, 132.
18. Kane, *GOCO Industrial Facilities*, 17.
19. Historic American Engineering Record, *Kansas Army Ammunition Plant*, HAER KS-4 (1984), 13, 17, 21–25. See also Steve Gaither, *The World War II Ordnance Department's Government-Owned Contractor-Operated (GOCO) Industrial Facilities: Kansas Army Ammunition Plant Historic Investigation*, U.S. Army Materiel Command Historic Context Series Report of Investigations Number 5A (Plano, TX: Geo-Marine, Inc., under contract DACA63-93-D-0014 to U.S. Army Corps of Engineers, Fort Worth District, February 1986).
20. Gaither, *Kansas Army Ammunition Plant*, 63.
21. Ibid., 63–64.
22. Goodwin and Associates, *AMC Facilities*, 121–123.
23. Thomson and Mayo, *Ordnance Production and Supply*, 204.
24. Leo P. Brophy and George J. B. Fisher, *The Chemical Warfare Service: Organizing for War*, in *The United States Army in World War II: The Technical Services* (Washington, DC: Office of the Chief of Military History, Department of the Army, 1959), 120–122; Brophy, Miles, and Cochrane, *The Chemical Warfare Service: From Laboratory to Field*, 256–258.
25. Brophy, Miles, and Cochrane, *Chemical Warfare Service: From Laboratory to Field*, 254–256, 277–278. For a list of all these facilities see ibid., Appendix A, 436–447.

26. Helen Brents Joiner, *The Redstone Arsenal Complex in the Pre-Missile Era: A History of Huntsville Arsenal, Gulf Chemical Warfare Depot, and Redstone Arsenal, 1941–1949* (Redstone Arsenal, AL: Historical Division, Army Missile Command, n.d.), 91–129. See also Goodwin and Associates, *AMC's World War II Facilities,* 200–203.
27. Bureau of Yards and Docks, *Building the Navy's Bases,* 1:323–353, 399.
28. Bureau of Yards and Docks, *Building the Navy's Bases,* 1:339–343.
29. Thomson and Mayo, *Ordnance Production and Supply,* 154–187.
30. Ibid., 68–103; "Ordnance Department Establishments, Active and Standby, February 1947," CMH Archives, file HRC 331, Ordnance Installations.
31. Historic American Engineering Record, *Watervliet Arsenal, Watervliet, New York,* HAER NY-1A (1985), Prints and Photographs Division, LC, Washington, DC, 38–46, 77–78; Historic American Engineering Record, *Watervliet Arsenal, Seacoast Gun Shop (Building 110, Big Gun Shop),* HAER No. NY-1B (1985), Prints and Photographs Division, LC, Washington, DC, 1–18.
32. Historic American Engineering Record, *Watervliet Arsenal,* 50–61; Historic American Engineering Record, *Watervliet Arsenal, Large Caliber Gun Tube Manufacturing Building (Building 135),* HAER No. NY-1J (1985), Prints and Photographs Division, LC, Washington, DC, 1–8.
33. Historic American Building Survey, "Navy Yard," HABS DC-442, Prints and Photographs Division, LC, Washington, DC, 1–6; *Ordnance Production* (Washington, DC: U.S. Naval Gun Factory, 1951), 1–8.
34. Joseph J. Mathews, "The New Naval Ordnance Plants," 1217–1220; Rowland and Boyd, *Bureau of Ordnance,* 252–253.
35. Thomson and Mayo, *Ordnance Production and Supply,* 243; Goodwin & Associates, *Army Materiel Command's Facilities,* 145. See also Kane, *GOCO Industrial Facilities,* 101.
36. Goodwin and Associates, *Army Materiel Command's Facilities,* 147; Historical Office, U.S. Army Tank-Automotive Command, "U.S. Army Tank-Automotive Command, Historical Overview: Lima Army Tank Plant, Lima, Ohio" (unpublished document, 1984, in TACOM files), 1.
37. Surplus Property Administration, *Shipyards and Facilities: Report of the Surplus Property Administration to the Congress* (Washington, DC: GPO, 1946), 5. One official list of private and naval shipyards on 1 July 1945 names 127 private yards; see Navy Department, Bureau of Ships, "Geographical List of Shipyards, NAVSHIPS (1851)" (Washington, DC, 10 July 1945), copy found in Naval Institute, file Shipyards—United States—General.
38. Surplus Property Administration, *Shipyards,* 6–7.
39. Grulich Architecture and Planning Services, "Historic Survey: Puget Sound Naval Shipyard, Bremerton, Washington" (Tacoma, WA, April 1986, on Navy contract N 624-85-C-9967; copy obtained at Naval Facilities Engineering Command, Planning and Engineering Division, Code 150, Legacy/HARP Program, Alexandria, VA), B-27.
40. Ibid., PSNS Inventories, facilities 701–705.
41. Bureau of Yards and Docks, *Building the Navy's Bases,* 1:194–196. Evidently the ways were subsequently demolished, as there is no record of them in Grulich Architecture and Planning Services, "Puget Sound Naval Shipyard."
42. Grulich Architecture and Planning Services, "Puget Sound Naval Shipyard," B-63-65.
43. Ibid. A good listing of the kinds of tools and equipment used in navy yard shops can be found in "The Industrial History of the Charleston Navy Yard, 1939–1945" (unpublished typescript manuscript, General Collections, Naval Historical Center, Washington, DC), Appendix 1, Tables 2 and 3. See also A.W. Carmichael, *Practical Ship Production* (2nd ed.; New York: McGraw-Hill Book Company, 1941), 169–188.
44. Grulich Architecture and Planning Services, "Puget Sound Naval Shipyard," B-63.

Chapter 4

From World War to Cold War, 1945–1953

Demobilization

After the surrender of Japan in September 1945, production ceased immediately in nearly all categories of armaments as the country began the process of demobilizing its armed forces and resuming a peacetime posture. Contracts were canceled, plants closed, and the defense workforce melted away to merge back into the civilian economy. With huge stockpiles on hand and no apparent need for continued production, the government moved quickly to dispose of the bulk of its plants, especially the "plancors" owned by the Defense Plant Corporation (DPC). A rapid disposal of the plants was considered important to the health of the nation's economy and to avoid having to abandon the facilities outright. After long years of depression and war, people were ready to start spending their wartime earnings, and new plants would be built if the war plants were not soon reconverted. The Surplus Property Administration, which had the responsibility of disposing of the plancors, reported to Congress in 1946: "Only to the extent that these plants can be put to use before similar capacity can be built . . . can they create jobs and facilitate the transition. Their greatest potential value will be lost if they are not disposed of quickly."[1]

The government naturally sought to sell the facilities to the contractors who had operated them during the war. Problems arose when the contractors did not want to buy the plants; some facilities were too specialized for civilian production or were simply not needed. Among the aircraft facilities, for example, disposal of the engine and accessory plants presented little difficulty. Being of a generic industrial character and located largely in areas with a heavy industrial concentration, they were easily reconverted for peacetime use. The airframe plants were harder to sell. They were of little value to the aircraft industry, which was already burdened with a great excess of production capacity and on the verge of a major contraction. Furthermore, some of the plants, such as Ford's facility at Willow Run, had been designed to take advantage of mass production techniques, which were of little use for the reduced postwar market. While the outlying feeder buildings could be adapted to manufacture other products, the large, high-bay assembly buildings were not practical for use in producing small goods.[2]

Similar problems hindered the effort to dispose of the surplus shipyards. The shipbuilding industry was faced with a major contraction of its own and could not absorb the excess facilities. Indeed, maintaining these surplus yards in operation would cause greater hardship on the prewar private yards, which did not have sufficient business for themselves. Like the airframe plants, many of the yards had been designed to mass produce ships, a useless feature in the postwar environment. However, shipyard facilities could be adapted to other uses, and they often included prime waterfront real estate.[3]

The ammunition plants were a special problem. With the exception of the ammonia works, which could help fill the burgeoning European demand for fertilizers, these plants did not have a civilian market for their products. Their very nature made it difficult if not impossible to convert them to any other peacetime uses. The buildings were widely spaced on huge tracts of land. Their facilities and equipment, whether for metal parts assembly, shell or bomb loading, or explosives manufacture, were unsuited to civilian production. They also were contaminated with chemicals, especially the powder and explosives works. Even their location, dispersed in rural areas far from population and industrial centers, made them unattractive to postwar investors. However, the Army planned to keep most of the ammunition plants, which helped mitigate the difficulty of their disposal.[4]

The most troublesome problems lay with the "scrambled" or "cats and dogs" facilities. These were plants in which government and private property were intermixed. During the mobilization, the government frequently paid for expansions to an existing plant, either by adding equipment, constructing new buildings, or buying adjacent land. This was especially common during the Emergency Period, when the government tried to limit the construction of entirely new plants by expanding the capacity of those that already existed. The government hoped and anticipated that after the war the contractor would purchase the government property, which would solve the problem. If the contractor refused, or if the two parties could not agree on a price, then perplexing problems arose. Machinery could be moved, but what could be done with government buildings on private land, or with government land with privately owned buildings on it?[5]

The problems did not revolve solely around the question of disposal. Accounting for the property was a nightmare, as the government had to be paid for the use of its facilities. A case in point was the Bethpage, Long Island, plant of the Grumman Corporation. Grumman produced fighters and torpedo bombers for the Navy, and its plant had expanded tremendously during the war. Grumman added more than 2.6 million square feet of floor space, with the Navy paying for all but a fraction of it. This expansion included an addition to Grumman's prewar plant and four new plants adjacent to it. After the war, the Navy sold two of those plants to Grumman but retained two, which were leased back to the company. The problems arose when Grumman, like many struggling aircraft companies in the lean postwar years, turned to the production, not just of civilian aircraft but of other civilian products, including an aluminum canoe of the company's own design. "At Bethpage," notes a historian of the company, "when it happened that a canoe hull was being formed on a stretchpress owned by Grumman in a plant owned by the Navy located on land owned by Grumman, the cost accounting became an exercise in creative mathematics."[6]

Ultimately, the government was forced to write off many of the facilities "as part of the inevitable cost of the war"[7] and sold them at a fraction of their wartime value. It expected to take a loss on the shipyards, for example, and did—the Navy's Bureau of Ships recouped just 30 percent of its investment. Many aircraft plants were never sold and remained in the government's inventory. Likewise, scrambled facilities remained scrambled, in some cases to the end of the Cold War.[8]

Most government-owned, government-operated (GOGO) plants remained in government hands, albeit at a very low level of operation. At arsenals, navy yards, air depots, and other such facilities, the emphasis was less on production than on research and on the preservation of the huge surplus stockpiles and inventories of ships, airplanes, cannons, small arms, and vast stores of ammunition. The Army's arsenals returned to their prewar status, continuing only sufficient production to preserve manufacturing know-how and to justify their existence. At the Watervliet Arsenal, for example, the workforce was cut in half, from 1,756 in September 1945 to 940 in June 1947. During that period, production was limited to a single shop, which turned out a few hundred 20-mm guns and several thousand trunnion blocks.[9] Employment at the Rock Island Arsenal declined from a peak of 10,000 in October 1943 to 1,483 in February 1946. As at Watervliet, shops were closed and the machines placed in standby, and all production work was concentrated in a single building. The main emphasis of Rock Island's efforts for the first year and a half after the war was the preservation and storage of weapons and the manufacture of spare parts; although in 1947 the arsenal did receive orders for production of components for small arms and artillery, as well as other miscellaneous items.[10]

Cutbacks were more severe at the Chemical Warfare Service's plants. Production ceased altogether at the Redstone Arsenal by late 1945, its only activity being the renovation and salvage of ammunition returned from overseas. The workforce was cut 80 percent before the end of 1945, from 3,048 in July to 605 by December. In 1947, the arsenal ceased operations altogether and went into standby status. The adjacent Huntsville Arsenal was deactivated and merged with Redstone by 1950. Both Pine Bluff and Rocky Mountain arsenals were placed on standby as well.[11]

While there was little new construction at these sites during the immediate postwar years, many of them did receive new equipment, especially machine tools, selected from the stocks left over from the war. Only rarely did renovations take on a more substantial character. A Maryland congressman, alarmed at the layoffs at the Naval Powder Factory and fearing that it would be closed altogether, persuaded the Navy to explore converting its main production capacity from smokeless powder, for which there was now little demand, to rocket propellant. In part because of this pressure, the Navy established pilot plants at Indian Head in 1947 to produce experimental new propellants for use in naval research. The new facilities included a nitroglycerine plant, a pilot plant for rolled sheet ballistite (a propellant), and a cast powder plant. Over the next 6 years, additional facilities were added and, with the onset of the Korean war, pilot lines became full production lines.[12]

The government also converted a few of the GOCOs into full government facilities. For example, Detroit Tank Arsenal was taken over by the Army. Here again, the facility was mainly used for storage; production was mostly limited to the manufacture of spare parts. In 1946 and 1947, the entire output of the plant (and indeed, of the country) for complete tanks was the modification of 20 M26 heavy tanks and the manufacture of 22 T29 and T30 heavy tanks.[13] Some of the ammunition plants were also redesignated as

Extrusion Press, Naval Propellant Plant, Indian Head, MD. These vertical presses extrude 4-in.-diameter high-energy base grains used in the Polaris A-3 missile. Source: Naval Institute Photographic Library, "Naval Propellant Plant," Annapolis, MD.

"arsenals," often after merging a loading plant with a nearby explosives or powder works. (These redesignated arsenals are not to be confused with the "old-line" manufacturing arsenals such as Watertown and Rock Island, which had more versatile facilities and workers.) Thus the Kankakee Ordnance Works and Elwood Ordnance Plant combined to form the Joliet Arsenal (IL), and the Hoosier Ordnance Plant and Indiana Ordnance Works formed the Indiana Arsenal. Other newly designated arsenals included the Red River Arsenal (TX), Radford Arsenal (VA), Ravenna Arsenal (OH), Twin Cities Arsenal (MN), and Milan Arsenal (TN).[14]

Although manufacturing and procurement were deemphasized during the postwar years, research and development proceeded at a rapid pace. Many promising new technologies had made their appearance in the latter stages of the war, such as rockets and jet aircraft, and the armed services moved quickly to initiate research programs. Meanwhile, some manufacturing plants were converted to research facilities. The production lines at the Naval Aircraft Factory at Philadelphia were shut down at the end of the war to avoid competing with private industry.* After 1945, the facility was devoted to research in engines, components such as catapults and arresting gear, materials, and aeromedicine.[15] Redstone Arsenal received a contingent of German rocket scientists in 1950 and became the center for missile research in the Army.[16] The research that was performed at these and other installations during the immediate postwar years would bear fruit in the early 1950s, when new weapons such as the F-86 Sabrejet would be rushed into production for the Korean War.

Preparedness Planning

The Army and Navy did not abandon their industrial base willy-nilly, although it may have seemed that way to some. In fact, the services remembered all too well the experience following World War I, when the government had in fact done so as if in the belief that the War to End All Wars would be just that. Whole defense-related industries had literally been abandoned in 1918, only to be recreated from scratch 20 years later at enormous expense. Even then, some of the damage was permanent, as many workers and managers with skills and experience were no longer to be found. For example, the art of manufacturing black powder had been lost permanently; although new plants were built to revive that industry during World War II, it was found that the powder never achieved the fine quality of that used in the previous war.[17]

So, in the middle and late 1940s, the services were determined to ensure access to essential facilities in the event of a new war, and they worked to counteract the overwhelming popular demand for immediate and total demobilization. In addition to the arsenals, depots, and other permanent installations, the services retained a number of the GOCO plants directly on standby. Whenever possible, the plants were leased to industry for civilian production on the condition that they could be called back during an emergency. Plants that were not needed immediately, such as ammunition plants, or that could not be sold or leased, such as some of the aircraft plants, were deactivated and maintained on contract by only a skeleton crew, if at all. Even for those facilities that were sold, the government often retained the right to buy them back in wartime. The number of such plants was very small in proportion to those fully disposed of by the government. Of the 364 facilities sponsored by the Navy's Bureau of Ships during the war, for example, only 30 were included in the postwar industrial preparedness program.[18]

The services took special care to retain a supply of machine tools. Machine tools were a critical element of production. Such tools are defined as "a power driven, complete metal-working machine, not portable by hand, with one or more tool-holding devices, used for progressively removing metal in the form of chips."[19] They operate by rotating the metal product against the cutting tool, as in a lathe; rotating the cutting tool against the metal, as in milling machines and drill presses; moving the tool longitudinally

---

*This was in spite of the Vinson-Trammell Act of 1934, which had decreed that at least 10 percent of all naval aircraft had to be procured from government-owned plants.

against the metal, as in the shaper; and moving the metal longitudinally against the tool, as in the planer. The more complex tools combined these operations.[20]

Again, the experience of World War I was an important lesson. A few tools had been packed away after 1918, to be brought back into use when mobilization began again. Although they were obsolete by the 1940s—they were unable to machine metal to the tolerances required by the newer airplanes, for example—these tools had been quite valuable for starting production and training workers during the early stages of mobilization. Nonetheless, the shortage of machine tools had been a critical bottleneck hindering production before 1943. Tools were supplied to manufacturers according to the priority assigned to the industry, with aircraft and antiaircraft production being given top preference. The government purchased the tools and supplied them to the contractors, which proved to be particularly effective because the government had the power to move the tools from one plant to another according to current needs.[21]

After the war, the government found itself in possession of thousands of such tools. The best ones were selected for installation at the permanent government facilities to replace tools that were old and worn from hard wartime use. This practice was an effective modernization program, allowing the beneficiaries to improve productivity and capabilities at a low cost to the government. Other selected tools were packed up and stored in central facilities as part of the War Reserve. The Navy, for example, stored its reserve at the Naval Ordnance Plant in South Charleston, WV. Whatever tools remained were sold off or otherwise disposed of.[22]

More active steps were also taken to make plans in the event of an emergency. Only four days after Japan's surrender in 1945, the Army and Navy Munitions Board (ANMB) was reconstituted, and it worked informally with the War Assets Administration to plan for the future. In 1947 the National Security Act supplanted the ANMB with the Munitions Board, a statutory agency within the Department of Defense with full jurisdiction "in all industrial matters with which the Armed Forces are concerned," especially in joint procurement planning. In that year, President Truman also created a civilian regulatory agency, the National Security Resources Board (NSRB), to take charge of industrial mobilization as the War Production Board had done in World War II. These two bodies worked separately to prepare industrial mobilization plans, assign priorities to the relevant industries, organize the distribution of critical raw materials in wartime, and supervise the peacetime stockpiling and maintenance of key munitions.[23]

In laws passed in 1947 and 1948, Congress also authorized the creation of a National Industrial Reserve, which consisted of government-owned plants that were not needed in peacetime and could be reconverted to civilian production, but which were considered essential to wartime production. These plants were sold under the "National Security Clause," which prohibited the new owners from altering the layout of the plants and required them to be ready to return the plant to war production within 120 days. Plants that could not be sold under these conditions were retained by the General Services Administration. The government also negotiated agreements with industry; for example, Westinghouse Electric Corporation agreed that, in the event of mobilization, only 10 percent of the company's Essington Steam Division in Philadelphia, a producer of steam turbines and reduction gears for the Navy, would be allowed to continue civilian production.[24]

The National Industrial Reserve formed only one part of the Industrial Plant Reserve, which represented all facilities deemed necessary in the early stages of mobilization. The services retained the plants they owned or had an interest in, including permanent installations (such as arsenals and navy yards) and the active and inactive plants and machine tools held on standby in their own Departmental Industrial Reserves. These latter included aircraft plants, ammunition and gun plants, and shipyards. In 1948, the Munitions Board reported that the Industrial Plant Reserve consisted of 27 permanent facilities, 158 standby plants in the Departmental Industrial Reserves, 182,000 machine tools, and 234 National Security Clause plants in the National Industrial Reserve. Of the standby plants, 48 were owned by the Army, 84 by the Navy, and 26 by the Air Force.[25]

The Korean Emergency

The American military industrial base was largely dormant when the North Korean army crossed the 38th Parallel into South Korea, touching off the Korean War. The United States was unprepared for the surprise attack. U.S. forces based in Japan rushed into action with World War II weapons and equipment. Production was expanded in most areas, but the delay was considerable, and in most instances—with tanks, guns, and ammunition, for example—the fighting ended in 1953 with the soldiers still using the same World War II issue; most of the new weapons and products were not ready, even after 3 years. Significant shortages of ammunition occurred in Korea, leading to the rationing of certain critical items such as howitzer and mortar shells. These shortages, although never quite as serious as some people suggested, nonetheless created a scandal that provoked a congressional investigation.[26]

The efforts at mobilization planning had been only partially successful. The NSRB never had much power or direction and, by the outbreak of war, it was merely an advisory committee to the President. The Munitions Board had too little money to do much stockpiling and was too timid to take away control of procurement and supply functions from the armed services. Neither the Munitions Board nor the NSRB cooperated with the other, and neither played a significant role in industrial coordination during the Korean conflict. That task was eventually assigned to the Office of Defense Mobilization.[27]

The plans prepared by the Munitions Board and the NSRB were of limited value for several reasons. First, the planners had assumed that the next war would be like the last one: an all-out affair, probably in Europe, with the Soviet Union as the likely opponent. No one expected that the United States would become involved in a limited land war in Asia. Neither did anyone expect that the U.S. forces would have to go into action well before they were ready. The 2-year mobilization of World War II had been leisurely by comparison. Then, once the fighting began in Korea, no one expected that it would drag on as long as it did, especially in the wake of the smashing victory at Inchon. The officers in charge of procurement were repeatedly told to expect that the war would end at a relatively near date. That date kept getting pushed back, and the exercise played havoc with the estimation of requirements.[28]

Furthermore, the Administration decided not to conduct a full-scale mobilization. The civilian economy was strong and healthy, and President Truman did not want to disrupt it unduly or risk losing public support for the war, which was never as strong as that for World War II. After the Chinese intervention in the war, the U.S. Government did assume control over some critical materials such as steel, copper, and aluminum, but not to the extent that it did in World War II, and defense production facilities found themselves competing with civilian industry for machine tools and products. The plans that had carefully laid out which firms would do what in the mobilization could not be applied. Often, companies that were expected to fulfill particular roles—to manufacture aircraft engines, for example, or metal parts for ammunition—were fully engaged in civilian production and were not interested in converting to military work. This created bottlenecks that seriously delayed production in industries that required a steady flow of components and that depended heavily on private manufacture. In the ammunition industry, for example, no plants were readily available to produce metal parts, which had been produced largely by private industry during the previous war. The Army established new government-owned, contractor-operated facilities for this work in Scranton, PA, and Riverside, CA, in 1951, but these plants did not begin production for nearly 2 years. The need to re-establish the metal parts industry seriously delayed ammunition production in the early phases of the war.[29]

Shell bodies being heat-treated, Scranton Army Ammunition Plant, Scranton, PA. Source: Scranton Army Ammunition Plant, Scranton, PA.

A second factor hindering the mobilization for Korea was that it took far longer to activate the idle plants than expected. The idea of having the plants available for production had been a good one, but the economy-minded government had allocated too little money to shut down and maintain the plants. Machine tools are precision instruments, and they require careful preparation for storage. This preparation involves flushing the fluids, cleaning the machinery, and treating it with preservatives. The government-owned machine tools laid away after World War II did not receive this treatment. The tools were not cleaned properly, were left in damp, unheated plants, and were packed in heavy grease that had to be painstakingly removed by disassembling the entire machine.[30]

The ammunition plants were in particularly bad shape. While the government had spent some money on other plants in the hopes of attracting buyers for them, it never had expected to sell the specialized powder and explosives works and loading plants. Virtually abandoned for 5 years, the facilities were in dreadful shape. It cost more than $600 million to rehabilitate as well as reactivate the 60 plants put back into service. Additionally, there were delays in obtaining equipment for them, as the plants had to compete with civilian producers for new machine tools. Ultimately, it took from 18 months to 2 years to get production at these plants up to a satisfactory level.[31]

A third factor affecting supplies was that the requirements were much higher than anticipated. The expenditure of ammunition was particularly high, as the United Nations forces relied on firepower to offset the heavy manpower advantages of the Communists on the battlefield. During one week in May 1951, 21 battalions fired more than 300,000 rounds of artillery ammunition. By comparison, 35 battalions advancing to relieve Bastogne in December 1944 fired only 94,000 rounds in 10 days. Many gun crews fired more than 250 rounds per gun each day; on 17 May 1951 the 38th Field Artillery Battalion fired an average of almost one round per gun every 2 minutes for 24 hours. In one 28-day period, X Corps fired 25,000 tons of ammunition, including 1,800 tons in 1 day.[32] The Navy, too, fired extensively at ground targets. By March 1953, Navy ships and airplanes had fired 310,000 tons of ammunition in Korea, only 23,000 tons short of the World War II total.[33]

In spite of the problems with mobilization, however, the production record during the Korean War was impressive. On 8 September 1950, President Truman signed the Defense Production Act, an important law that remains in effect today. Based on draft legislation prepared by the NSRB, the Act authorized the President to regulate the distribution of raw materials and to use Federal money to "make provision for loans . . . for the expansion of capacity, the development of technological processes or the production of essential materials." Furthermore, "when in his judgment it will aid the national defense," the President was authorized "to install additional equipment, facilities, processes or improvements to plants, factories and other industrial facilities." This Act not only promoted the mobilization for the Korean conflict, but it also formed the basis for government material assistance for defense contractors that was characteristic of the 1950s.[34]

The Air Force underwent significant expansion during the war, as Congress voted $10 billion to double its size from 48 to 95 wings. The production of aircraft rose from 2,600 in 1949 to 12,000 in 1953.[35] The Navy was nearly doubled as well, from 683 to 1,130 ships. To build this force, many standby plants and shipyards were reactivated. One such plant was the old Chance-Vought aircraft plant in Stratford, CT, which had sat vacant since the late 1940s when the company moved to Texas. The Air Force purchased the plant in 1951 and provided it to a contractor, the Avco Corporation, which created Bridgeport Lycoming Division (later Avco Lycoming, Stratford Division) to operate it. Bridgeport Lycoming repaired the plant (which had been badly damaged by a flood), greatly expanded the assembly areas, and installed machinery for the manufacture of aircraft engines. The company also built an aircraft test cell in 1953, consisting of large

Forging the Sword: Defense Production During the Cold War

Air Force Plant 43 at Stratford, CT, ca. 1960. Compare this photograph to that of 1943 (first figure). Note the extensive additions, especially to the main assembly buildings at center. Also note the jet engine test cells at left center (at the base of the causeway). Source: HAER No. CT-14, Stratford Army Engine Plant, p 45, Prints and Photographs Division, Library of Congress.

concrete chambers for the testing of engines before acceptance by the Air Force. For many years the plant produced airplane and helicopter engines, and later, reentry vehicles for the Titan and Minuteman missiles.[36]

The government had to offer the facilities because industry was very wary of overexpansion. The aircraft companies remembered too well the lean years of the late 1940s. The postwar market for civilian aircraft had proved weaker than expected, and by 1948 the industry, which had ranked first among all American industries during the war, had dropped to 44th. The fluid, episodic nature of the Korean conflict, which bedeviled military planners and logisticians, also discouraged long-range planning in industry. To provide an incentive to these companies to do defense work and to lure back nonaircraft companies such as automobile manufacturers to mass produce aircraft once again, the government offered the contractors the use of its idle facilities, often as branch plants.[37]

Furthermore, the government was anxious to avoid building new facilities if at all possible. The Air Force refused to supply funds for new construction when suitable existing space was available. With funding much more limited and uncertain than in World

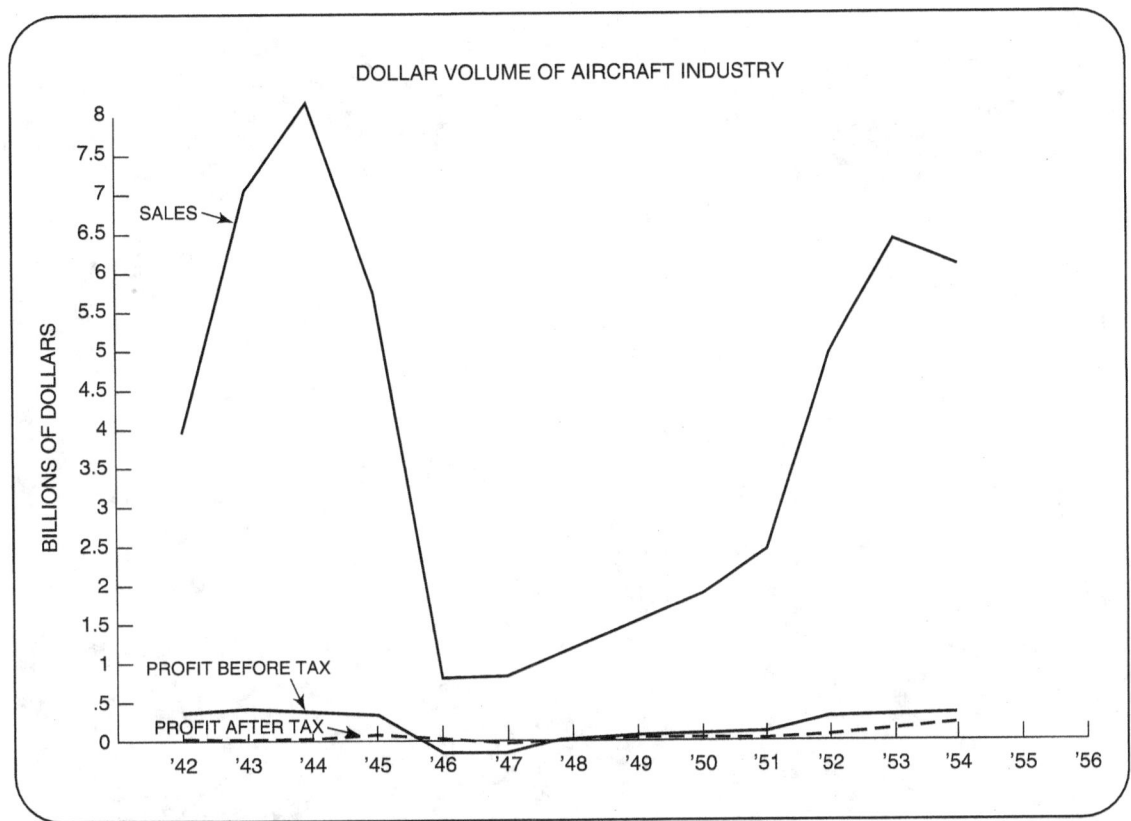

A chart illustrates the increase in aircraft sales during World War II and the Korean War, and the intervening slump of the late 1940s. Source: U.S. Congress, House Committee on Appropriations, Subcommittee for Special Investigations, *Aircraft Production Cost and Profits,* Hearings, 85th Cong., 1st Sess. (Washington, DC: GPO, 1957), p. 2835.

War II, the Air Force preferred to put its money into the new, more sophisticated machine tools then becoming available. Thus, the government supplied the equipment but expected the manufacturers to provide the floor space, and, as in World War II, it offered generous tax amortizing privileges as an incentive. It also encouraged the manufacturers to subcontract as much of the work as possible. In spite of their caution, the aircraft companies did respond. During World War II, they had invested less than 14 percent of the $1.556 billion spent on emergency building construction, but during the Korean conflict they financed almost three-quarters of the $1.085 billion spent. They also subcontracted heavily—sometimes more than 50 percent of a production order.[38]

Tank production was also expanded significantly. Old plants were reopened at American Locomotive and Fisher Body, and several new facilities began production, including the Cleveland Army Tank Plant and the Delaware Tank Plant. Whereas total production in 1950 was 1,742 tanks, the next year it was 2,232, and by 1953 it reached its Cold War high of 12,871 vehicles. Overall, 28,878 tanks were built from 1950 to 1954.[39]

Forging the Sword: Defense Production During the Cold War

Machining the race ring (on which the turret mounts) of an M-60 tank, Detroit Army Tank Plant, Warren, MI. Source: Historical Office, U.S. Army Tank-automotive and Armaments Command, Warren, MI, neg. no. 326.

Endnotes

1. Surplus Property Administration, *Aircraft Plants*, 34.
2. Ibid., 22–26.
3. Surplus Property Administration, *Shipyards*, 11–19, 24.
4. Surplus Property Administration, *Chemical Plants*, 19–21, 27–28, 34–35.
5. Surplus Property Administration, *Aircraft Plants*, 26; Surplus Property Administration, *Shipyards*, 24–25; Surplus Property Administration, *Chemical Plants*, 61.
6. Thruelsen, *Grumman Story*, 122, 237.
7. Surplus Property Administration, *Shipyards*, 16.
8. Gary E. Weir, *Forged in War: The Naval-Industrial Complex and American Submarine Construction, 1940–1961* (Washington, DC: Naval Historical Center, Department of the Navy, 1993), 151.
9. *A History of Watervliet Arsenal, 1813–1968* (Watervliet, NY: U.S. Army, Watervliet Arsenal, n.d.), 144, 146.
10. *A History of Rock Island and Rock Island Arsenal from Earliest Times to 1954* (3 vols.; Rock Island, IL: U.S. Army Rock Island Arsenal, n.d.), 3:481–485.

11. Joiner, *Redstone Arsenal Complex*, 129–134.
12. Carlysle, *Powders and Propellants*, 127–129.
13. Thornton and Prentiss, *The Detroit Arsenal*, 55–56; statistics on tank production supplied by Office of History, Tank-automotive and Armaments Command, Warren, MI.
14. "List of Ordnance Establishments, 1940–1945," in *Directory of Ordnance Establishments, 1942–1948*, U.S. Army Center of Military History, file HRC 331, Ordnance Installations.
15. Trimble, *Wings for the Navy*, 311–322.
16. Joiner, *Redstone Arsenal Complex*, 134.
17. Rowland and Boyd, *Bureau of Ordnance*, 201.
18. Surplus Property Administration, *Chemical Plants*, 20–21; Surplus Property Administration, *Shipyards*, 21–23; Surplus Property Administration, *Aircraft Plants*, 29–32; Cunningham, *The Aircraft Industry*, 182–183; Weir, *Forged in War*, 149–151.
19. Rowland and Boyd, *Bureau of Ordnance*, 433.
20. Ibid; Stanley Vance, *American Industries* (New York: Prentice-Hall, 1955), 133–141. A good description of common World War II-era machine tools can be found in Orlan William Boston, *Metal Processing* (New York: John Wiley & Sons, 1941).
21. Rowland and Boyd, *Bureau of Ordnance*, 434–444.
22. Rowland and Boyd, *Bureau of Ordnance*, 445–447; *A History of Rock Island*, 3:482–483.
23. "Mobilization Plans for Industry," *The Army Information Digest*, 6 (January 1951): 11–12; "Report of the Munitions Board," in *The First Report of the Secretary of Defense*, 1948, 93–94; Steven Rearden, *History of the Office of the Secretary of Defense, Vol. I: The Formative Years, 1947–1950* (Washington, DC: Historical Office, Office of the Secretary of Defense, 1984), 90–91, 129–130; Richard R. Deupree, "Army and Navy Munitions Board Activities," *The Military Engineer*, 39 (June 1947): 246–247.
24. "Report of the Munitions Board" (1948), 98–99; U.S. Senate, Committee on Armed Services, *National Industrial Reserve Act: Hearings*, 80th Cong., 2nd Sess. (Washington, DC: GPO, 1948), 1–8, 35–36; Weir, *Forged in War*, 152.
25. "Report of the Munitions Board" (1948), 99. In May 1950, on the eve of the Korean War, the Industrial Plant Reserve included 54 permanent installations and 400 other plants, of which 105 were idle and 268 were sold, leased, or in government use; "Mobilization Plans for Industry," 15.
26. Jerome G. Peppers, *History of United States Military Logistics, 1935–1985: A Brief Review* (Logistics Education Foundation Publishing, 1988), 186–187; Yoshpe and Franke, *Production for Defense*, 48; U.S. Senate, Committee on Armed Services, Preparedness Subcommittee No. 2, *Investigation of the Ammunition Shortages in the Armed Services*, hearings and report, 83rd Cong., 1st Sess. (Washington, DC: GPO, 1953). For a good summary account of the "ammunition problem" see Doris M. Condit, *History of the Office of the Secretary of Defense, Vol. II: The Test of War, 1950–1953* (Washington, DC: Historical Office, Office of the Secretary of Defense, 1988), 157–161; and James A. Huston, *The Sinews of War: Army Logistics, 1775–1953* (Washington, DC: Office of the Chief of Military History, U.S. Army [GPO], 1966), 630–634.
27. Rearden, *History of OSD*, 95–96, 129–131.
28. Huston, *Sinews of War*, 623–624.
29. Yoshpe and Frank, *Production for Defense*, 48–49; Condit, *The Test of War*, 498–501; Thornton, *Tanks and Industry*, 63–64; Department of the Army, Scranton Army Ammunition Plant, "Scranton Army Ammunition Plant Unit History," n.d. (carbon typescript in USAMHI Library, Installation File), 1–2; Historic American Engineering Record, *Riverbank Army Ammunition Plant*, HAER CA-28, Prints and Photographs Division, LC, Washington, DC, 28.
30. Kenneth E. Joy, "Machine Tools in Reserve," *Ordnance*, 38 (May–June 1954): 925–929.
31. U.S. Congress, Senate Committee on Armed Services, *Ammunition Shortages in the Armed Services*, hearings, 83rd Cong., 1st Sess. (Washington, DC: GPO, 1953); U.S. Congress, Senate Committee on Armed Services, *Investigation of the Ammunition Shortages in the Armed Services*, report, 83rd Cong., 1st Sess. (Washington, DC: GPO, 1953); Logistics Management Institute, *Condition and Operation of DoD Ammunition Production Facilities, Phase II, Task 68-19* (2 vols; Washington, DC: Logistics Management Institute, July 1970; hereafter cited as LMI, *Ammunition Production Facilities*), Appendix 5, 5.
32. Huston, *Sinews of War*, 631–632.
33. Rowland and Boyd, *Bureau of Ordnance*, 520.
34. Leon N. Karadbil and Roderick L. Vawter, "The Defense Production Act: Crucial Component of Mobilization Preparedness," in *Mobilization and the National Defense*, ed. Hardy L. Merritt and Luther F. Carter (Washington, DC: National Defense University Press, 1985), 38–40.
35. Charles D. Bright, *The Jet Makers: The Aerospace Industry from 1945 to 1972* (Lawrence, KS: The Regents Press of Kansas, 1978), 64.

36. Buchanan and Johnson, "Stratford Army Engine Plant," 37–42, 53.
37. Bright, *The Jet Makers,* 11–13, 63; Thruelsen, *Grumman Story,* 245; John S. Day, *Subcontracting Policy in the Airframe Industry* (Boston, MA: Division of Research, Harvard Business Shcool, 1956), 56.
38. Day, *Subcontracting Policy,* 45–48; Bright, *The Jet Makers,* 62–63.
39. Statistics on tank production supplied by the History Office, Tank-automotive and Armaments Command, Warren, MI.

Chapter 5

The Missile Era, 1953–1961

The New Look

The Korean ceasefire found the United States with an expanded publicly owned industrial base. As of June 1954, the government owned 288 plants, of which 249 were in the services' Departmental Industrial Reserve and 39 were left unsold in the National Industrial Reserve. Among these plants were:

- Explosives: 52
- Weapons: 49
- Shipyards: 48
- Aircraft: 47
- Metals: 39
- Chemicals: 11
- R&D and misc.: 42

Of the 233 active plants, 46 were government-operated, 100 contractor-operated, 64 leased for military production, and 23 leased for nonmilitary production. Fifty-five plants were inactive. The total replacement cost of these facilities was $8.66 billion.[1]

Unlike after its previous wars, the United States did not fully and immediately demobilize. Production and spending continued at a relatively high level. In this respect, the Korean War was the most important event in the history of Cold War production, and, indeed, was a watershed in American military history. After this war, the United States embarked on the first long-term peacetime program of military and industrial preparedness. No longer would the country virtually disarm after a war; instead, it would promote the concept of readiness. No longer was the question whether or not to produce, but what to produce and how much.

The emphasis on readiness and having industrial capabilities "in being" was only one hallmark of this period. Others were the shift in resources toward strategic systems such as bombers and missiles and the growing reliance on contractors (especially the increasingly large aerospace firms) for the design and production of complete systems instead of just components. In large part, these changes were a result of the advance of technology. The awesome power of nuclear weapons, especially the new hydrogen bomb, and the central role these weapons played in the Eisenhower Administration's "New Look" strategy of Massive Retaliation, placed increased emphasis on long-range delivery vehicles. The speed with which such vehicles could strike and the power of the weapons they carried reduced the available time for the country to mobilize and defend against an attack, especially after the Soviets successfully tested an intercontinental ballistic missile (ICBM) in

Forging the Sword: Defense Production During the Cold War

1957. As the Assistant Secretary of the Air Force for Materiel told Congress the following year, "The nuclear weapon, in long-range aircraft and in missiles, has now made the military threat a matter of hours or minutes and not one of years."[2] Thus, the United States could not afford a 2- or 3-year period of mobilization as before; a nuclear Pearl Harbor could well be fatal to the country.*

Meanwhile, the growing complexity of modern weapons was changing old notions of defense procurement. The World War II strategy of purchasing large numbers of weapons and vehicles and staggering quantities of ammunition was neither feasible nor desirable. Before the advent of missiles and nuclear weapons, saturation-type weapons—guns, bombs, and rockets—were used in large quantities. These weapons were mass produced and used large quantities of propellant, which represented the bulk of the cost. Missiles and nuclear weapons were much more lethal and expensive, so the government did not need to purchase as many of them. In these weapons, propellant was a very small part of the cost; the bulk of the expense was in the electronics in the missiles, fire-control and guidance systems, and launcher. Similar trends were occurring in the realm of aircraft, ships, and, to a lesser degree, tanks.[3]

The pattern set during World War II, whereby the government financed plants and equipment for the use of contractors, continued in the 1950s. The policy of the Department of Defense was to promote the use of private facilities, except "when it can clearly be demonstrated that private enterprise is unable, unwilling, or not organized to perform the service or provide the products necessary to meet current and mobilization requirements."[4] Few potential contractors were willing or able to invest in the plants and equipment at that time. The government did not directly build new plants for them, but it did permit them to use the ones it had built and improved during World War II and Korea, and it financed new construction through loans and tax incentives. Between 1950 and 1956, the services furnished their contractors with $3 billion worth of new facilities. For example, while the value of Boeing's company-owned facilities increased from $16 million in 1946 to $53 million in 1955, the value of the government's property used by Boeing during the same period grew from $7.4 million to $150 million. By 1959, the government's investment in the Martin Company, which worked on missiles such as the Titan and the Vanguard, was at least $78 million.[5]

Air Force Production and Facilities

The Air Force was at the cutting edge of the changes in procurement and production practices in the 1950s. This position was natural because the great technological changes that occurred during this era had the most impact on the Air Force's capabilities and mis-

---

*As early as 1947, an Army officer warned, "During World War II fully twenty-four months were spent in delaying actions on the battlefields while factories were built and equipped for the production of war materiel before full-scale counter-offensives could even be considered. Will atomic bombs, guided missiles, and similar paralyzing weapons still untried permit the two-year period of grace for our next generation?" (Alden D. Walker, "Caught With Our Plants Down," *The Military Engineer*, 39 [January 1947], 7).

sion. The Air Force inherited the strategic bombing mission of the Army Air Force of World War II, and, with the advent of nuclear weapons, the Air Force took center stage in military planning. In late 1953, the National Security Council issued Directive 162/2, which emphasized the importance of nuclear weapons and air power and which designated the Air Force as the first line of national defense. The "Balanced Force" concept of the late 1940s, in which the three services were maintained in roughly equal proportions to each other, gave way after Korea, as the Eisenhower Administration and the Joint Chiefs of Staff decided to increase the strength of the Air Force from 95 to 140 wings. Money flowed disproportionately to that branch of the armed services.[6]

As the first line of defense, the Air Force was particularly concerned about the faster pace of modern war. NSC Directive 162/2 had eliminated the customary buildup phase of war and projected that the first 90 days of the conflict would be decisive. Planners therefore shifted their emphasis from potential mobilization strength to a current military "force in being," which not only could go to war immediately but would itself deter an aggressor. Therefore, the Air Force would rely, not on standby warplant capacity, but on active production. As of December 1958, only 5 of the 80 plants owned by the Air Force were idle.[7]

More than the other services, the Air Force was affected by the growing complexity of weapons systems, and it took the lead in overhauling its procurement strategy. In particular, the Air Force was the first to adopt the "weapon system" concept and style of management. One definition of a weapon system was "a completely and integrally equipped aircraft, missile, or other flying device with all its airborne and ground equipment necessary to satisfy a military operational requirement." This concept reflected the philosophy that modern weapons were more than simply interchangeable tools; they were entire systems requiring specialized approaches to development, production, maintenance, training, and logistical support. Furthermore, the entire life cycle of the weapon had to be carefully managed, from conceptualization and development to eventual retirement from service. This "cradle-to-grave" approach to the management of technology first made its appearance in the Air Force in 1949, and it was officially instituted in 1951; but it was the report of the Air Force's Cook-Craigie Committee in 1954 that firmly established it.[8]

The weapon system concept reflected a revolutionary change in procurement practices. Before World War II, the traditional approach to aircraft procurement had been for the government to purchase generally standard aircraft components from a variety of manufacturers: the airframe from one company, the engine from another, instruments from a third, and so on. Many of the components were off-the-shelf purchases. That practice had already begun to change by the time of the Pearl Harbor attack, as the aircraft became more complex, the components more specialized, and the tolerances closer. After the war, the range of skills needed to design and assemble an aircraft greatly expanded, especially as electronic systems, or "avionics," became an increasingly critical element of jet aircraft design. By the mid-1950s, the entire aircraft was seen as a single, finely-honed system of well-integrated components, not simply a collection of parts. In the jet age, it was essential that the entire aircraft be designed, built, maintained, and operated with that in mind.[9]

Increasingly, the government was unable to perform the difficult, specialized technical work that was involved in aircraft development, and it came to rely on the prime airframe contractors to carry through all aspects of a weapons program, from design to production. In the new approach to aircraft design and production, all the elements going into the weapons system had to be developed according to an overall design and carefully scheduled program. The technique, introduced by the Germans during World War II, was partially applied in 1950 with the F-102 contract awarded to Convair. Two years later, it was applied fully in the B-52 program, again awarded to Convair. In 1953, the approach was formalized in "weapon system management," in which a single prime contractor was given responsibility for designing, manufacturing, and assembling the airplane. The prime contractor was also responsible for selecting the subcontractors and integrating their products into the system. A single Air Force officer, the "weapon system manager," had charge of the entire program and was responsible for supervising and approving the work. The Weapon System Program Office (WSPO) not only managed procurement and production, but served as a focal point for the program, coordinating the activities of the contractors, Air Force Headquarters, and the operational commands. This approach was applied to missile production as well.[10]

The Air Force significantly expanded its production facilities during the late 1950s. In spite of the buildup for Korea, most of its plants were idle at the end of the war in 1953. The Air Force sought to enlarge its industrial base, not only to meet the needs of its postwar expansion, but to create a reserve capacity two or three times that required for scheduled production. By 1954, 41 of the government's 47 aircraft plants were active contractor-operated or leased plants.[11] Whenever possible, the Air Force adapted its facilities for use in new aircraft programs. The Air Force lengthened runways to accommodate jet aircraft and constructed new, larger assembly areas. It also upgraded the equipment at many of these plants. The Department of Defense encouraged its agencies with custody of machine tools to replace obsolescent items. Because of the emphasis on current production and forces in being, the Air Force no longer needed the reserve tools it kept in storage, so it used them to replace the old or worn tools in the plants.[12]

The Air Force installed much new equipment, partly to accommodate such enormous new aircraft as the B-52, but also because of new manufacturing techniques. The 1950s saw revolutionary changes in the method of producing aircraft. Whereas airframe production during World War II had largely consisted of sheetmetal work, production in the 1950s involved much more machining of parts. The new jets, heavier and faster than the old propeller airplanes, required heavier skins and structural members. The aluminum skin of the B-47, for example, varied in thickness on different parts of the aircraft and had to be machined carefully to produce the proper taper. The structural members, made of strong, light, heat-resisting metals such as titanium, required extensive machining on high-powered, high-torque, low-speed machines, because such metals were much harder to cut than aluminum. While the techniques of assembling the aircraft had not changed much, the process had returned to the handcrafting methods of the 1930s because the airplanes were so complex and packed with electronic equipment. This process was a major factor in the skyrocketing costs of the new aircraft.[13]

The Air Force sought to develop new equipment and manufacturing processes. Immediately after World War II, the service developed some enormous presses of 30,000 tons, based on a German design, for stamping out large airframe sections. Several of these presses were installed in plants and used for many years. The Air Force also experimented with a reusable jig system for assembling aircraft, also designed by the Germans during World War II.[14] To improve speed and reliability in machining, the Air Force pioneered the use of automated machine tools. These machines were developed by the Massachusetts Institute of Technology for the Air Force starting in 1952. An early IBM* electronic computer made the necessary calculations and produced the required instructions, which were encoded on perforated or magnetic tape. The operator prepared the machine by setting the cutting tools in the proper position, clamped on the metal to be milled, and then fed in the tape. The machine performed the work automatically, cutting the metal to extremely fine tolerances. Such machines were in use by 1956. Three were installed in 1958 at the Republic Aviation Corporation plant at Farmingdale, NY, to help in the manufacture of F-105 fighters.[15]

Much of the Air Force's investment went into its missile program. In some respects, the production of missiles was similar to that of supersonic aircraft, using many of the same materials and manufacturing techniques. The body of the missile was made of sheet metal, with or without an interior supporting structure. The Atlas, for example, used no interior tank or supports. The outer skin itself served as the tank and was kept extremely rigid by tremendous pressure, like a steel balloon. On the other hand, the Titan was built like an airplane: its first stage consisted of a frame of welded aluminum, covered by a skin one-sixteenth of an inch thick.[16]

Yet the manufacture of missiles differed from that of jet aircraft in significant ways. Because missiles were largely made of sheet metal and extruded components, the plants did not require the large form presses and drop hammers of the aircraft plants. They also did not require the wide, open bays of the aircraft plants, although some of the larger missiles, such as the Saturn, were assembled vertically and thus required a tall structure with a very high ceiling. Components were manufactured to precise, exacting standards by automated machine tools, and, because of the delicacy and sensitivity of their electronic systems, they were assembled in dust-free, vibration-free plants under rigid temperature and humidity control. For the smaller missiles, at least, the plants more resembled laboratories than factories.[17]

A description of the manufacture of the Atlas is instructive. A plant in Pennsylvania produced the material for the skin, long stainless steel bands a yard wide and less than 40-thousandths of an inch thick, and sent it in rolls to the Atlas plant in San Diego, CA. Each band was joined at the ends to form a ring 10 feet in diameter and then mated with the others, edge over edge, the seams being carefully welded inside and out. As each missile tank was assembled, it was supported by special rings that held it sturdy because it had no integral supports of its own. When completed, the tank was filled with pressurized nitrogen gas, which stiffened the structure and smoothed the skin. It was then removed from the support rings and transferred to assembly docks where it was fitted with electronic equipment, plumbing lines, and a sustainer engine. The booster engine compartment was later rolled into place around the sustainer engine, while an adapter

---

*IBM = International Business Machines.

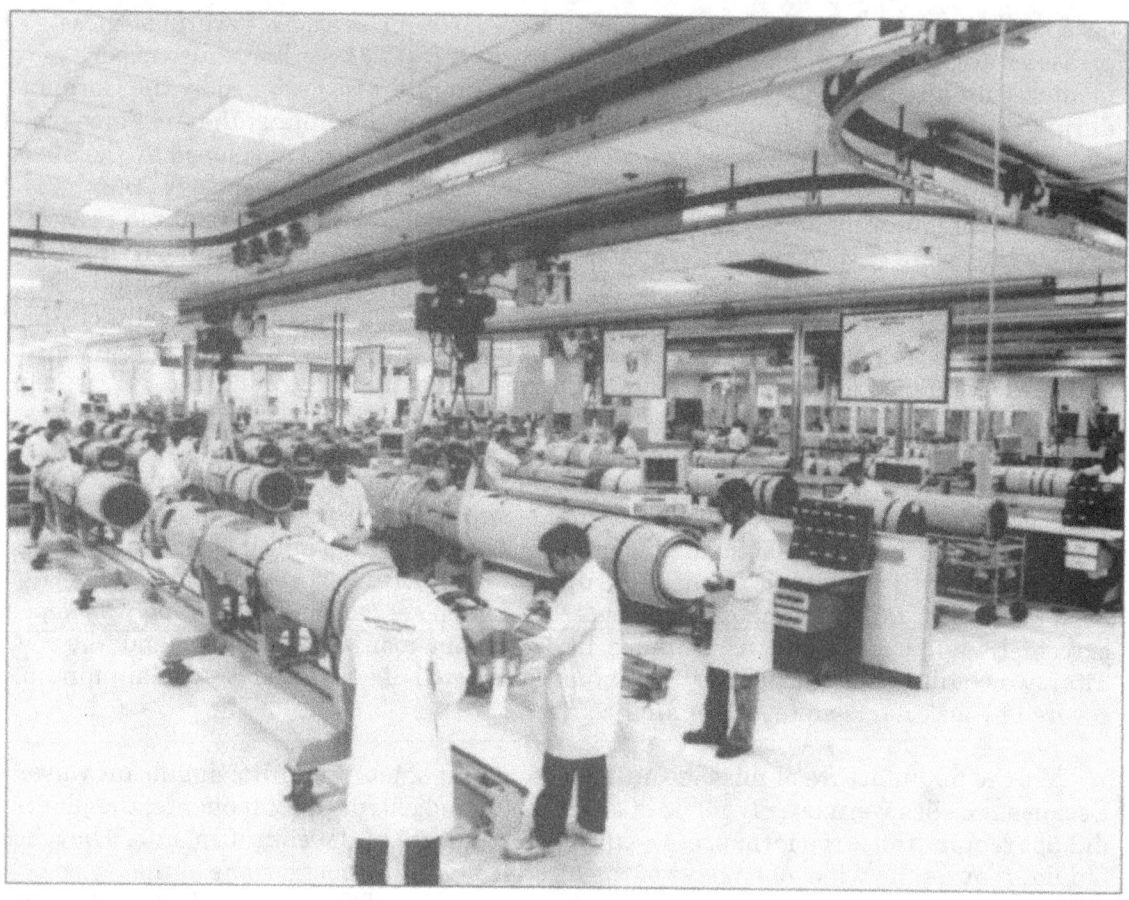

Manufacture of Tomahawk cruise missiles at General Dynamics, Convair Division, San Diego, CA. Source: Naval Institute Photographic Library, Annapolis, MD, file: "Weapon: U.S.: Missile: Tomahawk, Production."

section and a nose cone (produced by General Electric) were attached to the forward end of the tank.[18]

As much as possible, the Air Force tried to adapt existing plants, especially the idle aircraft plants, to missile production. Air Force Plant 19 in San Diego (the old Convair bomber plant) manufactured the first Atlas missiles, while Thor missiles were built in the old Douglas Aircraft plant in Santa Monica, CA. The Air Force expanded the facilities at Air Force Plant 16 in Downey, CA, to produce guided missiles, and it acquired the Blue-Bonnet powder plant from the Army in 1953 for the manufacture of propellant.[19]

Nonetheless, many of the old facilities were unsuitable for missile production, and the Air Force built new ones. Facilities for generating liquid oxygen and nitrogen were established near existing plants in Colorado, California, and Florida. Thor engines were built at

The Missile Era, 1953–1961

Stainless steel sheets used for the skin of the Atlas missile, manufactured in Pennsylvania and here being unrolled at the Atlas plant of the Convair Division, General Dynamics Corp., San Diego, CA. Source: Naval Institute Photographic Library, Annapolis, MD, file "Weapons: U.S.: Missile: Atlas."

The stainless steel sheets have been welded into bands, which are then welded to each other to form the tank of the Atlas missile. A single band is shown in the foreground; multiple band units are shown behind it. At right are the fixtures that hold the strips rigid until they are assembled into the completed tank. Source: Naval Institute Photographic Library, Annapolis, MD, file "Weapons: U.S.: Missile: Atlas."

Forging the Sword: Defense Production During the Cold War

A complete Atlas missile tank, 60-ft long, is being moved by cranes from the tank manufacturing area of the Convair plant to the final assembly area. The supports (seen on the incomplete assemblies) have been removed from the tank, which is held rigid by gas pressure. On the final assembly line, the tank will be mated to the propulsion section, and the control, guidance, telemetry, power supply, tracking, and other systems will be added. Source: Naval Institute Photographic Library, Annapolis, MD, file "Weapons: U.S.: Missile: Atlas."

Air Force Plant 65, a new facility near Neosho, MO.[20] Full production of the Atlas missile took place at a $40,000,000 plant built outside of San Diego. This plant consisted of 6 large buildings and 14 smaller ones on 252 acres. The manufacturing building was described as "an unimpressive box-like building."[21] Another popular account described the plant:

> There is no long production line . . . . During assembly the missiles sit side by side on raised docks designed so workers can crawl around, under, and over the giant birds as the need arises. As a missile is completed it is lifted gently by overhead cranes and placed on a sixty-four-foot trailer which stays with the missile until it is erected in firing position.

The incessant drumming of the rivet gun is gone, leaving the missile factory a comparatively quiet place, the dominating noises now being the whine of the power drill and the clang of the overhead cranes as they roll back and forth, speeding the flow of the heavier components to their rendezvous on the assembly docks.[22]

Navy Production and Facilities

During the 1950s and 1960s, the Navy experienced similar changes in its technology, the impact of which, although somewhat more subtle than those of the Air Force, were nonetheless revolutionary. The most important developments were in propulsion and weaponry. Nuclear propulsion gave Navy ships tremendous cruising range, limited only by the needs of the crew and of the rest of the ship. The Navy took to nuclear power readily; by 1956, only a year after the pathbreaking *Nautilus* underwent her trials, the Navy was planning or building 14 other nuclear submarines, a cruiser, and an aircraft carrier.[23] Nuclear power would affect the Navy as an institution as much as the ships themselves. For example, the emphasis on precision, so critical when dealing with such a sophisticated technology, permeated the thinking, not only of engineers of non-nuclear systems, but of naval administrators generally.[24]

The Navy was also quick to adopt missiles. During the late 1940s the Navy experimented heavily with guided missiles, and in 1951 converted an old battleship, the *Mississippi*, into a prototype Terrier missile ship. Other ships were converted, and in 1959 the first missile frigate, the *Dewey*, was launched.[25] More significant in terms of the Navy's mission was the development of the fleet ballistic missiles (FBMs) in the late 1950s. These missiles, the Polaris and later the Trident, when added to the nuclear-powered submarine, gave the Navy a greater offensive striking power of its own and ensured that the service would possess a solid share of the country's nuclear triad of bombers, ICBMs, and submarine-launched ballistic missiles (SLBMs). The nuclear-powered ballistic missile submarine was one of the most powerful symbols of the Cold War.[26]

Like Air Force jets, naval vessels were affected by the growing complexity of communication, navigation, and control systems. Electronic systems, including radar and sophisticated digital computers, proliferated aboard ship and came to represent as much as 40 percent of a new ship's cost.[27] A Navy study in 1958 revealed that the typical World War II-era destroyer, which had cost $8 million to build, had $12 million worth of electronic equipment installed since the war. Often the equipment developed by the several bureaus of the Navy Department proved incompatible, which further increased the expense. The growth in equipment costs coincided with a sharp rise in labor costs at shipyards. Limitations in funding after the Korean War meant the Navy could afford to build only about 20 ships per year, which was considered half of what was necessary to keep the active fleet at 800 ships. By 1958, the Navy was forced to cut back further on its shipbuilding and overhauling activities. The cost of modern technology had grown too high.[28]

Naval shipyards were also much affected by the new technology. Many, starved for new construction, were kept busy modifying ships. Puget Sound, for example, modified aircraft carriers for jets by installing steam-powered catapults and angled decks. Several shipyards were assigned to perform nuclear construction and maintenance, which required special facilities for the preparation and handling of reactors. Warships of all kinds were adapted to the use of nuclear propulsion. Most nuclear submarines, for example, were constructed at the Electric Boat Division of General Dynamics at Groton, CT, but 10 were produced at Portsmouth Naval Shipyard, NH, starting with the *Swordfish* in 1957. The yard also built a number of important conventional submarines, including the *Tang* in 1951, the *Albacore* in 1953, and the *Barbel* in 1959. In 1962, Portsmouth became the first complete nuclear submarine naval shipyard, with the capability of performing overhauls and repairs.[29]

The facilities at the navy yards themselves were also undergoing changes, as the needs of technology affected their character. For example, two old staples of any large metal-working industrial establishment, forges and foundries, were being closed down. Increasingly, the various components of a ship were made, not out of castings and forgings, but of metal plates and bars welded together. Galvanizing facilities were also shut down—the superstructures of ships were now being made of aluminum, not galvanized steel. Other shops that were no longer needed were sail lofts, pattern shops, and gas manufacturing plants.[30]

Similar changes were taking place among the Navy's ordnance facilities. Large guns were in good supply and no longer needed for the fleet, and new ships relied increasingly on guided missiles. Therefore, the Naval Gun Factory shifted its mission to the manufacture of sundry ordnance items. Some plant activities, such as the forge shop, were uneconomical and were shut down altogether.[31] The Navy did not need much smokeless powder either, and, by the late 1950s, the mission of the Naval Powder Factory at Indian Head was almost entirely directed towards the manufacture of rocket propellant. To reflect that fact, the name of the facility was formally changed in 1958 to the Naval Propellant Plant. Civilian employment at Indian Head declined from its Korean War peak of 3,000 in 1953 to 1,400 in 1958, almost the level before World War II. Work on propellant for the Polaris missile began in 1958, and by 1962 employment was back up to 3,300.[32]

Another Navy facility that made the transition to the missile age was Naval Ordnance Plant (NOP) Louisville, KY. In the years after World War II, NOP Louisville had been all but shut down until the Korean War granted it a reprieve. The plant's management concluded that, to avoid such a fate in the future, NOP Louisville needed to become a well-rounded, flexible facility capable of handling a wider variety of production tasks. During the war, the plant acquired additional lathes, milling machines, profilers, and other general-purpose tools, both new and used. It won some major jobs, including the manufacture of the Navy's 5"/54 gun mount and turrets for the Army's M-47 medium tank. In 1956 it began taking on missile work, including launchers and, later, rocket motors and warheads. Production at Louisville contributed to many programs, including surface-to-air missiles such as Tartar, Terrier, and Talos; surface-to-subsurface missiles such as Rat and Asroc; and air-to-air missiles such as Sidewinder and Sparrow. In 1960, the plant began to work on the launching system for the Polaris. As Louisville's work came to be geared increasingly towards missile work in the late 1950s and early 1960s, it reorganized its facilities, acquiring special-purpose, numerically controlled machine tools

Manufacture of Tomahawk cruise missiles by Convair, San Diego, CA. Note the clean, laboratory-like environment and the high-tech testing equipment.
Source: Naval Institute Photographic Library, Annapolis, MD, file "Weapons: U.S.: Missile: Tomahawk, Production."

like those used by the Air Force and creating an air-conditioned clean room for electronics work. The plant eagerly expanded its range of activities and, by 1966, was responsible for some $160 million in programs for all three services.[33]

The Navy continued to operate its ammunition production facilities, to replace the Korean expenditures, and to modernize the stockpile. By the late 1950s, the Navy's industrial base included 7 ordnance plants, 3 other ordnance factories (for guns, powder, and torpedoes), 6 Naval Ammunition Depots, and 24 contractor-operated Naval Industrial Reserve Ordnance Plants (NIROPs). The Navy operated most of these plants at a low level, to keep as many plants active as possible for the sake of preparedness.[34]

Six facilities produced propellant and explosives, although mostly on a small scale in pilot plants: the Naval Powder Factory at Indian Head, MD (GOGO); the Allegheny Ballistics Laboratory in Cumberland, MD, (GOCO), an experimental propellant research facility; the Naval Ordnance Test Station in China Lake, CA (GOGO), with a pilot plant of the manufacture of experimental types of explosives; NIROP-Henderson, NY (GOCO), manufacturing ammonium perchlorate for jet-assisted takeoff units; NIROP-Dresden, NY (GOCO), producing hydrogen peroxide for torpedoes; and NIROP-Glassmere, PA, making atomized aluminum powder for explosives. Five NIROPs made metal parts for gun ammunition, rockets and bombs; four NIROPs manufactured parts for proximity fuzes; and the depots, ordnance plants at Forest Park, IL and Macon, GA, and NIROP-Sacramento, CA, loaded and assembled the ammunition.[35]

Army Production and Facilities

Of the three services, the Army was the least affected by the new technology. The Army did make some adaptations to the atomic age. For example, it converted the Redstone Arsenal into a facility for conducting research and development (R&D) in rocketry; converted the Radford Arsenal (VA) and the Longhorn Ordnance Works (Karnak, TX) to the production of missile propellant; and obtained a reserve jet engine plant in Michigan from the Navy for the Redstone and Jupiter missile programs.[36] The Army also adapted a plant in Burlington, NC, for its Nike Ajax guided missile program. Originally built as a textile mill in 1927, the plant had been acquired by the government in 1942 for the manufacture of training aircraft and airframe components and for the rebuilding of tanks. In 1946 it was leased by the Western Electric Company, which made electronic equipment, including gun directors for the Navy. In 1952 the company began producing the guidance systems for the Nike Ajax and, later, the Nike Zeus. The facility also assembled and tested missiles, and was designated the Tarheel Army Missile Plant in 1963. The structures encompassed by the plant reflected its background. The original buildings were the standard, single-story, industrial types with sawtooth roofs and 50,000 and 70,000 square feet of floor space, respectively. During World War II, Albert Kahn Associates designed several additions to the plant, including a high-bay manufacturing facility. Western Electric further expanded the facility, adding several metal shed assembly buildings. For the missile program, the Army built a large two-story brick and concrete frame building as a test and assembly facility.[37]

Yet the Army depended less on sophisticated new weapon systems than the other services, and those that it did use, such as helicopters, were largely procured from industry using privately owned plants. By and large, the coming of the missile era had less impact on the Army's production base than on that of the Air Force or the Navy.

The Army also followed a different industrial strategy from the Air Force. For munitions, the Army did not need a high level of production. Indeed, for the first 5 years after the Korean armistice, the Army feared building up a large stockpile of items that could quickly become obsolescent, given the fast pace of technological change. The Army therefore sought to maintain the minimum stockpile sufficient to deter a potential enemy and to fight a limited war or, if necessary, the opening phases of a general war. It would balance this relatively small stockpile by maintaining its industrial base in such a shape as to be ready to resume operations in a very short time, so that the stocks could be replenished with the latest munitions before any shortage became severe.[38]

Learning the lesson of the Korean mobilization, the Army sought to keep as many plants in operation as possible, at the lowest level possible. For example, in the 19 active ammunition plants in 1957, only 50 of 183 production lines were kept operating. In

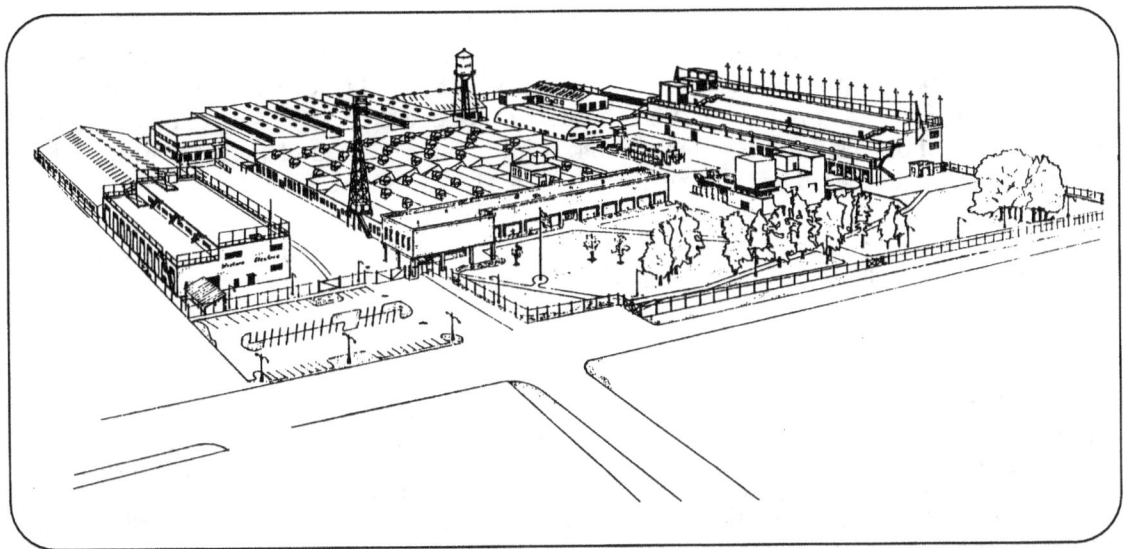

Tarheel Army Missile Plant, Burlington, NC. The Nike test buildings are shown at the right and left sides of the illustration. Source: HAER No. NC-15, Tarheel Army Missile Plant, p 26, Prints and Photographs Division, Library of Congress.

several idle explosives plants, the Army rehabilitated the TNT lines so that, upon emergency activation, the lines could be made operational as quickly as possible. The Army expected that these plants could be started up in 4 months, one-third the time required for Korea. The loading plants could be ready 2 months after that, in time to take the output from the explosives plants.[39]

In 1958, the Army's production base consisted of 74 plants, of which half were active. Of these 74 plants, 62 were managed by the Ordnance Department, including 35 engaged in or reserved for ammunition production; 11 in the tank-automotive program; 10 in weapons and fire-control programs, and 6 in the missile program. Of the rest, 9 belonged to the Chemical Corps, 2 to the Signal Corps, and 1 to the Quartermaster Corps. Of the 36 active plants, 17 were government-operated and 19 were contractor-operated; of the 38 inactive plants, 4 were to be GOGOs and 34 were to be GOCOs upon activation.[40]

By the end of 1958, the Army's procurement strategy had changed somewhat. The launch of Sputnik the previous year had made it evident that the industrial base was vulnerable to a devastating attack by nuclear ICBMs and that the government could not count on production under such circumstances. Therefore, the policy was to have sufficient stocks on hand to fight a war without the industrial base if necessary and to be able to fight a limited war with very little warning. Emphasis was still placed on maintaining the inactive production facilities in a high state of readiness, except for facilities needed only for a general war, which were to be maintained at a low level of readiness.[41]

Whatever the stated policy of the Army, the overriding fact is that, with the lion's share of defense dollars going to the Air Force and to the nuclear weapons and missile programs, the period from the end of the Korean War to the large-scale buildup in Vietnam was one of retrenchment. By 1958 the Army had declared 17 plants excess and was in the process of disposing of them. By 1964, it had disposed of another 19 plants. Part of this decline was the result of the Army's belief, as the Assistant Secretary of the Army for Logistics put it in 1957, that "consumption of conventional ammunition in a future war if atomics are used might be reduced by around 25 percent,"[42] but, for the most part, the disposal of these industrial sites seems to have been due to fiscal austerity.[43]

Endnotes

1. *Production,* vol. 13 of *The Economics of National Security* (Washington, DC.: The Industrial College of the Armed Forces, 1957), 76–78; hereafter cited as *Production* (ICAF). For somewhat different figures see the *Semiannual Report of the Secretary of Defense* (Washington, DC: GPO, 1955), 34.
2. Statement of Dudley C. Sharp, 2 Dec. 1958, in U.S. House Committee on Armed Services, Subcommittee on Special Investigations, *Utilization of Government-Owned Plants and Facilities,* hearings, 85th Cong., 2nd Sess. (Washington, DC: GPO, 1959; hereafter cited as HASC, *Utilization of Government-Owned Plants),* 1146. See also Termena et al., *Logistics,* 108–109.
3. U.S. House Committee on Armed Services, Subcommittee for Special Investigations, *Utilization of Naval Powder Factory, Indian Head, MD,* hearings and report (Washington, DC: GPO, 1958), 547–548.
4. Dept. of Defense Directive 4275.2, "Industrial Facilities Funded from Procurement and Production Appropriations," Nov. 1954 (rev. 6 Oct. 1956), as quoted in HASC, *Utilization of Government-Owned Plants,* 1088.
5. Yoshpe and Franke, *Production for Defense,* 44–45; *Production* (ICAF), 75–76; U.S. House Committee on Armed Services, Subcommittee for Special Investigations, *Weapons System Management and Team System Concept in Government Contracting: Hearings,* 86th Cong., 1st Sess. (Washington, DC: GPO, 1959; hereafter cited as HASC, *Weapons System Management),* 593; U.S. House Committee on Armed Services, Subcommittee for Special Investigations, *Aircraft Production Costs and Profits,* hearings, 85th Cong., 1st Sess. (Washington, DC: GPO, 1957), 1804–5.
6. Termena et al., *Logistics,* 110.
7. HASC, *Utilization of Government-Owned Plants,* 1146.
8. Michael H. Gorn, *Vulcan's Forge: The Making of an Air Force Command for Weapons Acquisition (1950–1985),* (Andrews AFB, MD: Office of History, Headquarters, Air Force Systems Command, 1989), 27–29; Lois E. Walker and Shelby E. Wickham, *From Huffman Prairie to the Moon: The History of Wright-Patterson Air Force Base* (Wright-Patterson AFB, OH: Air Force Logistics Command, n.d.), 362–363.
9. Bright, *The Jet Makers,* 67; HASC, *Weapons System Management,* esp. 4–21, 482–486.
10. HASC, *Weapon System Management,* 4–21, 482–486; Termena et al., *Logistics,* 128–130; Walker and Wickham, *Wright-Patterson,* 362–363, 382.
11. U.S. Senate Committee on Armed Services, Preparedness Subcommittee No. 1, *Aircraft Procurement,* hearings, 83rd Cong., 1st Sess. (Washington, DC: GPO, 1953), 6; *Production* (ICAF), 78.
12. Yoshpe and Franke, *Production for Defense,* 57; HASC, *Utilization of Government-Owned Plants,* 1147.
13. Bright, *The Jet Makers,* 120–126.
14. Ibid., 122–123.
15. Ibid., 123; Anne S. Harris, "History of the Air Force Plant Representative, Republic Aviation Corporation, Farmingdale, Long Island, New York, 1 January–30 June 1958," Air Force Historical Research Agency, document on microfilm at Air Force History Office library, Bolling AFB, Washington, DC, reel K2279, fr. 45–46.
16. Bright, *The Jet Makers,* 126.
17. Ibid., 126–131; G.R. Simonson, "Missiles and Creative Destruction in the American Aircraft Industry, 1956–1961," in *The History of the American Aircraft Industry: An Anthology,* G.R. Simonson, ed. (Cambridge, MA: M.I.T. Press, 1968), 233.
18. John L. Chapman, *Atlas: The Story of a Missile* (New York: Harper Brothers, 1960), 89–90.

19. HASC, *Utilization of Government-Owned Plants*, 1147, 1262, 1269.
20. Ibid., 1147, 1250.
21. Gladwin Hill, "Factory Opened for Atlas ICBM," *New York Times,* 12 July 1958.
22. Chapman, *Atlas,* 91.
23. Willis C. Barnes, "Korea and Vietnam," in *Naval Engineering and American Seapower,* Randolph W. King, ed. (Baltimore, MD: The Nautical and Aviation Publishing Company of America, Inc., 1989), 277.
24. Ibid., 279–80. See also Richard G. Hewlett and Francis Duncan, *The Nuclear Navy, 1946–1962* (Chicago, IL: University of Chicago Press, 1974); Francis Duncan, *Rickover and the Nuclear Navy: The Discipline of Technology* (Annapolis, MD: Naval Institute Press, 1990).
25. Barnes, "Korea and Vietnam," 288–289.
26. For the development of the Polaris, see ibid., 289–290; Harvey Sapolsky, *The Polaris System Development: Bureaucratic and Programmatic Success in Government* (Cambridge, MA: Harvard University Press, 1972).
27. Barnes, "Korea and Vietnam," 292–294.
28. U.S. House Committee on Armed Services, Special Subcommittee on Utilization of Naval Shipyard Facilities, *Utilization of Naval Shipyard Facilities,* hearings, 87th Cong., 1st Sess. (Washington, DC: GPO, 1961), 2803–2805.
29. *Portsmouth Naval Shipyard,* n.p.
30. HASC, *Utilization of Naval Shipyard Facilities,* 2743–2745.
31. HASC, *Utilization of Government-Owned Plants,* 1135–1136.
32. Carlisle, *Powder and Propellants,* 141–143.
33. "A History of the United States Naval Ordnance Plant, Louisville, Kentucky," OPNAV Report 5750–5, 1966, Naval Historical Center, IV 1–2, V 1–4, VI 1, VII 1, VII 1–3, IX 1–2, X 2, XII 6.
34. U.S. Senate Committee on Armed Services, Task Force of the Preparedness Investigating Subcommittee, *Proposed Closing of Certain Government-Owned Ordnance Plants,* hearings, 85th Cong., 1st Sess. (Washington, DC: GPO, 1957), 115–116,128–129, 134–135. There were actually 17 Naval Ammunition Depots, but only 6 were engaged in the production of ammunition; the rest were storage facilities. See LMI, *Ammunition Production Facilities,* appendix 7, 1.
35. Senate Committee on Armed Services, *Proposed Closing of Ordnance Plants,* 117–118.
36. Joiner, *Redstone Arsenal Complex,* 133–134; HASC, *Utilization of Government-Owned Plants,* 1104.
37. David G. Buchanan and John P. Johnson, *Historic American Engineering Record: Tarheel Army Missile Plant,* HAER No. NC-15, Prints and Photographs Division, LC, Washington, DC, 12–22, 29–30.
38. Senate Committee on Armed Services, *Proposed Closing of Ordnance Plants,* 35–47; Raymond J. Snodgrass, *Summary of Major Events and Problems of the Ordnance Corps,* July 1955–June 1956 (typed copy in CMH Archives), 86.
39. Senate Committee on Armed Services, *Proposed Closing of Ordnance Plants,* 86–87, 92–93, 98, 100, 107.
40. HASC, *Utilization of Government-Owned Plants,* 1105–1106.
41. Ibid., 1105.
42. Statement of Frank Higgins, 5 February 1957, in Senate Committee on Armed Services, *Proposed Closing of Ordnance Plants,* 5.
43. Snodgrass, *Summary of Major Events and Problems of the Ordnance Corps, July 1956–June 1957* (typed copy in CMH Archives), 8–9; *Annual Report of the Secretary of the Army,* FY 1964, in *Annual Report of the Secretary of War,* FY 1964, 178; HASC, *Utilization of Government-Owned Plants,* 1106.

Chapter 6

The Vietnam Era, 1961–1973

McNamara

The inauguration of President John F. Kennedy and his administration in 1961 promised major changes in the U.S. military. The new Secretary of Defense, Robert S. McNamara, brought new ideas such as rationalizing defense management by using modern, sophisticated planning and accounting techniques based on statistical analysis. During McNamara's tenure, historic changes in military organization took place, including changes in procurement organization, which came to be organized based on a systems approach. In 1962, the Army largely reorganized the seven technical services (including the Quartermaster Corps, Ordnance Corps, and Chemical Corps) into a series of commands. The services responsible for materiel production and procurement, including the Ordnance Corps and the Quartermaster Corps, were combined into a single organization, the Army Materiel Command (AMC). Seven subordinate commands were formed, among them Munitions Command (MUCOM), Weapons Command (WECOM), Missile Command (MICOM), and Mobility Command (MOCOM). MUCOM had charge of munitions facilities, including the Frankford, Picatinny, Edgewood, and later Pine Bluff and Rocky Mountain Arsenals. WECOM had charge of weapons production, including the Springfield, Watertown, and Watervliet Arsenals. MICOM had charge of missile production, including Redstone Arsenal, and MOCOM was responsible for tank production, including the Detroit Arsenal. Four years later, the Navy also reorganized, replacing its historic bureaus—Ships, Yards and Docks, Aeronautics, Ordnance, and so on—with systems commands: Naval Sea Systems (NAVSEA), Naval Air Systems (NAVAIR), Naval Ordnance Systems (NAVORD), Naval Facilities Engineering (NAVFAC).

McNamara also brought to his office a renewed determination to divest the government of its production facilities. This was not a new policy. Since the Korean War, the government had sought to reduce the number of facilities in its inventory, especially the older ones that were no longer useful or essential. The National Industrial Plant Reserve declined steadily during the 1950s, from its high of 236 plants in 1949 to only 13 plants by 1961. Some of these plants had been transferred to the Departmental Plant Reserve of the military services, but two-thirds had been taken out of reserve altogether because they were no longer needed. Meanwhile, contractors were increasingly expected to provide their own facilities.[1]

The disposal of government-held plants continued during the 1960s. The total number of industrial plants owned by the government (including the services) continued to decline, from 261 in 1960 to 216 in 1966. However, the government investment in plant equipment increased, from $7.6 billion in 1962 to $10.4 billion in 1967. Contractors could not or would not buy the tools, which were becoming more complex and expensive. They also feared being stuck with these specialized tools if the current program ended. As during the Korean War, the government was more willing to foot the bill for tools than for floor space.[2]

McNamara particularly questioned the need for the Navy's shipyards and the Army's arsenals, the very foundations of the traditional "arsenal system" of production. Ever since World War II, there had been too little commercial business to keep private shipyards open. Believing that the survival of the private yards was essential to America's military and economic strength, the government began directing more naval construction to those yards and away from the Navy shipyards. Between 1955 and 1961, 83 of the 107 new warships were built by private yards. By fiscal year 1961, 60 to 70 percent of total funding for naval construction (warships and nonwarships) was directed toward the private yards. The Navy's own yards were primarily relegated to maintenance and repair, although the overhaul of auxiliary ships such as tankers was also assigned to private yards in the late 1950s.[3] The Boston Shipyard, for example, started and finished only one new vessel after World War II, an LST.* The yard's primary activity was in servicing the fleet with repairs and overhauls; during the Korean War, it serviced more than 200 ships. Like the Gun Factory, it also busied itself with the manufacture of an assortment of miscellaneous items, such as anchors and chains, propellers, steam fittings, ammunition hoists, and dies and forgings for Watertown Arsenal.[4]

In general, the Navy shipyards were under severe criticism for being more expensive than private yards. Complaints were persistent that their labor costs were higher than those in private yards—which was not borne out by studies on the subject—and claims were made that the latter could do the work of construction, maintenance, and repair more economically. The Navy defended the navy yard complex, arguing that if its yards were uneconomical, it was because they could not pick and choose the work they wanted to perform. Each yard maintained a full complement of facilities to perform all necessary tasks, and even if not used in peacetime, these facilities would be essential in an emergency, when private yards could not be counted on.[5] Ultimately, few navy yards were actually closed, probably because they were large establishments employing almost a hundred thousand people across the country in 1961 (13,000 at the New York Navy Yard alone)[6] and, in many cases, they were critical to the local economy. The Navy did lose several shipyards during the 1960s and early 1970s, including Brooklyn and Boston, but these yards were old and their facilities too cramped and antiquated for the modern Navy. Other yards, including Portsmouth, were slated to be closed but later given a reprieve.

The Army's arsenals also came under heavy pressure. Although production had remained low during the postwar years (except during the Korean War), they continued in their role of preserving manufacturing expertise. Their peacetime function was largely research and development (R&D), with production left to contractors. For example, the Redstone Arsenal only carried the Redstone and Jupiter missiles through to production engineering. The Army then hired Chrysler to manufacture them in volume at a plant in Detroit. The arsenals determined how the products should be manufactured, making mockups and blueprints and operating low-volume pilot lines. In the late 1950s, for example, the Springfield Armory operated a pilot line for the new M-14 rifle. When the

---

*LST = landing ship tank.

Manufacture of 4-3/4 -in. anchor chain for the aircraft carrier U.S.S. Forrestal. A link is being removed from the furnace prior to being bent. Source: Naval Institute Photographic Library, Annapolis, MD, file " Boston Naval Shipyard."

production engineering was finalized, the Army contracted with industry for full production. By 1960, however, even this very limited production was threatened by the growing movement in the government to avoid competition with private industry. The arsenals appeared to violate the government policy not to make anything that could be provided by industry.[7] Furthermore, their research and development mission was jeopardized by the weapon system concept, which dictated that R&D should be performed by prospective manufacturers themselves. By 1958, 90 percent of the Army's R&D was already being performed by industry.[8]

Three arsenals were closed during this period. The industrial portion of Watertown Arsenal was closed in 1967, Springfield Armory followed a year later, and Frankford was closed in 1977. However, arsenals were politically well-connected, and closing them was every bit as difficult as a shipyard. The story of the closing of Frankford is indicative of the difficulty. In 1969, the Army declared its intention to move the R&D activities out of Frankford, to concentrate those activities in fewer installations and, in the words of the Armament Materiel Readiness Command's annual history, to "escape the low ceilings, bad lighting, cramped working space and the lack of air conditioning which, combined

Boston Naval Shipyard, Charlestown, MA. Source: Naval Institute Photographic Library, Annapolis, MD, file "Boston Naval Shipyard."

with an expensive heating system, made Frankford Arsenal an outmoded facility."[9] Local political leaders and the arsenal's unions launched a public campaign that helped prevent the transfer.[10]

Yet Frankford remained vulnerable because of the nature of the Army's reorganization under McNamara's supervision in 1962. That reorganization had consolidated the handling of materiel into systems, each under the responsibility of a specific organization. Frankford manufactured components for guns and ammunition, but was not responsible for any systems. In November 1974, the Army announced its intention to close the arsenal altogether. The City of Philadelphia worked hard to convince the Army to retain the proposed Armament Development Center, if not at Frankford, then at another site in the city. Congress was less sympathetic to the arsenal this time, but one congressman claimed the closure was illegal. Meanwhile, the city and the National Association of Government Employees brought a series of suits against the Army, the last of which was finally dismissed 2 years after the closure was first announced.[11]

Paradoxically, and contrary to the experiences of World War II and the Korean War, the mobilization for Vietnam accelerated the government's divestment of its own facilities. Resources were increasingly diverted to meet the needs of the war at the same time that distaste for public ownership of manufacturing facilities was reaching its height within the government. Defense officials expressed their determination to get the government out of production, which, they said, had a bad effect on free enterprise. Government ownership of facilities, it was said, eroded industry responsibility, subverted competition, and suffocated industry with bureaucracy. In 1966, a Department of Defense directive established its policy "to minimize Government ownership of industrial facilities insofar as possible in consonance with the need to assure economical support of essential defense production, maintenance, and research and development programs." The directive ordered that the government-owned portion of the industrial base would not exceed minimum needs over and above contractor-owned capacity. Private investment would be the normal means of providing for expansion. Government plants would be declared surplus as soon as not needed, although some facilities (such as ammunition plants) were exempted.[12]

The preference for private investment over public ownership of facilities had been official policy since the Korean War, but this time officials were determined to carry it out. "The application of our basic policy is going to be extremely firm with respect to new facilities," declared Robert H. Charles, the Assistant Secretary of the Air Force for Installations and Logistics, in 1967, "and we are going to seek every possible means of divesting ourselves of existing facilities for which government ownership is not required to protect current or emergency requirements."[13] In addition to shipyards and arsenals, a number of other facilities were closed down. The Air Force closed three modification depots (now called Air Materiel Areas, or AMAs): the Mobile AMA in Alabama, the San Bernardino AMA in California, and the Middletown AMA in Pennsylvania. The service also sold a number of its plants, reducing its inventory of facilities from 63 in 1964 to 48 in 1968. The Navy sold a number of plants in its Departmental Industrial Reserve, reducing its own inventory from 111 in 1964 to 78 in 1968.[14]

Vietnam

The large-scale U.S. intervention in Southeast Asia in 1965, and the subsequent escalation of the conflict, brought about another mobilization of the defense industrial base. Among government-owned plants, the munitions industry was particularly active. As in Korea, the requirements far exceeded what the planners had anticipated. As in Korea also, the war was not declared, the mobilization was limited, and the civilian economy was strong and healthy. The government again found itself competing with civilian industry for materials, equipment, and skilled labor, which drove prices up and caused initial shortages and delays in production. The services relied heavily on existing munitions stockpiles until production could get up to speed. Logistics planners were told to expect the war to be over by July 1967. Not only did this hamper the accurate formulation of requirements, but it helped dissuade potential commercial suppliers from taking up military production because they feared the war would be over just as they were hitting their peak.[15]

Forging the Sword: Defense Production During the Cold War

As the U.S. commitment in Southeast Asia deepened, the Army geared up its arsenals and reactivated its standby ammunition plants. The Watervliet Arsenal, for example, received orders for howitzers, tank guns, recoilless rifles, mortars, and grenade launchers. Although most of the arsenal's production lines had been closed in the years after Korea, the machines had been well maintained and stored so as to facilitate their reactivation. By 1967, employment there reached 4,000 workers.[16]

At the start of the buildup in 1965, only 11 of 25 ammunition plants were in operation. Three years later, all but one was. By 1969, the peak year of production, the GOCO plants had 147 lines in operation and employed 121,062 workers.[17] The effort to reactivate the ammunition plants was not without difficulty. Some of the plants had been maintained reasonably well in the years following Korea, but many others were not. Funding cutbacks had reduced the level of maintenance at the latter facilities to a very minimal level of "protective surveillance." Nonetheless, the process of rehabilitating and activating plants went more smoothly than for Korea. It took a TNT plant only 3 months to start up as opposed to 8 months in 1950, and it took 8 months to reach full production as opposed to 20 in 1950.[18]

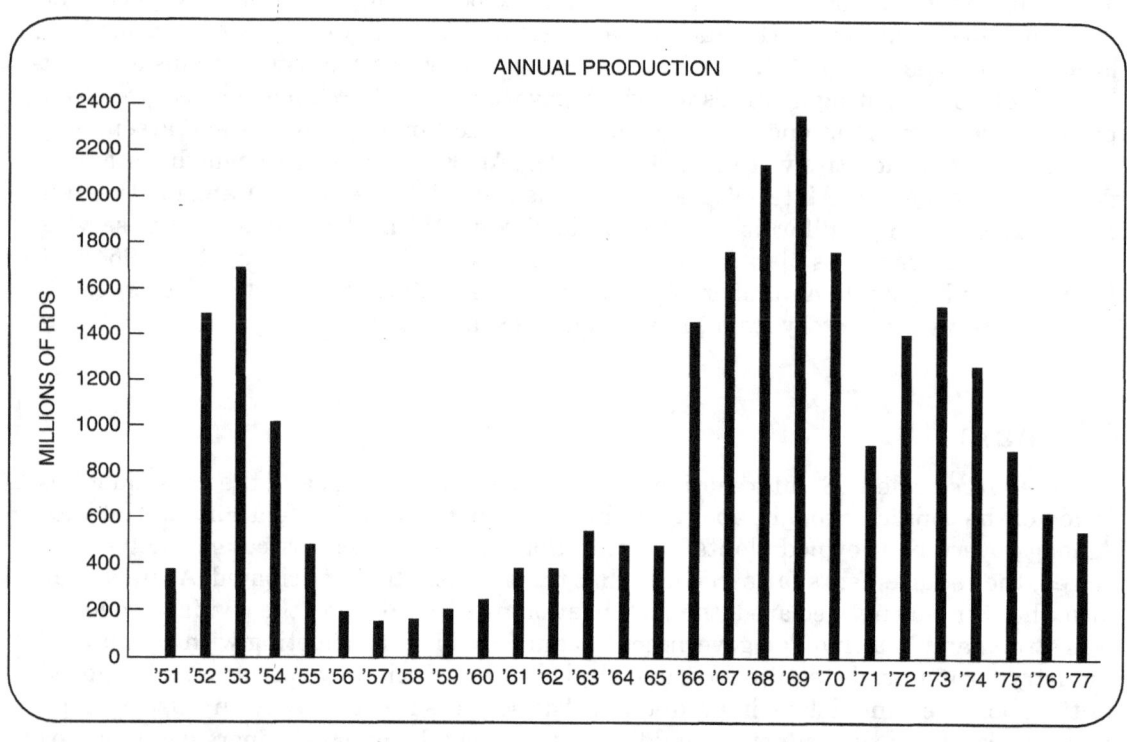

Small arms ammunition production at Lake City Army Ammunition Plant, 1951-1977. Note the peaks for the wars in Korea and Vietnam. Source: U.S. Army Armament Materiel Readiness Command, *Lake City Army Ammunition Plant, Annual Historical Review, 1 October 1977-30 September 1978,* Appendix N, U.S. Army Military History Institute, Carlisle Barracks, PA.

The Vietnam Era, 1961–1973

As the American military effort in Southeast Asia began to decline after 1969, with troops being withdrawn and ground combat greatly reduced, demands for rifle and artillery ammunition dropped off precipitously. From 1971 to 1973, production of 155-mm high-explosive (HE) shells dropped almost in half, from 4 million to 2.3 million rounds; and production of 175-mm HE shells dropped even more, from 791,000 to 182,000 rounds. Only 18 of the ammunition plants were still active by the time of the ceasefire. However, bombing continued at increasingly high levels during these years, as part of President Richard Nixon's effort to force the North Vietnamese to the bargaining table. Thus, production of 750-pound general-purpose bombs rose sharply from 1971 to 1973, from 489,000 to 758,000 per year.[19]

Endnotes

1. National Industrial Reserve, *Thirteenth Annual Report to the Congress,* 1 April 1961 (copy located in National Defense University Library, Fort Leslie J. McNair, Washington, DC); Yoshpe and Franke, *Production for Defense,* 45.
2. Yoshpe and Franke, *Production for Defense,* 50–56.
3. HASC, *Utilization of Naval Shipyard Facilities,* 2714–2715.
4. Frederick R. Black, *Charlestown Navy Yard, 1890–1973* (Boston: Boston National Historical Park, National Park Service, 1988), 661, 665, 706–707, 715–721.
5. John W. Dolan, Jr., "The Naval Shipyard Complex," *Naval Engineers Journal* 82 (December 1970): 26. See also the Navy's testimony in HASC, *Utilization of Naval Shipyard Facilities,* passim.
6. HASC, *Utilization of Naval Shipyards,* 2815.
7. HASC, *Utilization of Government-Owned Plants,* 115.
8. Bright, *The Jet Makers,* 67.
9. U.S. Army Armament Materiel Readiness Command (ARMCOM), *Annual Historical Review, FY 1977* (Rock Island, IL: Historical Office, ARMCOM, n.d.; copy found at USAMHI Library), 1:29.
10. Ibid., 29–34.
11. Ibid., 35–40.
12. DoD Directive 4275.5, "Industrial Facility Expansion and Replacement," 14 November 1966, as quoted in Yoshpe and Franke, *Production for Defense,* 50–51.
13. As quoted in ibid., 51–52.
14. Annual Reports of the Secretaries of the Army, Navy, and Air Force, 1964 and 1968.
15. Pepper, *United States Military Logistics,* 229–230; James V. Murray and John Swantek, eds., *The Watervliet Arsenal, 1813–1993: A Chronology of the Nation's Oldest Arsenal* (Washington, DC: Dept. of the Army, 1993), 260.
16. Murray and Swantek, *Watervliet Arsenal,* 342–345, 362.
17. Pepper, *U.S. Military Logistics,* 230; Historical Office, HQ U.S. Army Armament Command, *Annual Report of Major Activities, U.S. Army Munitions Command,* Dover, New Jersey, Fiscal Year 1973 (Rock Island, IL: U.S. Army Armament Command, 27 June 1974; hereafter cited as MUCOM, *Annual Report;* copy found in CMH Archives, Histories File), 476.
18. LMI, *Ammunition Production Facilities,* 17–21, appendix 5, 5–6.
19. MUCOM, *Annual Report,* 1973, 475–476.

Chapter 7

The End of the Cold War, 1973–1989

Modernization

The period between the Vietnam ceasefire in 1973 and the end of the Cold War in the late 1980s was marked by two contradictory trends, both reflecting, directly or indirectly, the aftermath of the conflict in Southeast Asia. On the one hand, many U.S. government facilities underwent extensive modernization—in most cases, the first since the Korean War or even World War II. Particularly affected were the ammunition complexes and shipyards. Yet, on the other hand, there was a general decline of the nation's defense production base, both private and government-owned. This decline was characterized by the loss of facilities—through divestment or bankruptcy—and a slackening in the pace of technological advancement, brought about largely by the decrease in industrial investment. By 1980, the situation approached a crisis, which the Reagan buildup only partially alleviated. The American shipbuilding industry, for example, all but collapsed during this period.

The efforts towards modernization began in the late 1960s, at least partly because of problems that manifested themselves during the Vietnam buildup. The focus of these efforts was on the ammunition plants and the shipyards. The mobilization for Vietnam was hindered, although not seriously, by the antiquated ammunition facilities. For example, Twin Cities Army Ammunition Plant (AAP),* a producer of small arms ammunition, had difficulty manufacturing the new 5.56-mm and 7.62-mm rounds because the machinery then in place was designed for 0.30- and 0.50-caliber ammunition. Some needed equipment was not available, and much of the old was worn and required extensive repair.[1]

Furthermore, the manufacturing processes had not been improved since the Korean War—or earlier, in some cases. At small arms ammunition plants, for example, the machinery had been installed during World War II and represented World War I technology. The layout of the assembly lines, with the components manually transported between the production areas, was inefficient. The production rate of 100 rounds per minute at the Twin Cities AAP was far too slow for the current firing rate of 6,000 rounds per minute in combat. Newer technology available by the early 1970s could achieve a production rate of 1,200 rounds per minute.[2]

Modernization began in the late 1960s. In 1970, the U.S. Army Munitions Command (MUCOM) completed a study of the munitions production base, and immediately

---

*All Army ordnance plants and works were redesignated "Army Ammunition Plants" in 1963.

launched a major program to overhaul it. In 1973, after criticism of its management by the General Accounting Office, the Army assigned a single project manager to oversee all of the modernization efforts. The Project Manager's Office was transformed into the U.S. Army Munitions Production Base Modernization Agency (MPBMA) in 1979 and had charge of the modernization programs throughout the 1980s.[3]

The modernization programs were intended to provide new, more up-to-date equipment and increase the amount of automation. The arsenals received much needed renovation. At Watervliet Arsenal, a major focus of the modernization effort, a new rotary forge was installed in 1975 to improve the hot forging of thick-walled cannon barrels and the cold forging of thin-walled barrels (i.e., mortars and recoilless rifles). This forge was to be a central component of a new integrated production line that would automate the process of heating and forging the barrels.[4] Another major effort at Watervliet was the Renovation of Armament Manufacturing, or Project REARM, which was intended to improve cannon manufacturing capabilities. The effort included such work as a new $4.3 million shop floor control system to manage inventory and 160,000 lines of tooling. By 1990, the 10-year, $300 million program had increased the arsenal's productivity 27 percent. By this time, the arsenal was using state-of-the-art numerically controlled machine tools, advanced shop control technology, and a flexible manufacturing system to produce such new weapons as the German-designed 120-mm M256 gun for the M1A1 Abrams Main Battle Tank. The Rock Island Arsenal had a similar REARM project.[5]

The government-owned, contractor-operated (GOCO) plants also underwent extensive renovation. The first projects approved were at nitric acid and TNT plants.[6] At Radford AAP, for example, a new TNT line was installed in 1968, the first since World War II. The facility had a capacity of 50 tons per day.[7] In the mid-1970s, the Continuous Automated Single-Base Line was installed at Radford. This $50 million facility completely automated the manufacture of two high-explosive propellants used in artillery shells. The key feature was the use of computers to control the mixing of the explosives, thereby permitting workers to stay out of the plant area altogether. The sensory control of the plant was much more stringent than in typical industrial control systems and allowed the plant to be shut down in the event of even the slightest variation from normal conditions. During the 1980s, a similar multi-based line was installed.[8]

Another modernization program was the Small Caliber Ammunition Program (SCAMP), which involved the installation of new lines to mass produce small arms ammunition, especially 5.56-mm rounds for the M-16 rifle. After considering the acquisition of new machines for the manufacture of such ammunition, the Army decided instead to overhaul the entire manufacturing process rather than make piecemeal, incremental changes. The new system was to use automated, continuously moving lines for a higher rate of production. The various processes—manufacture of bullets and cases, loading and assembling of rounds, insertion of the primer, and so on—were to be performed by equipment submodules that could be replaced quickly for repair and maintenance without halting production. Output was to be 1,200 components per minute. One account described this system as "a breakthrough in the production and inspection of small caliber ammunition. It is an ultra high speed, fully automated process using the latest industrial technology such as solid state electronics, fiber optics and lasers."[9] The SCAMP Management Office was opened at Frankford Arsenal in 1970, and the first contracts for the equipment were let a year later. Both Lake City (MO) AAP and Twin Cities AAP took part in the program.[10]

The most notable development in this period was the construction of a new ammunition plant, the first since the Korean War. The Mississippi AAP in southern Mississippi was established to manufacture a new artillery round, the 155-mm M483 shell, which contained a cargo of grenades as a submunition. Mississippi was to be the first integrated ammunition plant, with facilities for fabricating the metal parts and the cargo as well as loading, assembling, and packing the shells. It boasted state-of-the-art automated lines that had been developed by Frankford and Picatinny Arsenals during the early 1970s. Construction began in 1978, and the plant became operational in the mid-1980s.[11]

The Navy also launched its own modernization efforts. During the mid-1960s, the service developed a master plan to modernize the shipyards that were not closed. Between 1965 and 1971, the Navy spent $300 million in improvements. In 1968 it proposed to spend $800 million on an 8-year Shipyard Modernization Program to incorporate the latest shipbuilding techniques in its yards.[12] At Portsmouth Naval Shipyard, for

Aerial view of the Mississippi Army Ammunition Plant, Picayune, MS. The metal parts plants are in the foreground; the load, assemble, and pack (LAP) plant is behind it. Source: Mississippi Army Ammunition Plant, Picayune, MS.

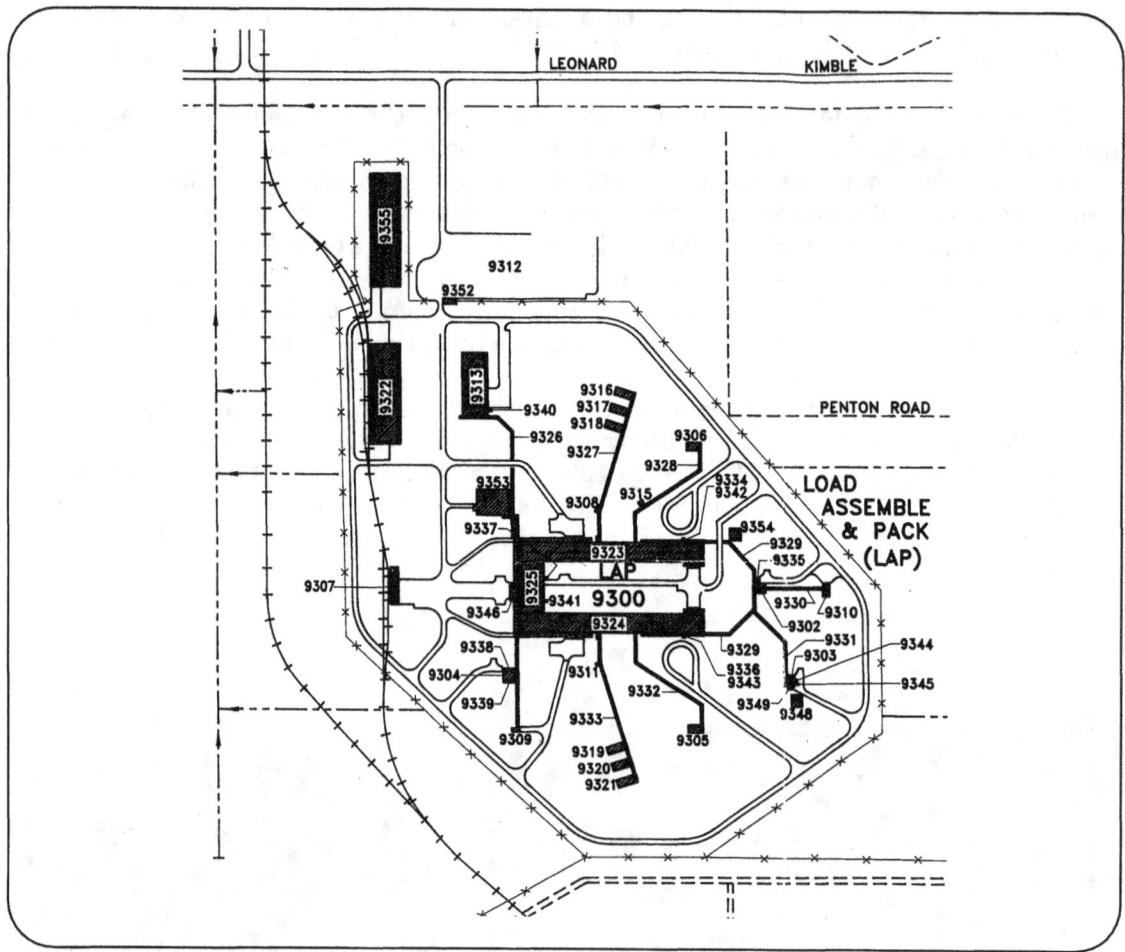

Layout of the LAP plant, Mississippi Army Ammunition Plant. The most dangerous operations are performed in separate buildings connected to the main plant building by covered walkways.
Source: Mississippi Army Ammunition Plant, Picayune, MS.

example, a modernization plan was developed that called for $75 million to be spent on more than 50 projects over 15 years.[13] During the 1970s, the Navy began renovation efforts in its ammunition depots as well. At McAlester Naval Ammunition Depot, for example, the Navy began work on the "A" Plant, which was intended to be a high-volume, fully automated bomb line.[14]

Decline of the Industrial Base

In spite of efforts at upgrading the government-owned production base, the defense industrial base as a whole suffered a decline, especially during the 1970s. In part, this decline was a continuation of the ongoing process of disposing of government facilities. Criticism of government ownership of production facilities had increased during the

The End of the Cold War, 1973–1989

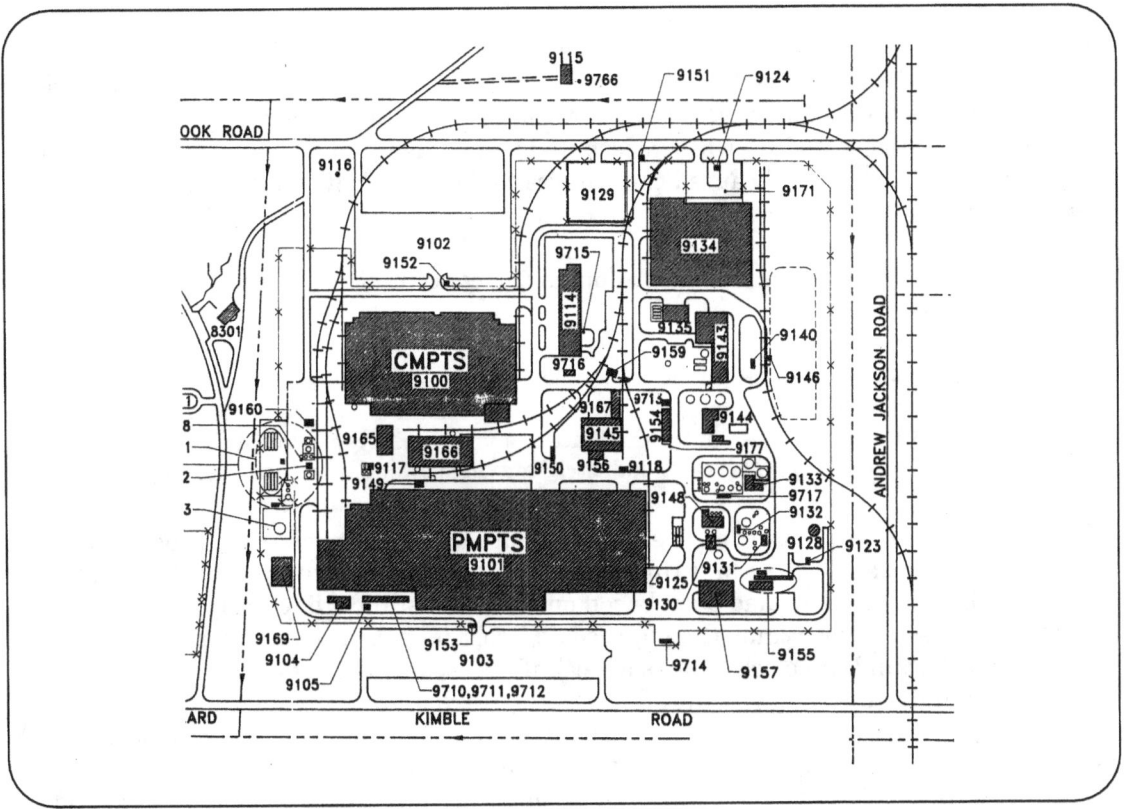

Layout of the metal parts manufacturing facilities at Mississippi Army Ammunition Plant, showing the cargo metal parts (CMPTS) and the primary metal parts (PMPTS) plants. Source: Mississippi Army Ammunition Plant, Picayune, MS.

tensions of the Vietnam Era. In 1967, the Congressional Subcommittee on Economy in Government of the Joint Economic Committee held hearings on military procurement, and the following year it issued a highly critical report condemning the lax government controls over the disposition of its property. In March 1970, the Department of Defense issued a directive establishing a program to phase out its facilities.[15] Renewed attempts to sell the Air Force plants during the 1970s and 1980s were partially successful, but about a dozen could not be sold, usually because the government and the occupying contractor could not agree on a price.

During the 1970s, the Navy got out of the business of producing ordnance munitions altogether. In 1975, the Secretary of Defense designated the Army as the "Single Manager" for the procurement of ammunition, meaning that the Army would be responsible for the procurement, production, and distribution of ammunition for all three services. The Navy's three primary ammunition-producing facilities, Hawthorne Naval Ammunition Depot (NAD), Crane NAD, and McAlester NAD, were transferred to the Army in 1978. Hawthorne was converted to a GOCO and turned over to a contractor; Crane and McAlester continued to be operated by the government.

The problems were not limited to the disposal of facilities, however, but were general throughout the defense industrial base. These problems stemmed from several causes, not the least of which was the belt tightening that occurred after Vietnam. The defense budget dropped sharply during the 1970s, putting severe limitations on procurement. The scarcity of defense dollars was exacerbated by the rising inflation rate, which led to labor unrest and strikes and caused contractors to demand that inflationary adjustments be worked into their contracts.

In addition, mobilization planners adopted the concept of the "short-war scenario." As one critic explained it:

> This concept holds that a short intense war will be fought which will end quickly or escalate to the use of selected strategic nuclear weapons. Under these conditions, the settlement would occur before any effect could be felt from the existence of an industrial capacity which would be turned to support of the war effort. Therefore, industrial staying power . . . has been deemphasized.[16]

This short-war philosophy led the Department of Defense to change its basic policy on the production base for the first time since World War II. Up to this point, peacetime production in a given plant had been based on the 1-8-5 standard: one shift, 8 hours per day, 5 days a week. In wartime, the plant could boost its output by adding shifts and running the lines around the clock, 7 days a week if necessary. This ability to increase production by merely enlarging the workforce, without expanding the facilities themselves, was known as "surge capability." Surge production had long been built into mobilization planning, although, as we have seen, it was not always well executed. In 1977, however, the Department of Defense, believing that surge was unnecessary in a short war (and seeking to save money), decided that it would maintain only enough production capacity to meet the needs of the Five-Year Defense Plan (FYDP)—a peacetime standard. So for example, if one plant could meet the FYDP requirements by running multiple shifts, that alternative was preferred over maintaining two plants on a one-shift basis.[17]

The Army endured labor troubles and restive contractors because of the uncertainties of the post-Vietnam era and the high inflation rate of the 1970s. However, it was perhaps the Navy that suffered the most during this time. The period from 1973 to 1980 was, as commentator Joseph F. Yurso described it, "one of decline, turmoil, and conflict in the field of naval engineering."[18] During the 1970s, the size of the active fleet declined precipitously, from almost 1,000 ships in 1969 to fewer than 500 by 1980—the smallest number since 1940. Many of these ships were of World War II vintage and were finally being retired. Yet ship construction had also dropped off, because of the war in Southeast Asia. From 1963 to 1967, the Navy had programmed 250 new ships, or 50 per year. After 1967, however, the needs of the war were soaking up defense dollars, as was an expensive conversion of the Polaris missile submarines to carry the Poseidon missile. By the early 1970s, the Navy was authorized to build only 13 ships per year, far too few to maintain even the reduced fleet. "The Navy," Yurso noted, "found itself forced to a course of action amounting to unilateral naval disarmament if left uncorrected."[19]

To make matters worse for the Navy, the private yards were enjoying their biggest peacetime boom in their history, thanks to the Merchant Marine Act of 1970. After having pleaded poverty to force the closure of three Navy shipyards and the end of new

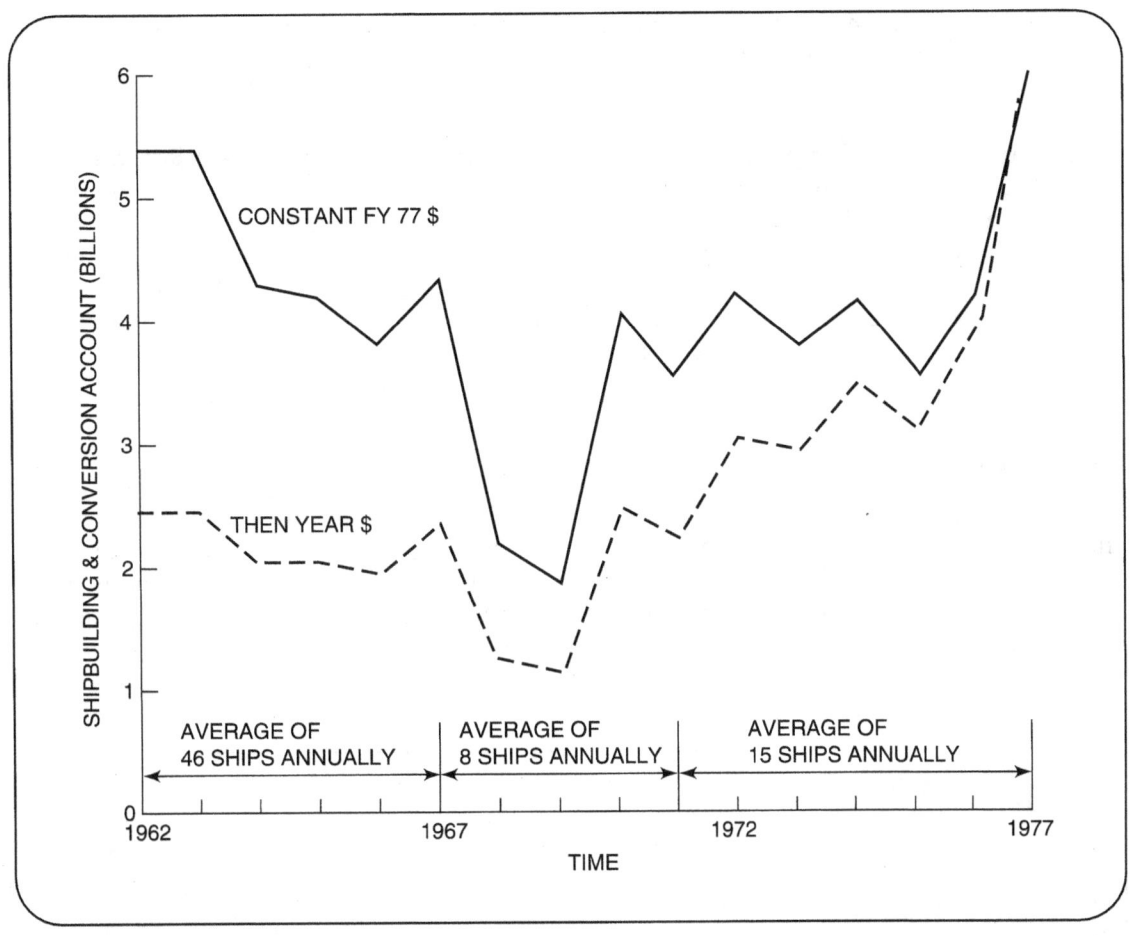

Navy shipbuilding, 1962–1977. Source: Naval Institute Photographic Library, Annapolis, MD, file "Ship construction."

construction at the others, the private yards now demanded more favorable terms from the government or refused Navy work altogether.[20] The Navy did take delivery of the huge nuclear-powered Nimitz-class aircraft carriers starting in 1975, but with the closing of Boston Naval Shipyard and the privately owned New York Shipbuilding Corporation, only one yard in the country, Newport News Shipbuilding and Drydock Company in Virginia, had the facilities to handle such work.[21]

The Reagan Buildup

By 1980, the state of the nation's defense industrial base caused considerable alarm. As early as 1975, Congress had noted the poor condition of the naval construction program.[22] By the end of the decade, several important studies had been made on the problems of the industrial base and the decline of mobilization planning. A congressional

Forging the Sword: Defense Production During the Cold War

committee held hearings on the subject, and the Defense Science Board held a summer study, as it had in 1976. Several writers, most notably Jacques Gansler, worked hard to publicize the problem.[23]

The 1981–1986 buildup during the administration of President Ronald Reagan provided short-term relief to certain sectors of industry. For example, the new administration announced plans for a 600-ship Navy and appointed a strong Secretary of the Navy, John Lehman, to reorganize the service and lead the expansion. Included in this effort was the reactivation of the old World War II-era battleships such as the New Jersey and the Iowa.[24] Procurement funding increased dramatically for other major weapons systems as well, including tanks, missiles, and especially aircraft.

Conclusion

The trend towards closure of facilities has continued—indeed, accelerated—since the end of the Cold War in 1989. Intensifying budgetary pressures have combined with a declining and unclear military threat to cause the government to close or sell many other plants. If not for the expense of environmental evaluation and cleanup, the government

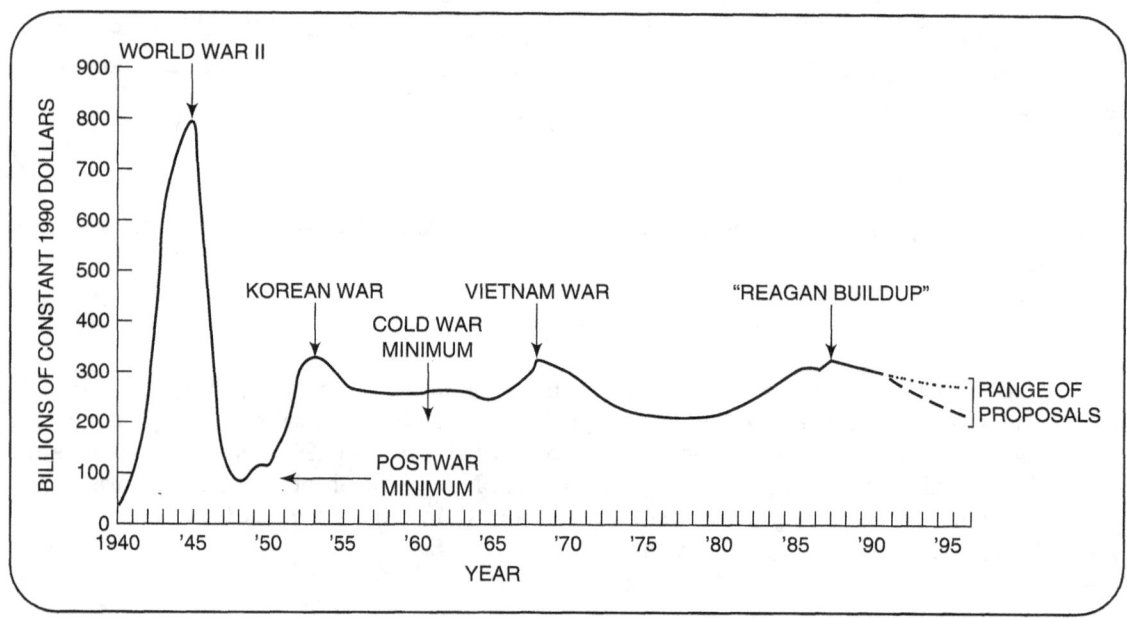

Chart showing defense spending in constant 1990 dollars. Note the peaks during World War II, the Korean War, the Vietnam War, and the Reagan buildup; also note the drop that occurred during the late 1940s and the relatively high level of spending after the Korean War. Source: U.S. Congress, Office of Technology Assessment, *Redesigning Defense: Planning the Transition to the Future U.S. Defense Industrial Base,* OTA-ISC-500 (Washington, DC: GPO, 1991), p. 29.

The End of the Cold War, 1973–1989

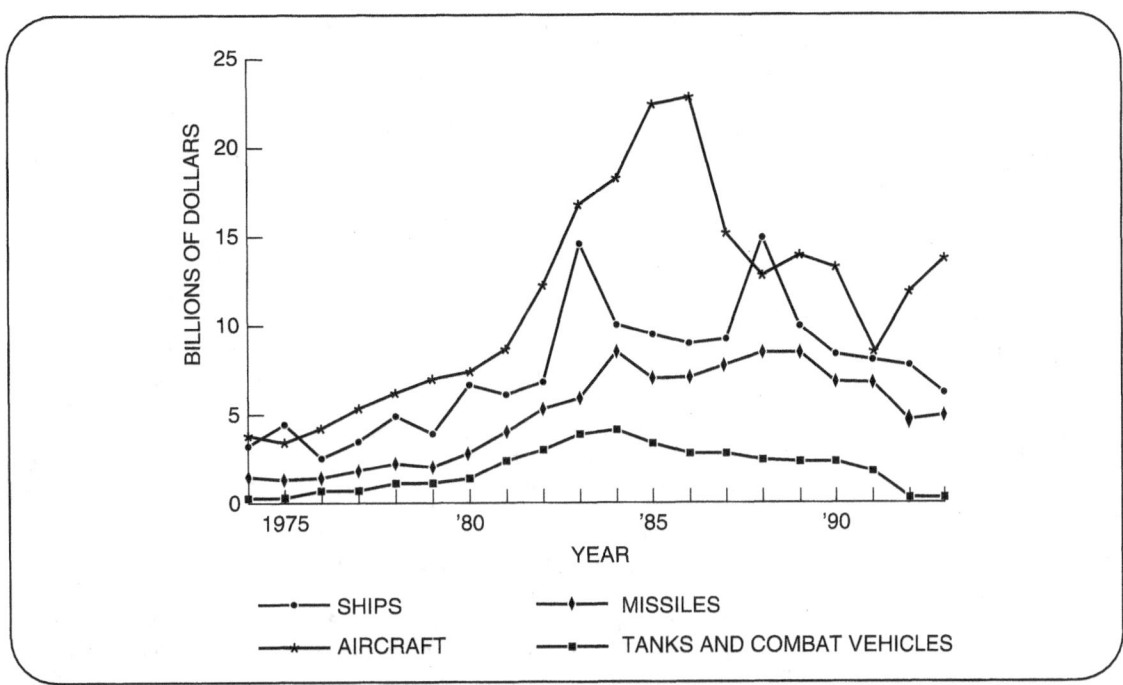

Figure 42. Procurement of major weapon systems, Fiscal Years 1974–1993, in constant 1991 dollars. Source: U.S. Congress, Office of Technology Assessmen, *Redesigning Defense: Planning the Transition to the Future U.S. Defense Industrial Base,* OTA-ISC-500 (Washington, DC: GPO, 1991), p. 56.

might keep very few industrial establishments. As it is, many installations have already been closed as a result of several rounds of activity by the Base Realignment and Closure Commission, bringing a new word into the language: to be "BRACCed" or closed down. Half of the Navy's eight remaining shipyards are being closed, and several of the Air Force's GOCO plants are being sold. Ammunition and ordnance plants are also being disposed of. The current policy is for those plants that are not sold to pay for their own upkeep through rental of the facilities to industry; they are now (in 1996) engaged in seeking tenants and awaiting the possibility of further closures.

Endnotes

1. Twin Cities Army Ammunition Plant, *Annual Report of Major Activities,* 1 July 1973–30 June 1974, CSHIS-6(R2) (copy found in USAMHI Library), 16.
2. Ibid.; MUCOM, *Annual Report,* 1973, 541–542.
3. U.S. Army Production Base Modernization Activity, *Annual Historical Review, Fiscal Year 1987,* RCS: CSHIS-6-R3 (Picatinny Arsenal, NJ: U.S. Army Production Base Modernization Activity, 1987; copy found in USAMHI Library), 1–3.

4. Headquarters, U.S. Army Armament Command, *Annual Report of Major Activities (RC: CSHIS-6(R2)), U.S. Army Armament Command, Rock Island, IL, FY 1975* (Rock Island, IL: U.S. Army Armament Command, 1975; copy found in USAMHI Library; hereafter cited as ARMCOM, Annual Report), I, 356–358; Historical Office, U.S. Army Armament Materiel Readiness Command, *U.S. Army Armament Materiel Readiness Command, Annual Historical Review, FY 1977* (Rock Island, IL: U.S. Army Armament Materiel Readiness Command, 1977; copy found in USAMHI Library; hereafter cited as ARRCOM, *Annual Historical Review),* 180–181.
5. ARRCOM, *Annual Historical Review,* FY 1977, I, 178–180; ARRCOM, Annual Historical Review, FY 1980, 72; "Watervliet Arsenal, Albany, N.Y.," *Ordnance* (November 1990), p 36.
6. U.S. Army Production Base Modernization Activity, *Annual Historical Review, Fiscal Year 1987,* 1.
7. "TNT Plant Dedicated," clipping attached to Radford Army Ammunition Plant, *Historical Summary, FY 1968* (copy found in USAMHI Library).
8. Robert F. Jackubi and William P. Mulokey, "Army's Automated Propellant Plant," *The Military Engineer,* 67 (May–June 1975): 148–150; Ashley M. Neville and Debra A. McLane, *The World War II Ordnance Department's Government-Owned Contractor-Operated (GOCO) Industrial Facilities: Radford Ordnance Works Historic Investigation,* U.S. Army Materiel Command Historic Context Series, Report of Investigations Number 6A (Plano, TX: Geo-Marine, Inc., under contract to U.S. Army Corps of Engineers, Fort Worth District, Contract No. DACA63-93-D-0014, February 1996; copy found at Corps of Engineers Historical Office), 96.
9. ARRCOM, *Annual Historical Review,* FY 1980, 78.
10. Ibid.; Twin Cities Army Ammunition Plant, *Annual Report, 1 July 1973–30 June 1974,* 17–19; ARRCOM, *Annual Historical Review,* FY 1977, I 176.
11. Jeffrey A. Hess, *Historic American Engineering Record: Mississippi Army Ammunition Plant,* HAER MS-4, Prints and Photographs Division, LC, Washington, DC, 17–25; "Mississippi Army Ammunition Plant," *Ordnance* 62 (March–April 1978): 479, 499.
12. "Navy Plans Shipyard Modernization" *Proceedings of the Naval Institute,* 94 (December 1968), 154; Nathan Sonenshein, "U.S. Shipbuilding and Repair—Future Prospects," *Naval Engineers Journal,* 82 (December 1970), 24.
13. *Portsmouth Naval Shipyard,* n.p.
14. U.S. Army Armament Materiel Readiness Command/U.S. Army Armament, Munitions and Chemical Command, *Annual Historical Review,* FY 1983, RCS: CSHIS-6 R# (Rock Island, IL: U.S. Army Armament, Munitions and Chemical Command, 1983; hereafter cited as ARRCOM/AMCCOM, *Annual Historical Review),*15. The program at McAlester was not very successful; see ibid., 15–17.
15. "Aerospace Industries Association, *Government-Owned Facilities and Property* (Washington, DC: Aerospace Industries Association, July 1971; copy found in NDU Library), 1–3.
16. Harry F. Ennis, "Peacetime Industrial Preparedness for Wartime Ammunition Production (Past, Present and Future)," in *The U.S. Defense Mobilization Infrastructure: Problems and Priorities,* Robert L. Pfaltzgraff, Jr., and Uri Ra'anan, eds. (Hamden, CT.: Archon Books, 1983), 56–57.
17. Defense Science Board, *Report of the Defense Science Board 1980 Summer Study Panel on Industrial Responsiveness* (Washington, DC: Office of the Under Secretary of Defense for Research and Engineering, Jan. 1981; copy found in NDU Library), 12–13, 22, 107.
18. Joseph F. Yurso, "Decline of the Seventies," in *Naval Engineering and American Seapower,* 325.
19. Ibid., 325–327, 355–356.
20. Ibid., 329–340.
21. Ibid., 341–342.
22. Ibid., 356–357.
23. Ennis, "Peacetime Industrial Preparedness," 63; U.S. House Committee on Armed Services, Defense Industrial Base Panel, *The Ailing Defense Industrial Base: Unready for a Crisis,* hearings and report, 96th Cong., 2nd Sess. (Washington, DC: GPO, 1980); Defense Science Board, *Industrial Responsiveness;* Jacques Gansler, *The Defense Industry* (Cambridge, MA: M.I.T. Press, 1980); Gansler, "A Ten-Point Program for the Defense Industry," *Sea Power,* 24 (March 1981): 32–47; Gansler, "Rebuilding the Arsenal," *Sea Power,* 24 (September 1981): 31–38.
24. John R. Baylis, "The Six Hundred Ship Navy and Merchant Marine Doldrums," *Naval Engineering and American Seapower,* 361–362.

Defense Production During the Cold War: A Bibliography

Miscellaneous References

The Army Library. *Mobilization: Preparedness, Manpower, Industrial; A Selective Bibliography.* Washington, DC: The Army Library, 1980.

Coletta, Paolo E., ed. *United States Navy and Marine Corps Bases.* Westport, CT: Greenwood Press, 1985.

Shrader, Charles R. *U.S. Military Logistics, 1607–1991: A Research Guide.* New York: Greenwood Press, 1992.

Records Repositories

Performing documentary research in the history of government-owned manufacturing facilities is problematical. Because such facilities belonged to one or the other of the three services, they left behind records of varying quantity, quality, and accessibility. Furthermore, many of the records of the government-owned, contractor-operated (GOCO) plants are in the hands of the contractors. This account focuses largely on records in public hands. It discusses the records in general terms, describing the particular places where records can be found. Pertinent World War II records are described, as well as Cold War-era records. Records relating to specific sites are listed in the Appendix.

The National Archives has a particularly extensive set of records relating to arsenals, ammunition plants, and shipyards because these sites nearly all dated from World War II or earlier, and the records from those periods are more accessible than for the Cold War. A scattering of Cold War records can be obtained for the 1950s and sometimes the 1960s, but the bulk of that era's records are still retained by the services in the Washington National Record Center (WNRC) or in their own files.

Archives I, Washington, DC. The downtown branch of the National Archives holds the bulk of the World War II-era records. Particularly relevant for Cold War industrial research are the Completion Reports of the Construction Division of the Office of the Chief of Engineers, U.S. Army Corps of Engineers (Record Group 77, series 391). These reports include descriptions and plans of all the facilities erected by or under the supervision of the Corps of Engineers and, before December 1941, by the Quartermaster General's Office, including the Army and Air Force GOCO plants.

Archives II, College Park, MD. Archives II includes many records of interest to researchers studying defense production and production facilities. Some of these records are still in the process of being transferred from the Suitland Branch of the National Archives and are not yet available. Among the records of the Office of the Secretary of Defense (OSD) are those of the Office of the Assistant Secretary (Property and Installations) (see entry 179, Correspondence relating to the Acquisition, Expansion, Maintenance, and Disposal of Military Real Property, 1951–1953) and the records of the Munitions Board.

For Army production and facilities, a particularly strong concentration of records can be found in the Records of the Office of the Chief of Ordnance (Record Group 156), especially the correspondence, reports, and other records of the Industrial Division (entries 1239–1332) during the late 1940s and 1950s. Subdivisions include the Ammunition Branch, Guided Missile Branch, Weapons and Fire Control Branch, and Automotive Branch. The records of the Historical Branch of the Executive Division (entries 646–654) includes histories and related documents concerning Ordnance plants and works during World War II and the years immediately after. Other relevant records (mostly World War II-era) include: Ordnance-Sponsored Reconstruction Finance Corporation "PLANCOR" Files, 1941–1945 (entry 774); Records relating to Ordnance-Owned and Contractor-Operated Facilities, 1941–1945 (entry 775); Records Relating to Government-Owned and Government-Operated Facilities, 1945–1953 (entry 776); Records Relating to Facilities Expansion, 1940–1948 (entry 794); Histories Concerning the Office of the Chief of Ordnance and the Development of Ordnance Materiel and Production Facilities, 1942–1944 (entry 948); and Records Relating to the Expansion of Production Facilities, 1942–1944 (entry 949). Finally, the Executive Office Division includes Histories of Ordnance Installations and Activities, 1946–1954, arranged alphabetically by name of installation. Many of these records are still classified, however.

Other relevant Army records might be found in: the Records of the Office of the Inspector General (Record Group 159), which includes correspondence and reports relating to inspections; the Records of the Chemical Warfare Service (Record Group 175), for information on the CWS arsenals and plants; and the Records of U.S. Army Commands, 1942– (Record Group 338), which has records relating to individual installations, although many of these have been transferred to regionalized archives (see below).

Records of the Navy and the Air Force are somewhat sketchier. Relevant Air Force Records might be found in the Records of the Air Force Staff (Record Group 341), which includes material on manufacturing and real estate. The Records of the Secretary of the Air Force (Record Group 340) is a large collection with few good finding aids. Naval records can be found in Record Group 19 (Bureau of Ships), Record Group 71 (Bureau of Yards and Docks), Record Group 74 (Bureau of Ordnance), and Record Group 72 (Bureau of Aeronautics). Researchers examining specific facilities will want to explore Record

Group 181 (Naval Districts and Shore Establishments). These have largely been transferred to the Regional Archives, as indicated in the Appendix.

Regional Archives. In recent years many Federal records have been "regionalized," that is, transferred to or deposited in archives in the region where they originated. These records include many documents related to specific installations, including industrial plants. These archives are part of the National Archives system. The following is a list of regional archives (the location of specific record collections are listed in the Appendix):

1. New England Region (Waltham, MA)
2. Northeast Region (Bayonne, NJ)
3. Mid-Atlantic Region (Philadelphia, PA)
4. Southeast Region (East Point, GA)
5. Great Lakes Region (Chicago, IL)
6. Central Plains Region (Kansas City, MO)
7. Rocky Mountain Region (Denver, CO)
8. Pacific Sierra Region (San Bruno, CA)
9. Pacific Southwest Region (Laguna Niguel, CA)
10. Pacific Northwest Region (Seattle, WA)
11. Alaska Region (Anchorage, AK)
12. Southwest Region (Fort Worth, TX)

Washington National Record Center. Most records dating from the 1960s onward—and many earlier records as well—remain in the custody of the military services or the Department of Defense. The bulk of them are retained in the Washington National Record Center at Suitland, MD. They are held there until transferred into the custody of the National Archives. Access to these records requires the permission of the originating agency.

Army History Offices. Historical records relating to the Army's industrial installations, including unit histories, are scattered. Some records are held at the U.S. Army Center of Military History (CMH) in Washington, DC. The records held in the archives there are collected primarily to support CMH research projects and consist of a smattering of items. Essentially two sets of holdings exist, the histories file and the subject files. The subject files contain relatively few items pertaining to production and nothing from the Cold War period. The histories file includes a few odd annual histories and special studies. Most of them have not yet been declassified and are still restricted, including the annual historical summaries of the U.S. Army Munitions Command, FY 1964–1970 and FY 1973. Only the last one has been declassified.

The U.S. Army Military History Institute (USAMHI) at Carlisle Barracks, PA, holds no official records, but it does have a collection of manuscripts and oral histories. The latter include the Tank-Automotive Command Papers, 1963–1990, which includes oral histories of former commanders and program managers of TACOM; and the Materiel Command Papers, 1964–1990, which includes oral histories of general officers and civilians who served with the Army Materiel Command (AMC). One box of papers relates to the Sacramento Air Logistics Center. More useful is the collection of annual histories held in the library at USAMHI, which is described in the section below on "Command Histories."

Other records are held in the historical offices of the Army commands. The AMC (Alexandria, VA) has some files with a scattering of documents, but more records are held by its subcommands, which have cognizance over the facilities themselves. These AMC subcommands include: the Industrial Operations Command (IOC, Rock Island, IL), which controls the Army Ammunition Plant complex; Missile Command (MICOM, Redstone Arsenal, AL), with records relating to missile production; and Tank-automotive and Armaments Command (TACOM, Warren, MI), with records relating to tank production. The holdings include historical records, including reports, photographs, and copies of annual unit histories.

Air Force History Offices. The Air Force has a more centralized system than the Army. Its historical records are all held at the U.S. Air Force Historical Research Agency (USAFHRA) at Maxwell AFB, AL. Copies are available on microfilm at the Library of the Air Force History Office (AFHO), Bolling AFB, Washington, DC. These records include reports, correspondence, and histories from various installations, including a few reports relating to the Air Force's GOCO plants. The following are some of the relevant records (reports are included in the appropriate section of this bibliography; records relating to specific sites are listed in the Appendix):

Department of the Air Force. "Aircraft Program Data Furnished the Senate Armed Services Subcommittee on Air Force, March 1956" (K168.1501–16; see also –17 and –18).

Department of the Air Force, Deputy Chief of Staff, Materiel, "Memoranda and Position Statements Prepared for Submission before the Symington Subcommittee, March–May 1956" (K168.1501–30).

Department of the Air Force, "Presentation of the Aircraft Production Program to the Aircraft Industries Association, 16 January 1952" (K168.15–35).

Directorate of Materiel Programs, Deputy Chief of Staff, Materiel, "History, January–June 1958: USAF Production Program, FY 1959" (K144.01).

Directorate of Production, Deputy Chief of Staff, Supply and Logistics, "History, July–December 1963" (K144.01, v 5).

Directorate of Statistical Services, *Production Digest: Aircraft, Guided Missiles, Aircraft Engines,* 1956– (K134.399–47).

Secretary of the Air Force, "History, January–June 1952: The Difficulties Encountered in the Heavy Press Program," p. 245 (K168.02).

The History Office at Headquarters, Air Force Materiel Command (Wright-Patterson AFB, OH) also has an archive of relevant materials that include a set of Industrial Planning Project Reports produced between 1946 and 1947 by the Army Air Forces Field Procurement Offices. These reports, 30 to 100 pages long, provide information about the construction, layout, and operation of a sampling of the GOCO plants during World War II.

Navy Historical Center. The Navy has the most centralized collection of historical records, which is located at the Navy Historical Center at the Navy Yard, Washington, DC. These records consist, for the most part, of annual histories (see "Command Histories" below) relating to specific shore installations. The library, which has a good collection of published sources relating to naval history, also holds a small number of unpublished histories dating from the end of World War II, including those of the Charleston and Norfolk Navy Yards; in addition, a few documents and reports relating to the Naval Gun Factory are held in the Special Collections Department (see the Appendix).

Congressional Hearings and Reports

Among the better sources of information on defense production and production facilities are the congressional hearings and resulting reports. In their testimony, witnesses often provided considerable background information relating to facilities, plans, and procedures, although one may wade through literally thousands of pages in order to locate pertinent or useful information. The following list represents some of the more worthwhile sources.

U.S. Congress. House Committee on Appropriations. *Disposition of Real Property Assets at Aberdeen Proving Ground and Edgewood Arsenal, Maryland [and] Contractor Bidding Procedures.* Hearings, 92nd Cong., 2nd Sess. Washington, DC: GPO, 1973.

———. House Committee on Armed Services. *Report With Respect of Naval Shipyards and Their Essentiality to National Defense.* 87th Cong., 1st Sess. Washington, DC: GPO, 1961.

———. Defense Industrial Base Panel. *The Ailing Defense Industrial Base: Unready for a Crisis.* Hearings and Report. 96th Cong., 2nd Sess. Washington, DC: GPO, 1980.

———. *Capability of U.S. Defense Industrial Base.* Hearings, 96th Cong., 2nd Sess. Washington, DC: GPO, 1980.

———. Seapower Subcommittee. *Current Status of Shipyards, 1974.* Report, 93rd Cong., 2nd Sess. Washington, DC: GPO, 1975.

———. *Status of Shipyards.* Hearings, 91st Cong., 2nd Sess. Washington, DC: GPO, 1970.

———. *Status of Shipyards.* Report, 91st Cong., 2nd Sess. Washington, DC: GPO, 1971.

———. Special Subcommittee on Utilization of Naval Shipyard Facilities. *Utilization of Naval Shipyard Facilities.* Hearings, 87th Cong., 1st Sess. Washington, DC: GPO, 1961.

———. Subcommittee on Seapower and Strategic and Critical Materials. *Hearing on Shipbuilding Programs.* Hearings, 95th Cong, 1st Sess., 25 May 1977. Washington, DC: GPO, 1977.

———. Subcommittee for Special Investigations. *Aircraft Engines Production Cost and Profits.* Hearings, 85th Cong., 1st Sess. Washington, DC: GPO, 1957.

———. *Aircraft Production Cost and Profits.* Hearings, 85th Cong., 1st Sess. Washington, DC: GPO, 1957.

———. *Replies to Questionnaires on Aircraft Production Costs and Profits.* 85th Cong., 1st Sess. Washington, DC: GPO, 1957.

———. *Utilization of Government-Owned Plants and Facilities.* Hearings, 85th Cong., 2nd Sess. Washington, DC: GPO, 1958.

———. *Weapons System Management and Team System Concept in Government Contracting.* Hearings, 86th Cong., 1st Sess. Washington, DC: GPO, 1959.

———. House Committee on the Budget. Task Force on National Security and International Affairs. *Shipbuilding, Ship Maintenance, and Claims.* Hearings, 95th Cong., 1st Sess., 4–5 October 1977. Washington, DC: GPO, 1977.

———. House Committee on Government Operations. *Negotiated Sale of a Government-Owned Defense Plant Near Laramie, Wyo.* Hearings, 84th Cong., 1st Sess. Washington, DC: GPO, 1955.

———. Joint Committee on Defense Production. *Defense Industrial Base.* Hearings, 94th Cong., 2d Sess. Washington, DC: GPO, 1977.

———. Senate Committee on Armed Services. *Ammunition Shortages in the Armed Services.* Hearings, 83rd Cong., 1st Sess. Washington, DC: GPO, 1953.

———. *Investigation of the Ammunition Shortages in the Armed Services.* Report, 83rd Cong., 1st Sess. Washington, DC: GPO, 1953.

———. *National Industrial Reserve Act of 1948.* Hearings and report, 80th Cong., 2nd Sess. Washington, DC: GPO, 1948.

———. Preparedness Investigating Subcommittee. *Proposed Closing of Certain Government-Owned Ordnance Plants.* Hearing, 85th Cong., 1st Sess. Washington, DC: GPO, 1957.

———. Preparedness Subcommittee No. 1. *Aircraft Procurement.* Hearings, 83rd Cong., 1st Sess. Washington, DC: GPO, 1953.

———. Senate Committee on Military Affairs. *Progress of Plant Disposal.* Report, 79th Cong., 2nd Sess. Washington, DC: GPO, 1946.

———. *War Plants Disposal.* 3 vols.; Washington, DC: GPO, 1945.

———. *War Plants Disposal—Aircraft Plants.* Hearings, 79th Cong., 1st Sess. Washington, DC: GPO, 1945.

Miscellaneous Reports and Documents

A number of reports shed light on the defense industrial base at various times. While information can be gleaned from them, they are usually too brief to be of use. This is especially true of the reports of the General Accounting Office. A worthwhile source are the annual reports of the Secretary of Defense (1947–), which give a sense of the policies of the Department of Defense regarding mobilization planning and the government ownership of facilities. These reports usually include the reports of the secretaries of the Army, Navy, and Air Force, which often—but not always—discuss the status of the facilities they own, again in fairly brief terms. Mention should also be made of the reports of the Surplus Property Administration in 1945–1946, which provide an excellent, concise overview of the status of the government-owned production base at the end of World War II.

During the 1950s, the Air Force Materiel Command prepared a number of special historical studies on production and logistics. These studies, which are all still classified, are housed at the History Office of the Headquarters, Air Force Materiel Command, Wright-Patterson Air Force Base, OH. Copies are also deposited with the Air Force Historical Research Agency, Maxwell AFB, AL.

Few historical studies are available relating to Cold War production facilities. The Air Force's Aeronautical Systems Center, Office of Environmental Management, Compliance Division (ASC/EMC), is developing Historic Building Inventories for all nine remaining GOCO plants, including Cultural Resources Management Plans (CRMP) for the four plants projected for retention. These studies should be completed in the spring of 1997 and are maintained by ASC/EMC, 1801 Tenth Street, Suite 2, Wright-Patterson AFB, OH 45433-7626.

A number of studies relating to World War II facilities are of interest for Cold War Research. Geo-Marine, Incorporated, prepared an excellent set of studies on the Army's GOCO plants. These studies include a contextual overview (see Kimberly Kane, *Historic Context . . .*) and nine detailed studies of specific ammunition plants, including Badger Army Ammunition Plant (AAP), Indiana AAP, Joliet AAP, Kansas AAP, Radford AAP, Ravenna AAP, Twin Cities AAP, Holston AAP, and Lake City AAP (see the Appendix). These studies provide valuable information on the design, construction, management, and technology in these plants. They are available from the U.S. Army Corps of Engineers, Fort Worth District, and can also be found at the Corps of Engineers' historical library at Fort Belvoir (Alexandria, VA).

R. Christopher Goodwin and Associates, Inc., prepared a historic contextual overview of all World War II facilities currently (1996) in the inventory of the AMC, which includes not only the ammunition plants, but the arsenals, tank factories, Chemical Warfare Service installations, and Naval ammunition depots. This study is available from the Baltimore District of the Corps of Engineers and can also be found at the Corps of Engineers' historical library. Goodwin and Associates also prepared *National Historic Context for Department of Defense Installations, 1790–1940* (Deborah K. Cannan, et al.), which provides further background on a wide range of facilities, not just those relating to production. These volumes can be obtained from the Baltimore District of the Corps of Engineers and also from Naval Facilities Engineering Command (NAVFAC), Planning and Engineering Division, Code 150, Legacy and HARP Programs, Alexandria, VA. Many reports prepared under the Legacy and HARP (Historical and Archaeological Resource Protection) Programs, especially those relating to the Navy, are available at NAVFAC, which also maintains files on Navy installations.

An extremely useful set of reports were those sponsored under the Historic American Building Survey/Historic American Engineering Record (HABS/HAER) Program, copies of which are housed in the Prints and Photographs Division, Library of Congress, Washington, DC. These documents include HABS studies, usually brief descriptions of structures with many photographs, and HAER reports, with more extensive written descriptions and historical analysis of the sites. Nearly all Army sites, including ammunition plants and arsenals, are represented by HAER reports. A few other sites, notably shipyards and miscellaneous factories, are also included. The Army studies, prepared in 1984 by Building Technology, Inc., are an invaluable source of background information, site descriptions, and illustrations, although they do not quite extend to the end of the Cold War.

Air Coordinating Committee. "Report to the Air Coordinating Committee of the Subcommittee on Demobilization of the Aircraft Industry," 11 October 1945. K178.2914-3, Air Force Historical Research Agency, Maxwell AFB, AL.

Air Materiel Command. "Development and Production of Fighter Aircraft for USAF." K201-60, Air Force Historical Research Agency, Maxwell AFB, AL.

Air Materiel Command. "Development and Production of Heavy Bomber Aircraft for USAF." K201-64, Air Force Historical Research Agency, Maxwell AFB, AL.

Air Materiel Command, Aeronautical Systems Center, Manufacturing Methods Division. "Breaking the Producibility Barrier: A Summary of Manufacturing Methods Projects, 1956–1958, AMC TR 58-1. K215.1704-1 (NC), Air Force Historical Research Agency, Maxwell AFB, AL.

Aerospace Industries Association of America. *Government-Owned Facilities and Property: Industry/Government Relationship*. Washington, DC: Aerospace Industries Association of America, 1971 (copy located at National Defense University Library, Fort Leslie J. McNair, Washington, DC).

Bibliography

Air Force Association. *The Fourth Pillar: Reconstitution and the Industrial Base in the Future of the U.S. Military.* Air Force Association, 1 June 1993 (copy located at National Defense University Library, Fort Leslie J. McNair, Washington, DC).

Alling, Frederick, et al. *History of the Air Material Command Support of the Far East Air Force in the Korean Conflict, June–November 1950.* Wright-Patterson AFB, OH: Historical Division, Air Materiel Command, 1950. (Classified; located at Headquarters, Air Force Materiel Command, Wright-Patterson AFB, OH.)

Bickner, Robert E. *Changing Relationship Between the Air Force and the Aerospace Industry.* Santa Monica, CA: Rand Corp., July 1964.

Bowes, Marianne. *Cost Differences in Public and Private Shipyards.* Research Contribution CRC 442. Alexandria, VA: The Public Research Institute, Center for Naval Analyses, 1981 (copy located at Naval Historical Center Library, Navy Yard, Washington, DC).

British Ammunition Productivity Team. *Ammunition: Report of a British Productivity Team on Ammunition Which Visited the United States of America in 1952.* London: British Productivity Council, 1953 (copy located at National Defense University Library, Fort Leslie J. McNair, Washington, DC).

Brunner, Gerti L., and George R. Hall. *Air Force Procurement Practices, 1964–1968.* Santa Monica, CA: Rand Corp., April 1968.

Cannan, Deborah K., et al. *National Historic Context for Department of Defense Installations, 1790–1940: Final Report.* 4 vols. Frederick, Maryland: R. Christopher Goodwin and Associates, Inc., August 1995, under contract DACW31-89-D-0059 to the U.S. Army Corps of Engineers, Baltimore District.

Clammer, Wilbur H. *Allocation and Control of the Materials for Aircraft Production, 1948–1955.* Wright-Patterson AFB, OH: Air Materiel Command, 1956. K201-87, Air Force Historical Research Agency, Maxwell AFB, AL.

Civil Aeronautics Administration, *Military and Civil Aircraft and Engine Production Report, 1950.* CAA Report 101. K196-12, Air Force Historical Research Agency, Maxwell AFB, AL.

DeHaven, Ethel M. *History of the Air Force Industrial Readiness Concepts, 1945–1957.* Wright-Patterson AFB, OH: Historical Division, Air Materiel Command, 1957. (Classified; located at Headquarters, Air Force Materiel Command, Wright-Patterson AFB, OH.)

Greenberg, Edward. *Government-Owned Plant Equipment Furnished to Contractors: An Analysis of Policy and Practice.* Rand Research Memorandum RM-6024-1-PR. Santa Monica, CA: Rand Corp., 1969 (copy located at National Defense University Library, Fort Leslie J. McNair, Washington, DC).

Kane, Kimberly L. *Historic Context for the World War II Ordnance Department's Government-Owned Contractor-Operated (GOCO) Industrial Facilities, 1939–1945.* U.S. Army Materiel Command Historic Context Series, Report of Investigations Number 1. Plano, TX: Geo- Marine, Inc., October 1995, under contract DACA63-93-D-0014 to the U.S. Army Corps of Engineers, Fort Worth District.

Logistics Management Institute. *Condition and Operation of DoD Ammunition Production Facilities, Phase II, Task 68-19.* 2 vols. Washington, DC: Logistics Management Institute, 1970 (copy located at National Defense University Library, Fort Leslie J. McNair, Washington, DC).

Morrison, Clifford. *History of the Industrial Preparedness Planning, 1916–1950.* Wright-Patterson AFB, OH: Historical Division, Air Materiel Command, 1953. (Classified; located at Headquarters, Air Force Materiel Command, Wright-Patterson AFB, OH.)

Morrow, Ardath. *History of Heller Associates Study of USAF Materiel Management Organizations, Aug 1948–Feb 1951.* Wright-Patterson AFB, OH: Historical Division, Air Materiel Command, 1951. (Classified; located at Headquarters, Air Force Materiel Command, Wright-Patterson AFB, OH.)

Novick, David. *The What and the How Are Both Essential to Munitions Production.* Rand Corp. Paper P-273. Santa Monica, CA: Rand Corp., 1952 (copy located at National Defense University Library, Fort Leslie J. McNair, Washington, DC).

R. Christopher Goodwin and Associates, Inc. *Historic Context for the Army Materiel Command's World War II Facilities: Final Report.* Frederick, MD: R. Christopher Goodwin and Associates, Inc., March 1996, under contract DACAW31-89-D-0059 to the U.S. Army Corps of Engineers, Baltimore District.

Reconstruction Finance Corporation. Office of Surplus Property. *Second Advance Listing of Government-Owned Industrial Plants, to be disposed of by Reconstruction Finance Corporation.* Washington, DC: Office of Surplus Property, Reconstruction Finance Corp., 1945.

Reguere, Miguel Angel, "An Economic Study of the Military Air Frame Industry." New York: New York University, October 1957. K112.1-8, Air Force Historical Research Agency, Maxwell AFB, AL.

Self, Mary. *History of the Development of Guided Missiles, 1946–1950.* Wright-Patterson AFB, OH: Historical Office, Air Materiel Command, 1951. (Classified; located at Headquarters, Air Force Materiel Command, Wright-Patterson AFB, OH.)

Snyder, E. Clifford. *History of Production Problems During the Air Force Buildup, 1950–1954.* Wright-Patterson AFB: Historical Division, Air Materiel Command, 1956. (Classified; located at Headquarters, Air Force Materiel Command, Wright-Patterson AFB, OH.)

———. *History of USAF Supply Program and Problems, 1945–1949.* Wright-Patterson AFB, Ohio: Historical Division, Air Materiel Command, Jan. 1956. (Classified; located at Headquarters, Air Force Materiel Command, Wright-Patterson AFB, Ohio.)

U.S. Advisory Committee on Fiscal Organization and Procedures. *Accounting and Management of Inventory of Government-Owned Industrial Facilities and Equipment in the Department of Defense.* Inventory Activities Working Group Report. Washington, DC: n.p., 1954.

———. *Findings of the Survey: Army, Navy, Air Force. Appendix to Report on Accounting and Management of Inventory of Government-Owned Industrial Facilities and Equipment in the Department of Defense.* Washington, DC: n.p., 1954.

U.S. Bureau of the Census. *Census of Manufactures, 1972: Ordnance and Accessories, N.E.C.* Washington, DC: U.S. Department of Commerce, Social and Economic Statistics Administration, Bureau of the Census, 1975.

———. *Census of Manufactures, 1987, Preliminary Report: Industry Series. Ordnance and Accessories, N.E.C.* Washington, DC: U.S. Department of Commerce, Social and Economic Statistics Administration, Bureau of the Census, 1989.

U.S. Congress. Office of Technology Assessment. *Redesigning Defense: Planning the Transition to the Future U.S. Defense Industrial Base.* OTA-ISC-500. Washington, DC: GPO, 1991 (copy located at National Defense University Library, Fort Leslie J. McNair, Washington, DC).

U.S. Department of Defense. *Annual Reports of the Secretary of Defense.* Washington, DC: GPO, 1948– .

———. Advisory Committee on Fiscal Organization and Procedures. Report of the Industrial Activities Working Group. Washington, DC: n.p., 1954.

———. Defense Science Board. *Report of the Defense Science Board 1980 Summer Study Panel on Industrial Responsiveness.* Washington, DC: Office of the Under Secretary of Defense for Research and Engineering, January 1981 (copy located at National Defense University Library, Washington, DC).

———. Office of the Coordinator of Shipbuilding, Conversion and Repair. *Shipbuilding and Ship Repair Industry of the United States: The Annual Report of the Coordinator of Shipbuilding, Conversion and Repair, Department of Defense.* Washington, DC: Department of Defense, 1984.

U.S. General Accounting Office (GAO). *Army Contracting Practices for Conventional Ammunition at its Government-Owned, Contractor-Operated Plants.* Report GAO/NSIAD-85-8; B-216610. Washington, DC: GAO, 1984.

Forging the Sword: Defense Production During the Cold War

———. *Army Procurement: Contracting for Management and Operation of Government-Owned Ammunition Plants.* Report GAO/NSIAD-88-72. Washington, DC: GAO, 1988.

———. *Army's Programs for Procuring Ammunition and Modernizing Ammunition Plants.* Report LCD-75-441. Washington, DC: GAO, 1975.

———. *Assessing Production Capabilities and Constraints in the Defense Industrial Base.* GAO/PEMD-85-3/B-217381. Washington, DC: GAO, 1985.

———. *Construction of Industrial Facilities at Government-Owned Plants Without Disclosure to the Congress: Department of the Navy, Department of the Air Force.* Report B-140389. Washington, DC: GAO, 1970.

———. *DOD's Industrial Preparedness Program Needs National Policy to Effectively Meet Emergency Needs: A Report to the Congress.* PLRD-81-22. Washington, DC: GAO, 1981.

———. *Government Support of the Shipbuilding Industrial Base, Maritime Administration, Department of Defense.* Report PSAD-75-44/B-118779. Washington, DC: GAO, 1975.

———. *Management of Department of Defense Industrial Plant Equipment Can Be Improved.* Washington, DC: GAO, 1976.

———. *Need for Improvements in Controls over Government-Owned Property in Contractors' Plants, Department of Defense.* Washington, DC: GAO, 1967.

———. *Review of the Administration of Government-Owned Property in Possession of Defense Contractors.* Washington, DC: GAO, 1957.

———. *Review of Readiness of Idle Ammunition-Production Facilities, Department of the Army.* Washington, DC: GAO, 1966.

U.S. Office of Defense Mobilization. Advisory Committee on Production Equipment. *Production Capacity: A Military Reserve; A Report to the Director of Defense Mobilization.* Washington, DC: GPO, 1953.

U.S. Surplus Property Administration. *Aircraft and Aircraft Parts: Report to the Congress.* Washington, DC: GPO, 1945.

———. *Aircraft Plants and Facilities. Report of the Surplus Property Administration to the Congress, January 14, 1946.* Washington, DC: GPO, 1946.

———. *Chemical Plants and Facilities. Report to the Congress.* Washington, DC: GPO, 1945.

———. *Magnesium Plants and Facilities. Report of the Surplus Property Administration to the Congress, December 7, 1945.* Washington, DC: GPO, 1945.

———. *Report to Congress on Disposal of Government Iron and Steel Plants and Facilities. October 8, 1945.* Washington, DC: GPO, 1945.

———. *Synthetic Rubber Plants and Facilities. Interim Report of the Surplus Property Administration to the Congress. January 14, 1946.* Washington, DC: GPO, 1946.

———. *Shipyards and Facilities: Report of the Surplus Property Administration to the Congress, January 31, 1946.* Washington, DC: GPO, 1946.

U.S. War Production Board. *Official Munitions Production of the United States by Months, July 1, 1940–August 31, 1945.* Washington, DC: Civilian Production Administration, 1947.

Zimmerman, Sarah. *Procurement in the United States Air Force, 1938–1949,* vol. 1: *Purchasing Phases;* vol. 2: *Production Phases.* Wright-Patterson AFB, OH: Historical Division, Air Materiel Command, 1950.

Command Histories

For most of the Army and Navy sites, and a few of the Air Force sites, some sort of command histories can be found. These histories contain a varying degree of information. Some will only have a basic chronology of the year's events; others include photographs, clippings, and narrative descriptions of the site and its activities. Command histories for Navy sites can be found at the Operational Archives Branch of the Naval Historical Center, Washington Navy Yard, Washington, DC. These usually consist of a general history of the site up until 1958, with annual supplements being added thereafter. Similarly, Army sites produced annual histories starting in 1968; the first of this series, for the ammunition plants at least, give a brief accounting of the history of each site up until 1968. These histories can be found at the History Office of the Industrial Operations Command, Rock Island, IL, and the library of the U.S. Army Military History Institute (USAMHI) at Carlisle Barracks, PA. Command histories at the USAMHI can be borrowed through Inter-Library Loan. The Air Force Historical Research Agency (AFHRA) also has a few biannual or quarterly reports from the Plant Representative Offices or detachments of the Contract Management Division at the individual Air Force plants. These reports are available in hardcopy at AFHRA, Maxwell AFB, AL, and on microfilm at Bolling AFB, Washington, DC. The individual unit histories on file at AFHRA, USAMHI, and the Naval Historical Center are listed in the Appendix under the name of the relevant site.

In addition to the site histories, USAMHI has a number of annual histories of the various commands that were responsible for the production of munitions. These histories are listed here.

Armament Command
    2 vols. (FY 1975)
Armament Materiel Readiness Command
    6 vols. (FY 1976–1980, 1983)

Armament, Munitions, and Chemical Command
    11 vols. (FY 1983–1991, 1993–1994)
Ballistic Missile Agency
    2 vols. (January–June 1960, July–December 1961)
Bell Plant Activity
    1 vol. (October 1963–June 1969)
Defense Clothing & Textile Supply Center
    2 vols. (FY 1964–1965)
Defense Industrial Plant Equipment Center
    2 vols. (FY 1969, 1971)
Defense Industrial Supply Center
    5 vols. (FY 1963, 1968–1971)
Electronics Command
    4 vols. (FY 1971–1972, 1976–1977)
Lockheed Plant Activity
    1 vol. (FY 1969)
Materiel Command (and Materiel Development & Readiness Command)
    18 vols. (FY 1963, 1970–1981, 1988, 1990–1993)
    Operational Reports Lessons Learned (3 vols.)
    Ammunition Center (2 vols.)
Mobility Command
    1 vol. (FY 1965)
Ordnance Missile Command
    5 vols. (January–June 1960 - January–June 1962)
Production Base Modernization Agency
    6 vols. (FY 1982–1983, 1986–1989)
Tank-Automotive Command
    13 vols. (FY 1970, 1972, 1981–1984, 1986, 1988–1989, 1991–1994
    Miscellaneous (2 vols.: Information Brochure; Historical Overview)
Tank-Automotive Materiel Readiness Command
    4 vols. (FY 1977–1980)

Books

Beazer, William F., William A. Cox, and Curtis A. Harvey. *U.S. Shipbuilding in the 1970s.* Lexington, MA: Lexington Books, 1972.

Bethlehem Steel Company. *An Introduction to Shipbuilding, Prepared and Made Available by Shipbuilding Division, Bethlehem Steel Co. Training within Industry, Labor Division, War Production Board, Washington, DC.* Washington, DC: GPO, 1942.

Boston, Orlan William. *Metal Processing.* New York: John Wiley & Sons, 1941.

Bright, Charles D. *The Jet Makers: The Aerospace Industry from 1945 to 1972.* Lawrence, KS: The Regents Press of Kansas, 1978.

Brophy, Leo P., and George J.B. Fisher, *The Chemical Warfare Service: Organizing for War.* Part of the *United States Army in World War II: The Technical Services.* Washington, DC: Office of the Chief of Military History, Department of the Army, 1959.

Brophy, Leo P., Wyndham D. Miles, and Rexmond C. Cochrane. *The Chemical Warfare Service: From Laboratory to the Field.* Part of the *United States Army in World War II: The Technical Services.* Washington, DC: Office of the Chief of Military History, Department of the Army, 1959.

Carmichael, A.W. *Practical Ship Production.* ed. New York: McGraw-Hill Book Co., 1941.

Carrison, Daniel J. *The United States Navy.* New York: Praeger, 1968.

Chapman, John L. *Atlas: The Story of A Missile.* New York: Harper Brothers, 1960.

Clark, Asa A., IV, and John F. Lilley. *Defense Technology.* New York: Praeger, 1989.

Cole, Brady M. *Procurement of Naval Ships: It Is Time for the US Navy to Acknowledge Its Shipbuilders May Be Holding a Winning Hand.* National Security Affairs Monograph 79-5. Washington, DC: National Defense University, Research Directorate (GPO), 1979.

Condit, Doris M. *The History of the Office of the Secretary of Defense, Vol. II: The Test of War, 1950–1953.* Washington, DC: Historical Office, Office of the Secretary of Defense, 1988.

Connery, Robert H. *The Navy and the Industrial Mobilization in World War II.* Princeton, NJ: Princeton University Press, 1951.

Cunningham, William Glenn. *The Aircraft Industry: A Study in Industrial Location.* Los Angeles: L.L. Morrison, 1951.

D'Arcangelo, Amelio M., ed. *Ship Design and Construction.* New York: The Society of Naval Architects and Marine Engineers, 1969.

Day, John S. *Subcontracting Policy in the Airframe Industry.* Boston: Division of Research, Harvard Business School, 1956.

Dobbs, Judy. *A History of the Watertown Arsenal, Watertown, Massachusetts, 1816–1967.* Watertown, MA: Army Materials and Mechanics Research Center, 1977.

Drewes, Robert W. *The Air Force and the Great Engine War.* Washington, DC: National Defense University Press, 1987.

Duncan, Francis. *Rickover and the Nuclear Navy: The Discipline of Technology.* Annapolis, MD: Naval Institute Press, 1990.

Ennis, Harry F. *Peacetime Industrial Preparedness for Wartime Ammunition Production*. Washington, DC: National Defense University, Research Directorate [GPO], 1980.

Farley, James J. *Making Arms in the Machine Age: Philadelphia's Frankford Arsenal, 1816–1870*. University Park, PA: Pennsylvania State University Press, 1994.

Fine, Lenore, and Jesse A. Remington. *The Corps of Engineers: Construction in the United States*. Part of the *United States Army in World War II: The Technical Services*. Washington, DC: Office of the Chief of Military History, United States Army, 1972.

Fogelson, Robert M. *America's Armories: Architecture, Society, and Public Order*. Cambridge, MA: Harvard University Press, 1989.

Fox, J. Ronald. *The Defense Management Challenge: Weapons Acquisition*. Boston: Harvard Business School Press, 1988.

Franklin, Roger. *The Defender: The Story of General Dynamics*. New York: Harper and Row, 1986.

Gansler, Jacques S. *The Defense Industry*. Cambridge, MA: MIT Press, 1980.

Gill, Timothy. *Industrial Preparedness: Breaking with an Erratic Past*. Washington, DC: National Defense University Press [GPO], 1984.

Goodwin, Jacob. *Brotherhood of Arms: General Dynamics and the Business of Defending America*. New York: Times Books, 1985.

Gorn, Michael H. *Vulcan's Forge: The Making of an Air Force Command for Weapons Acquisition, (1950–1985)*. 2 vols. Andrews AFB, MD: Office of History, Headquarters, Air Force Systems Command, 1989.

Gregory, William H. *The Defense Procurement Mess*. Lexington, MA : Lexington Books, 1989.

Herb, Charles Oliver, ed. *Ordnance Production Methods: A Collection of Articles Published in Machinery, Describing Manufacturing Operation on Rifles and Small Arms, Machines Guns, Bullets, Shells, Cartridge Cases, Guns, Bombs, Tanks, and Other Weapons of War*. New York: Industrial Press, 1951.

Hewes, James E. *From Root to McNamara: Army Organization and Administration, 1900–1963*. Washington, DC: Center of Military History, U.S. Army (Washington, DC: GPO, 1975).

Hewlett, Richard G., and Francis Duncan. *The Nuclear Navy, 1946–1962*. Chicago: University of Chicago Press, 1974.

Holley, Irving Brinton, Jr. *Buying Aircraft: Materiel Procurement for the Army Air Forces.* Part of the *United States Army in World War II: Special Studies.* Washington, DC: Office of the Chief of Military History, Dept. of the Army, 1964.

Huston, James A. *The Sinews of War: Army Logistics, 1775–1953.* Washington, DC: Office of the Chief of Military History, U.S. Army [GPO], 1966.

King, Randolph W., ed. *Naval Engineering and American Seapower.* Baltimore, MD: The Nautical and Aviation Publishing Company of America, Inc., 1989.

Krary, S.F., et al. *Technology of Machine Tools.* Toronto: McGraw-Hill of Canada, 1969, 1977.

Levenson, Leonard George. *Wartime Development of the Aircraft Industry.* Washington, DC: GPO, 1944.

Libicki, Martin C. *Industrial Strength Defense: A Disquisition on Manufacturing, Surge, and War.* Washington, DC: Mobilization Concepts Development Center, Institute for National Strategic Studies, National Defense University, 1988.

Lilley, Tom, et al. *Problems of Accelerating Aircraft Production during World War II.* Boston, MA: Division of Research, Graduate School of Business Administration, Harvard University, 1947; repr. Elmsford, New York: Maxwell Reprint Co., 1970.

Markusen, Ann, et al. *The Rise of the Gunbelt: The Military Remapping of Industrial America.* New York: Oxford University Press, 1991.

Merritt, Hardy L., and Luther F. Carter. *Mobilization and the National Defense.* Washington, DC: National Defense University Press, 1985.

Mihalak, Joseph. *Management of Tank-Automotive Items During the Technical Services Era, 1899–1962.* Warren, MI: U.S. Army Tank-Automotive Command, 1983.

Mullins, James P. *The Defense Matrix: National Preparedness and the Military-Industrial Complex.* San Diego, CA: Avant Books, 1986.

Nagle, James F. *A History of Government Contracting.* Washington, DC: George Washington University Press, 1992.

Peppers, Jerome G. *History of United States Military Logistics, 1935–985: A Brief Review.* Huntsville, AL: Logistics Education Foundation Pub., 1988.

Pfaltzgraff, Robert L., Jr., and Uri Ra'anan, eds. *The U.S. Defense Mobilization Infrastructure: Problems and Priorities.* Medford, MA: Archon Books, 1983.

Rae, John B. *Climb to Greatness: The American Aircraft Industry, 1920–1960.* Cambridge, MA: MIT Press, 1968.

Rearden, Steven. *History of the Office of the Secretary of Defense, Vol. I: The Formative Years, 1947–1950.* Washington, DC: Historical Office, Office of the Secretary of Defense, 1984.

Rosen, Steven, comp. *Testing the Theory of the Military-Industrial Complex.* Lexington, MA: Lexington Books, 1973.

Rowland, Buford, and William B. Boyd. *U.S. Navy Bureau of Ordnance in World War II.* Washington, DC: Bureau of Ordnance, Dept. of the Navy, 1954.

Sapolsky, Harvey M. *The Polaris System Development: Bureaucratic and Programmatic Success in Government.* Cambridge, MA: Harvard University Press, 1972.

Simmons, Henry T. *The Aircraft Industry.* Cambridge, MA: Bellman Publishing Co., 1958.

Simonson, George R., ed. *History of the American Aircraft Industry: An Anthology.* Cambridge, MA: MIT Press, 1968.

Smith, Ralph Elberton. *The Army and Economic Mobilization.* Part of the *United States Army in World War II series.* Washington, DC: Office of the Chief of Military History, Dept. of the Army, 1959.

Stout, Wesley Winans. *Bullets by the Billion.* Detroit, MI: Chrysler Corp., 1946.

Termena, Bernard J., Layne B. Peiffer, and H. P. Carlin. *Logistics: An Illustrated History of AFLC and Its Antecedents, 1921–1981.* Wright-Patterson Air Force Base, OH: Office of History, Headquarters, Air Force Materiel Command, n.d.

Thomson, Harry C., and Lida Mayo. *The Ordnance Department: Procurement and Supply.* Part of the *United States Army in World War II: The Technical Services.* Washington, DC: Office of the Chief of Military History, Dept. of the Army, 1960.

Thruelsen, Richard. *The Grumman Story.* New York: Praeger, 1976.

U.S. Army Industrial College. *Procurement and Production.* U.S. Army Industrial College War Readjustment Course. Washington, DC: Army Industrial College, 1944.

U.S. Army Materiel Command. *Army Materiel Command Evolution, 1962–1993.* Alexandria, VA: Historical Office, Headquarters, U.S. Army Materiel Command, 1993.

U.S. Army Materiel Command. *Arsenal for the Brave: A History of the United States Army Materiel Command, 1962–1968.* Washington, DC: n.p., 1969.

U.S. Army Materiel Command. *Historical Summary, Fiscal Year 1963– .* Washington, DC: AMC, 1963– .

U.S. Bureau of Yards and Docks. *Building the Navy's Bases in World War II: History of the Bureau of Yards and Docks and the Civil Engineer Corps, 1940–1946.* 2 vols. Washington, DC: GPO, 1947.

Vance, Stanley. *American Industries.* New York: Prentice-Hall, 1955.

Vawter, Roderick L. *Industrial Mobilization: The Relevant History.* ICAF Studies in Mobilization and Defense Management. Washington, DC: National Defense University Press, 1983.

Walker, Lois E., and Shelby E. Wickham. *From Huffman Prairie to the Moon: The History of Wright-Patterson Air Force Base.* Wright-Patterson AFB, OH: Air Force Logistics Command, n.d.

Weir, Gary E. *Forged in War: The Naval–Industrial Complex and American Submarine Construction, 1940–1961.* Washington, DC: Naval Historical Center, Dept. of the Navy, 1993.

Wesley, Frank Carver, and Cate, James Lea, eds. *The Army Air Forces in World War II.* 7 vols. Chicago: The University of Chicago Press, 1948–1958; repr. Washington, DC: Office of Air Force History [GPO], 1983.

White, Eston S. *Defense Acquisition and Logistics Management.* National Security Management Series. Washington, DC: National Defense University Press, 1984.

Whitehurst, Clinton H., Jr. *The U.S. Shipbuilding Industry: Past, Present, and Future.* Annapolis, MD: Naval Institute Press, 1986.

Woods, George Bryant. *The Aircraft Manufacturing Industry: Present and Future Prospects.* New York: White, Weld and Co., 1946.

Yoshpe, Harry B., and Charles F. Franke. *National Security Management: Production for Defense.* Washington, DC: Industrial College of the Armed Forces, 1968.

Articles

Alden, John D. "The Case For Navy Shipyards?" *Naval Engineers Journal,* 77 (August 1965): 660–664.

"The Army Learns from Industry." *Army Information Digest,* 4, no. 12 (December 1949): 18–22.

"The Arsenals." *Ordnance,* 45 (July–August 1960): 55–57.

Clark, Dorothy K. "Ammunition in Korea." *Ordnance,* 46 (May–June 1962): 833–835.

Crawford, D.J. "A Tank Isn't Born Overnight." *Armor*, 60, no. 4 (1951): 6–11.

Crist, Russell A. "Production and Policy (in the Manufacture of Defense Equipment)." *Ordnance*, 45 (March–April 1961): 626–629.

Dolan, John W., Jr. "The Naval Shipyard Complex." *Naval Engineers Journal*, 82 (December 1970).

Gansler, Jacques S. "Rebuilding the Arsenal." *Sea Power*, 24 (Sept. 1981): 31–38.

———. "A Ten-Point Program for the Defense Industry." *Sea Power*, 24 (March 1981): 32–47.

Halser, Ashley, Jr. "Shipyards: Biggest Weakness in Our War Potential?" *U.S. Naval Institute Proceedings*, 77 (July 1951): 737–743.

"How Army's Arsenal System Works." *Armed Forces Management*, 6 (October 1959): 15–17.

Joy, Kenneth E. "Machine Tools in Reserve." *Ordnance* 38 (May–June 1958): 925–929.

Karadbil, Leon N., and Roderick L. Vawter. "The Defense Production Act: Crucial Component of Mobilization Preparedness." In *Mobilization and the National Defense*, ed. Hardy L. Merritt and Luther F. Carter. Washington, DC: National Defense University Press, 1985.

Kemp, Robert A., and James C. Blewster. "The Army's Production Base: Cornerstone of America's Future Survival." *Army Logistician*, 2, no. 6 (November–December 1970): 4–9.

"Last Chance for U.S. Shipbuilders?" *Sea Power*, 27 (December 1984): 18–31.

McCone, J.A. "The Hard Facts of Aircraft Production." *Air Force*, 34 (November 1951): 28–29.

"Machinability Speeds Production." *Aviation Age*, 16, no. 5 (Nov. 1951): 6–10.

Martin, William H. "Industry and the Arsenals." *Army*, 9 (March 1959): 28–32.

Mathews, Joseph J. "The New Naval Ordnance Plants." *U.S. Naval Institute Proceedings*, 70 (October 1944): 1216–1221.

Maynard, Lemuel. "Mobilizing Munitions." *The Quartermaster Review*, 30, no. 6 (1951), 115–117.

Mitchell, Donald W. "Mobilization Progress." *Current History*, 23, no. 133 (1952), 139–143.

"Mobilization Plans for Industry." *Army Information Digest,* 6, no. 2 (1951), 11–21.

"Moving the Production Line." *Aviation Age,* 17, no. 6 (June 1952): 43–45.

"Navy Plans Shipyard Modernization." *U.S. Naval Institute Proceedings,* 94 (December 1968): 154.

Nelson, H.B. "Emphasis on Production." *Quartermaster Review,* 30 (May–June 1951): 7–9.

Newton, Clarke. "How To Make Tanks in a Hurry." *Colliers,* 128, no. 22 (1951): 24–25 & 60–62.

"Ordnance in Korea." *Ordnance,* 35 (November–December 1950): 201–203.

"The Patton 48." *Armor,* 61, no. 4 (1950): 32–33.

"Production Flow—From Plans to Planes." *Air Force,* 35, no. 5 (May 1952): 21.

Reday, Joseph Z. "Industrial Mobilization in the U.S." *U.S. Naval Institute Proceedings,* 79, no. 10 (1953): 1065–1075.

Richards, Ed. "A Bibliography of Sources for Defense (Industry) Information." *Data,* 6 (September 1961): 23–26.

Sapolsky, Harvey M. "Equipping the Armed Forces." *Armed Forces and Society,* 14, no. 1 (Fall 1987): 113–128.

"Senate Group Hits Production Lag." *Army Navy Journal,* 89, no. 14 (1 December 1951): 422, 425.

"Solons Tour Plants to Find Bottlenecks." *Air Force Times,* 12, no. 39 (3 May 1952): 5.

Sonenshein, Nathan. "U.S. Shipbuilding and Repair—Future Prospects." *Naval Engineers Journal,* 82 (December 1970): 13–30.

"Squeezing the Air Power Pipeline, How the Air Force Cuts the Delivery Time of Aircraft Engines." *Air Force,* 35, no. 5 (May 1952): 32–33.

"Study Defense Production." *Army-Navy Journal,* 88, no. 8 (21 October 1950): 218.

"Tank Production." *Armor,* 59, no. 5 (1950): 32–33.

"Two Messages to Congress: Breathtaking Production Figures and the American Aircraft Industry." *Interavia,* 6, no. 2 (1951): 98–99.

Walton, Francis. "Industry in the Cold War." *Ordnance,* 44 (January–February 1960): 588–91.

Warner, W.W. "Arsenals in Action." *Army Information Digest,* 6, no. 9 (1951): 39–44.

"War Readiness Plans Call for Fast Buildup." *Air Force Times,* 16, no. 2 (31 December 1955).

Watson, Mark S. "Ammunition Expenditure in Korea." *Ordnance,* 37 (September–October 1952): 254–55.

Appendix:

Industrial Facilities Owned by the Department of Defense, 1996

ALABAMA

Redstone Arsenal
Huntsville, AL

Redstone Arsenal sits on 40,000 acres, and includes administrative buildings, laboratories, flight test ranges, and other specialized buildings and equipment.

The center was built in World War II as three separate installations for the Chemical Warfare Service: the Huntsville Arsenal, the Redstone Ordnance Plant, and the Gulf Chemical Warfare Depot. The Redstone Rocket Test Stand, built in 1953, was placed on the National Register of Historic Sites in 1976. It was an important facility in the development of the Jupiter C and the Mercury-Redstone vehicles that launched the first American satellite and the first American manned spaceflight. It is headquarters of the U.S. Army Missile Command (MICOM), which manages the Army's missile and rocket program. The missile program began in 1950 under Wernher von Braun and his team of German scientists. The 500-mile surface-to-surface Redstone missile was developed here. It was the first of the large U.S. ballistic missile systems to become operational.

Sources:

Mike Baker, *Redstone Arsenal: Yesterday and Today*. U.S. Government Printing Office, 1993.

Historic American Engineering Record No. AL-9, Prints and Photographs Division, Library of Congress, Washington, DC.

Internet: http://www.redstone.army.mil/history/home.htm (includes a chronology of events and a number of photographs).

Prentice M. Thomas, Jr., *Cultural Resources Investigations at Redstone Arsenal, Madison County, Alabama*. New World Research, Inc., 1980.

Helen Brents Joiner, *The Redstone Arsenal Complex in the Pre-Missile Era: A History of Huntsville Arsenal, Gulf Chemical Warfare Depot, and Redstone Arsenal, 1941–1949*. Redstone Arsenal, AL: Historical Division, Army Missile Command, n.d.

David S. Akens, *Rocket City, USA,* Huntsville, AL: Strode Publishers, 1959.

Erick Bergaust, *Rocket City, U.S.A.: From Huntsville, Alabama to the Moon,* New York: Macmillan, 1963.

Helen Brents Joiner and Elizabeth C. Jolliff, *The Redstone Arsenal Complex in its Second Decade, 1950–1960.* Redstone Arsenal, AL: Army Missile Command, Historical Division, 1969.

Record Group 156, Records of the Office of the Chief of Ordnance, entry 646, Executive Division, Historical Branch, Histories (World War II), boxes 157–159, National Archives II, College Park, MD.

Record Group 338, Records of U.S. Army Commands, Records of Posts, Camps, and Stations: Redstone Arsenal, 1941–1950 (some boxes classified). National Archives II, College Park, MD.

ARIZONA

Air Force Plant 44
Tuscon, AZ

Air Force Plant 44 is southwest of Tucson and is operated by Hughes Aircraft. It covers 2,900 acres (95% government-owned) and 2.1 million square feet (51% government-owned, including the manufacturing space and Final Assembly and CheckOut [FACO] facilities).

The main plant complex was built in 1951 by the Del Webb Corporation for Hughes Aircraft Co. Hughes then sold the plant to the U.S. Air Force (USAF), but continued to operate it. At that time it was the prime production plant for the Falcon family of air-to-air missiles. In 1954, the plant was expanded by adding land and building the FACO facility for the Navy's Walleye Missile. Test cells and explosive storage magazines for the Phoenix and AMRAAM programs were added later. In the mid-1980s, over 1,900 acres were transferred to the state, Tucson, and the Air National Guard. At that time, AFP 44 supported the TOW, Maverick, Phoenix, ARBS (Angle Rate Bombing System), and AMRAAM programs. The FACO facility is used for Maverick and TOW missile assembly.

Sources:

Aeronautical Systems Division, Facilities Management Division, "USAF Industrial Plant Ownership Responsibilities," Wright-Patterson AFB: Air Force Systems Command, [1986?], 35–38.

History, Arizona Air Procurement District, January–June 1955, K204.602, Air Force Historical Research Agency, Maxwell AFB, AL.

ARKANSAS

Pine Bluff Arsenal
Pine Bluff, AR

Pine Bluff Arsenal is 8 miles northwest of Pine Bluff, AK, and 30 miles southeast of Little Rock. It includes 14,943 acres and 952 buildings, which provide 3.3 million square feet of floor space, including storage bunkers. It also has 42 miles of railroad track and 2 million square yards of roads and paved surfaces.

The facility was established in November 1941 as the Chemical Warfare Arsenal; it was renamed Pine Bluff Arsenal 4 months later. Its original mission was as a manufacturing center for magnesium and thermite munitions. The arsenal produced its first incendiary grenade on 31 July 1942. During World War II and the years following, the arsenal's manufacturing capabilities continued to expand. The expansion included facilities to manufacture and store various types of chemical-filled weapons. Arsenal-produced conventional munitions were used in the Korean and Vietnam wars. During the war years, the arsenal produced millions of grenades, bombs, and shells as well as millions of pounds of mustard and Lewisite. While the arsenal manufactured these agents during World War II and remains a storage site for a portion of our nation's chemical defense stockpile, it has never produced a lethal nerve agent. Pine Bluff was also the site of the Production Development Laboratories, responsible for manufacturing and loading biological munitions. President Nixon banned biological weapons in 1969 and manufacturing ceased. In 1972, this part of the complex was renamed the National Center for Toxicological Research, removed from the jurisdiction of the Arsenal and placed under the Department of Health, Education, and Welfare. Currently, it manufactures chemical, smoke, riot control, incendiary, and pyrotechnic mixes and munitions. Limited production facilities also are used to manufacture chemical defense items such as clothing and protective masks. Pine Bluff is the only active site at which white phosphorous-filled weapons are loaded. The arsenal is also a storage site for 12 percent of the nation's chemical munitions. There are plans to destroy that stockpile onsite by incineration.

Sources:

Historic American Engineering Record No. AR-2, Prints and Photographs Division, Library of Congress, Washington, DC.

http://www-ioc.army.mil/elements/pinebl.html

Seymour M. Hersh, *Chemical and Biological Warfare: America's Hidden Arsenal.* Garden City, NY: Doubleday and Co., 1969.

"Pine Bluff Arsenal Profile." Unpublished report prepared by the U.S. Army Armament Materiel Readiness Command, 1983, PBA Administrative Archives.

Pine Bluff Arsenal, annual histories (1970–1972, 1976–1988), U.S. Army Military History Institute Library, Carlisle Barracks, PA.

Record Group 338, Records of U.S. Army Commands, Records of Posts, Camps, and Stations: Pine Bluff Arsenal, 1941–1950, and 1943–1950 (classified). National Archives II, College Park, MD.

CALIFORNIA

Air Force Plant 42
Palmdale, CA

Air Force Plant 42 is at Palmdale, CA, north of Pasadena in Los Angeles County. It is operated by Lockheed, Rockwell International, Northrop, and Nero. It has over 6,600 acres (the government owns 85%) and includes approximately 4.2 million square feet of floor space (the government owns 45%). The site includes multiple high bay buildings and airfield access with flyaway capability. The facility also has one of the heaviest load-bearing runways in the world.

The Palmdale Airport began as a U.S. Army Air Corps base in 1940. It was used during World War II as an emergency landing strip and for B-25 transition training. The base was sold as surplus to Los Angeles County in 1946. The concept for AFP 42 originated in the challenge of flight testing high performance jet aircraft over heavily populated areas. In 1951, the USAF purchased the site and awarded a contract to Lockheed Aircraft to develop the master plan for the site. The plan was to construct a facility that would meet the requirements of full war mobilization and augment the industrial production potential of the major airframe manufacturing industry in southern California. With USAF encouragement, Lockheed signed a lease in 1956 for 237 acres to use Palmdale Airport for final assembly and flight testing. The site supported multiple contractors. During the 1980s, it was used by Lockheed to produce the U-2/TR-1 and support the SR-71. Northrop produced the F-5E, and Rockwell supported the B-1B.

Sources:

Aeronautical Systems Division, Facilities Management Division, "USAF Industrial Plant Ownership Responsibilities," Wright-Patterson AFB, OH: Air Force Systems Command, [1986?], 31–34.

History, Air Force Contract Management Division, January–June 1971, K243.0708-47, Air Force Historical Research Agency, Maxwell AFB, AL.

History, Air Force Contract Management Division, July–December 1973, K243.0708-47, Air Force Historical Research Agency, Maxwell AFB, AL.

History, Air Force Contract Management Division, July 1974–December 1976 (with chronology, 1917–1976), K243.07 V.3, Air Force Historical Research Agency, Maxwell AFB, AL.

History, Air Force Contract Management Division, January–December 1979, K243.0708-50, Air Force Historical Research Agency, Maxwell AFB, AL.

History, Air Force Contract Management Division, January–December 1979, K243.0708, Air Force Historical Research Agency, Maxwell AFB, AL.

History, Air Force Contract Management Division, January–December 1983, K243.07 Annex 1, Air Force Historical Research Agency, Maxwell AFB, AL.

History, Air Force Contract Management Division, January–December 1986, K243.07 V.3, Air Force Historical Research Agency, Maxwell AFB, AL.

History, Air Force Aeronautical Systems Division, January–December 1986, K243.011 V.5, Air Force Historical Research Agency, Maxwell AFB, AL.

History, Air Force Contract Management Division, January–December 1988, K243.07 V.1, Air Force Historical Research Agency, Maxwell AFB, AL.

Sacramento Air Logistics Center, "Contractor Joint Tenancy at Air Force Plant 42, Palmdale, CA," 1958, K205.104–27, Air Force Historical Research Agency, Maxwell AFB, AL.

Air Force Plant 19

San Diego, CA

Air Force Plant 19 is northeast of San Diego, CA. It covers 2,850 acres (the government owns only 2%) and 6.3 million square feet of floor space (the government owns 25%). Operated by General Dynamics, the plant has a high bay area for aircraft assembly and specially configured areas for Atlas/Centaur tank assembly.

Construction of AFP 19 began November 1940, and the plant opened in 1941. It was built as an assembly plant for the B-24 Liberator bomber, to augment primary design and assembly at the Lindberg Field Plant. Employment at the plant peaked at 45,000 in 1942. At the end of World War II the plant was sold as surplus. In 1957 the government reacquired the plant and constructed four support buildings for Atlas missile manufacturing and assembly. During the 1980s, the plant performed fabrication, minor assembly, and subassembly work for the Ground Launched Tomahawk Cruise Missile, Transporter Erector Launcher (TEL), and Launcher Control Center. It also supported Atlas/Centaur and Shuttle/Centaur tanks and Atlas refurbishment. In 1996 the plant was transferred to the Navy, where it continues production under the Command, Control, and Ocean Surveillance Center.

Source:

Aeronautical Systems Division, Facilities Management Division, "USAF Industrial Plant Ownership Responsibilities," Wright-Patterson AFB, OH: Air Force Systems Command, [1986?], 23–25.

Air Force Plant 70
Sacramento, CA

Air Force Plant 70 is east of Sacramento and is operated by Aerojet General Strategic Propulsion Co. The site covers about 13,000 acres (only 1% government-owned) and includes 372,000 square feet of floor space (only 7% government-owned). The government's production facilities are highly integrated into those belonging to the contractor.

In the early 1950s, Aerojet General Strategic Propulsion Co. moved into the Sacramento area to create a testing site for hazardous rocket motor and engine operations, which had previously been conducted at a facility at Azusa, CA. Aerojet General deeded 52 acres to the government, which built two temporary buildings (with a design life of 5 years) to support the Titan missile. Later the site was used to manufacture and support the Minuteman program. In 1969, the property was declared excess, and McClellan AFB acquired the facility to use the buildings for a warehouse and a photo lab. In 1975, the facility was transferred to the Air Force Systems Command. In the early 1980s, Aerojet General was awarded the MX Missile contract. The USAF attempted to sell the facility to Aerojet General, but the company refused the offer. As of 1986, AFP 70 supported the MX Peacekeeper (95%) and the Titan and Minuteman (5%) programs. Aerojet General's Sacramento operations also supported: the AIM-9 Sidewinder, the RIM-24 Tartar, UGM-84 Harpoon, MIM-23 Hawk, AIM-7 Sparrow, AUM-45 Shrike, GBU-22 Paveway II, Astrobee, AIM-54 Phoenix, LGM-25 Titan, Shuttle, Mark-56 Quickstrike, the Minuteman Motor, Polaris, and Small ICBM.

Sources:

Aeronautical Systems Division, Facilities Management Division, "USAF Industrial Plant Ownership Responsibilities," Wright-Patterson AFB, OH: Air Force Systems Command, [1986?], 42–43.

History, Sacramento Air Logistics Center, FY 1986, K205.10–37 V.9, Air Force Historical Research Agency, Maxwell AFB, AL.

Barstow Marine Logistics Center
Barstow, CA

Barstow Marine Logistics Center is 120 miles from Los Angeles, adjacent to the city of Barstow in the Mojave Desert. The site consists of 5,387 acres divided into three areas: Nebo (Little Shepherd), Yermo (Desert Flower), and the rifle-pistol range.

Begun in June 1942 as a Navy supply depot, the facility was turned over to the Marines in December 1942. The Marine Corps activated the depot on 4 January 1943. During the early part of the Korean War, it operated 24 hours a day to equip the First Marine Division for the Inchon-Seoul campaign. During the war, 200 pieces of mobile equipment left the repair facility each day. Since 1954, it has been responsible for logistics for the Marine in the Pacific Ocean Area and Far East. During the Vietnam War it provided 70% of the supplies received by the Marines in the Far East. Its current mission is to procure, maintain, repair, rebuild, store, and distribute supplies and equipment.

Source:

U.S. Marine Corps, History and Museums Division, "Command Chronologies-California-Marine Corps Logistics Base, Barstow."

Long Beach Naval Shipyard
Los Angeles, CA

Long Beach NSY is 7 miles from Los Angeles International Airport.

The property was first leased to the Federal government in 1935, but most construction occurred during World War II. The shipyard was closed in 1950, then reactivated in 1951 for the Korean War. By 1952, an attack carrier and destroyer escorts had transferred there. The shipyard also hosted minesweepers and MSTS* ships. Supply and fuel depots at the site were reactivated in 1955. Additional ships were ported at the shipyard, and other ships were refurbished for transport overseas. In 1974, base realignment downgraded the shipyard to a naval support activity, and dozens of ships were transferred elsewhere. However, the base was again upgraded to a Naval Station in 1979. During the 1980s, two battleships were refurbished at the shipyard. Long Beach NSY was scheduled to close as of 1996.

Sources:

"Command History U.S. Naval Base Los Angeles/Long Beach, California, 1946," and annual supplements. Operational Archives, Naval Historical Center, Washington Navy Yard, Washington, DC.

U.S. Naval Station Long Beach Historical Report, Annual Reviews, 1959–1973. Some of the annual reviews have annexes which include photographs, rosters, ships company weekly listings, etc.

Record Group 181, Records of Naval Districts and Shore Establishments in the Regional Archives, miscellaneous records of Long Beach/Los Angeles Naval Base (incl. Central Subject Files, 1948–1953). National Archives—Pacific Sierra Region, San Bruno, CA.

---

*MSTS = Military Sea Transportation Service.

Forging the Sword: Defense Production During the Cold War

Mare Island Naval Activities
Vallejo, CA

Mare Island Naval Activities is at the northern end of San Francisco Bay, 30 miles from the City of San Francisco. The property consists of more than 2,500 acres. The complex had four separate functions: shipyard, ammunition depot, hospital (building later converted for training facilities) and Marine barracks.

The oldest naval base on the west coast, Mare Island was founded in 1853. During World War II, it repaired 1,227 ships and built 391 new ships. In 1948, it was designated as a major overhaul and repair facility for submarines. In 1965, Mare Island and San Francisco Naval Shipyard were merged and renamed San Francisco Bay Naval Shipyard. With sites at Mare Island and Hunters Point, it was the largest Naval Shipyard in the world. The San Francisco Bay Naval Shipyard was disestablished in February 1970. Hunters Point was closed in 1973. Mare Island was (in 1996) scheduled to close.

Sources:

Arnold S. Lott, *A Long Line of Ships: Mare Island's Century of Naval Activity in California,* Annapolis, MD: U.S. Naval Institute, 1954.

Sue Lemmon and E.D. Wichels, *Sidewheelers to Nuclear Power: A Pictorial Essay Covering 123 Years at the Mare Island Naval Shipyard,* Annapolis, MD: Leeward Publication, Inc. 1977.

Historic American Building Survey No. CA-1543, Prints and Photographs Division, Library of Congress, Washington, DC.

Historic American Engineering Record No. CA-3, Prints and Photographs Division, Library of Congress, Washington, DC.

Mighetto and Youngmeister, AIA."Historic Survey of Mare Island Naval Complex, Intermediate Inventory," MSS, Mare Island Naval Complex, 1985.

National Register of Historic Places, National Park Service. "Mare Island Naval Shipyard," MSS, National Register, National Park Service, 1986.

Quarterly Summary of Mare Island Naval Shipyard, 2nd, 3rd, and 4th quarters, 1947; Command History to 31 December 1958 with updates each year 1959–1964. Command History 1 January 1969 through 31 January 1970. Mare Island Naval Shipyard Command History, yearly 1970–1973. Operational Archives, Naval Historical Center, Washington Navy Yard, Washington, DC.

Legacy/HARP files, Naval Facilities Engineering Command, Planning and Engineering Division, Code 150, Alexandria, VA.

Record Group 181, Records of Naval Districts and Shore Establishments in the Regional Archives, miscellaneous records of Mare Island Navy Yard (mostly 19th and early 20th c., but some World War II and Cold War correspondence). National Archives—Pacific Southwest Region, Laguna Niguel, CA.

Riverbank Army Ammunition Plant
Riverbank, CA

Riverbank AAP is in the northern San Joaquin Valley, 6 miles northeast of Modesto and 90 miles east of San Francisco. It includes 132 buildings, 19 from the original construction period, and covers 168 acres. Some acreage is currently leased to nonmilitary concerns.

Riverbank AAP was constructed in 1942 and began operation as an aluminum reduction facility in 1943. During World War II, its annual production of aluminum, a critical component for aircraft manufacture, was 96 million pounds. The plant was closed in 1944 as requirements for aircraft declined. During the Korean War it was reopened and converted to an Army ammunition plant for the manufacture of steel cartridge cases. It was the largest shell-casing plant at that time, operated by Norris Industries. Construction activities and the installation of six production lines were assigned to Bechtel Corp. The site was closed again in 1958 but reopened in 1966 to produce shell and mortar casings and related metal parts for the Vietnam War. It was again operated by Norris Industries in association with Bechtel Corp. It was classified as inactive in 1981. Norris Industries is the current contractor, and the plant is in maintenance or layaway of standby facilities. Current tenants include American Safety Products and LMC-West.

Sources:

Internet: http://www-ioc.army.mil/elements/riverban.htm
http://www.openterprise.com/rvbnhome.htm
http://www-ioc.army.mil/iocfact/RBAAP.HTM

Historic American Engineering Record No. CA-28, Prints and Photographs Division, Library of Congress, Washington, DC.

"Riverbank Aluminum Plant," Report prepared in the Office of the County Engineer for the Stanislaus County Board of Supervisors, August 1, 1950. Modesto-Stanislaus Library, Modesto, CA. Contains a site plan, building descriptions, and photographs.

"Sect'y of Army Inspects Remodeled Aluminum Facility; Operations Are Top Secret." *The Stockton Record,* September 20, 1952.

Army Ammunition Plant Profile, Riverbank AAP," n.d. Government files, RBAAP. An information brochure that provides historical and production overviews.

Riverbank Army Ammunition Plant, annual histories (1968–1970, 1972–1973, 1976–1981), U.S. Army Military History Institute Library, Carlisle Barracks, PA.

Sacramento Air Logistics Center
McClellan AFB, CA

Sacramento ALC is in the northeast section of Sacramento.

The site was established in 1937 as Sacramento Air Depot; the name changed to McClellan Field in 1939 and to McClellan AFB in 1947. During World War II the depot was engaged in modifying aircraft as well as providing maintenance and repair support for the Army Air Forces. Air Force Materiel Command assumed control of the facility in 1946. The base was used for storing surplus aircraft in the postwar period. Facilities were completed in 1956 to accommodate the 8th Air Division (later replaced by the 552nd Airborne Early Warning and Control Wing). Control of the facility came under the newly established Air Force Logistics Command in 1961. It provided mission support for BMEWS, SAGE, and interceptor backup systems during the Vietnam War. Aircraft overhaul facilities were completed between 1971 and 1977, and a depot radar systems and overhaul facility was completed in 1977. Currently, it is one of five centers for the Air Force Materiel Command. It has assumed world-wide responsibility for the management of Air Force electrical components, communications-electronics systems, fluid drive accessories, and tactical shelters. In 1988, the base was assigned the F-15 Eagle workload. In 1992, it provided alternate support for the KC-135, and full responsibility for the A-10, F-111, F-117 Stealth, and F-22.

Source:

Maurice A. Miller, general editor, *McClellan Air Force Base, 1936–1982: A Pictorial History*. McClellan AFB, CA: Office of History, Sacramento Air Logistics Center, 1982.

COLORADO

Air Force Plant PJKS
Denver, CO

Air Force Plants PJKS—the name is derived from the initials of the builders—is southwest of Denver, CO. It is operated by Martin Marietta Aerospace and covers almost 5,500 acres (only 8% government owned), which includes 3.5 million square feet of floor space.

Martin Marietta Aerospace deeded the land for Air Force Plant PJKS in 1957. Test facilities were constructed for the research and development (R&D) of the Titan I weapon system. Portions of this land were cleared for construction of test Complexes "A" and "B," which were comprised of four static firing test stands, blockhouses, field support buildings, a Cold Flow Laboratory, and Central Support Building. Complex "A" was used for the Titan II, which required additional construction of systems test and components test facilities from 1960–1964 for R&D of toxic hypergolic fuels. The test stands were deactivated in 1964. As of 1986, the plant primarily supported the MX Peacekeeper and the Titan III. The facility also includes the only U.S.-based hydrazine purification process.

Source:

Aeronautical Systems Division, Facilities Management Division, "USAF Industrial Plant Ownership Responsibilities," Wright-Patterson AFB: Air Force Systems Command, [1986?], 51–53.

Rocky Mountain Arsenal
Commerce City, CO

Rocky Mountain Arsenal is a few miles northeast of downtown Denver and has 17,238 acres. Many of the original production lines have been removed and many of the buildings remodeled.

Rocky Mountain Arsenal was opened in 1943 under the Chemical Warfare Service. From 1945 to 1950, the site was used for reconditioning and demilitarization of mustard shells. During the Korean War, it produced white phosphorous-filled munitions and incendiary cluster bombs. From 1953 to 1957, it produced GB nerve gas for which a new facility was constructed. In 1970, chemical warfare material was disposed of here. Its current mission is contamination cleanup.

Sources:

Historic American Engineering Record No. CO-21, Prints and Photographs Division, Library of Congress, Washington, DC.

History of Rocky Mountain Arsenal. Unpublished report, 1980. RMA Administrative Archives.

Cal Queal, "The Many Secrets of Rocky Mountain Arsenal." *Denver Post—Empire Magazine.* April 13, 1969.

Tom Rees, "Nerve Gas Detoxification Begins at Arsenal." *Rocky Mountain News.* October 30, 1973.

U.S. Arsenal, Rocky Mountain, *Operations under Army Industrial Fund.* Denver, CO: n.p., 1951.

Rocky Mountain Arsenal Army Ammunition Plant, annual histories (1968, 1970–1971, 1976–1982, 1984–1986), U.S. Army Military History Institute Library, Carlisle Barracks, PA.

Department of the Army, "Summary History of Rocky Mountain Arsenal, Denver, Colorado, 1942–1967," MSS, Installations File, U.S. Army Military History Institute Library, Carlisle Barracks, PA.

Department of the Army, *Rocky Mountain Arsenal, Denver, Colorado: Guide and Directory.* San Diego, CA: Military Publishers, Inc., 1968 (Installation File, U.S. Army Military History Institute Library, Carlisle Barracks, PA.).

Record Group 338, Records of U.S. Army Commands, Records of Posts, Camps, and Stations: Rocky Mountain Arsenal, 1942–1950. National Archives II, College Park, MD.

CONNECTICUT

New London Naval Submarine Base
New London, CT

On the east bank of the Thames River near Groton, CT, New London Naval Submarine Base is the birthplace of the submarine force. It was originally a Navy yard, converted to a submarine base in 1916, and greatly expanded in World War II. The advent of nuclear power required an improvement in training and support facilities. By 1959, New London had become the largest submarine base in the world with 8,210 active personnel. In 1969, the base also took on logistical and training responsibilities for fleet ballistic missile submarines. In 1974, the Naval Submarine Support Activity was established. By 1979, the base supported the new Los Angeles and Ohio class submarines. Major units today include Supervisor of Shipbuilding, Conversion and Repair, and Naval Submarine Support Facility.

Sources:

Historic American Engineering Record No. CT-37, Prints and Photographs Division, Library of Congress, Washington, DC.

Ecology and Environment, Inc., "Cultural Resource Assessment: Naval Submarine Base, New London/Groton, Connecticut." MSS, Naval Submarine Base, 1992.

G.W. Lautrup, "U.S. Naval Submarine Base, New London, Conn.: Command History, 1959." MSS, Nautilus Memorial Submarine Force Library and Museum, Groton, CT.

Stratford Army Engine Plant
Stratford, CT

Stratford Army Engine Plant is on the Housatonic River and includes 115 acres of land and 44 buildings.

This facility was originally known as the Sikorsky Aero Engineering Corporation, which opened in 1929. The company changed its name to Sikorsky Aviation Corporation in 1934. It produced a number of airplanes for the Navy and the Marine Corps, as well as for private companies, but had financial difficulties during the Great Depression. Chance Vought Aircraft, another subsidiary of the Sikorsky parent company (United Aircraft) was brought in to make use of some of the facilities. The name was changed to Vought-Sikorsky Aircraft Division in 1939, and many improvements were made to the facility. During World War II the Stratford plant produced the Corsair, a high speed fighter, for the Navy. The facilities were expanded between 1942 and 1944. When the war ended, Chance Vought began vigorous research on jet aircraft. The Navy offered the company an unused plant in Texas and the operation moved to Dallas in 1948. This move left the Stratford plant vacant, and soon afterward, flooding from the nearby river damaged much of the facility. The Air Force purchased the facility in 1951 and renamed it Air Force Plant No. 43. Avco Corporation became the contractor, repaired the damaged buildings, and built dikes. The plant then began manufacturing aircraft engines. In 1961, it began producing helicopter engines. Also in the 1960s, it began producing engines for hydrofoils and hovercraft. In 1976, the plant was transferred from the Air Force to the Army and renamed the Stratford Army Engine Plant. One of Avco's engines was selected for the new Abrams XMI Main Battle Tank. The Abrams tank engines were still in production in the 1980s, as were helicopter engines.

Sources:

Historic American Engineering Record No. CT-14, Prints and Photographs Division, Library of Congress, Washington, DC.

Avco Corporation, *Avco Corporation, The First Fifty Years: 1929–1979.* Greenwich, CT: Avco Corporation, 1979.

Gerand P. Moran, *Aeroplanes Vought,* 1917–1977. Temple City, CA: Historical Aviation Album, 1978.

Stratford Army Engine Plant, Installation and Activity Brochure. Stratford, CT: DARCOM, 1980.

United Technologies, *The Helicopter History of Sikorsky Aircraft,* Stratford, CT: Sikorsky Aircraft, 1981.

DISTRICT OF COLUMBIA

Washington Navy Yard
Washington, DC

The Washington Navy Yard is in southeast DC on the Anacostia River.

Forging the Sword: Defense Production During the Cold War

The yard was established in 1800, burned during the War of 1812, but rebuilt shortly afterward. The site was unsuited for shipyard activities—the Anacostia River tended to fill its bed—so the Washington Navy Yard increasingly focused on the production of armaments and machinery for the fleet. By the 1880s, the site had become the main source of weapons for the Navy, and by the turn of the century, it had the facilities to produce the great 16-inch guns of the battleships. During World Wars I and II, the Navy yard continued as the leading source of heavy armaments. It also provided a number of other heavy and light manufacturing services for the Navy, with its forge shops, foundry, and machine shops. In 1945, it was designated the Naval Gun Factory. During the early years of the Cold War, the Navy Yard continued as a ship repair center, but demand had lessened for the kind of ordnance and other products that the factory manufactured. In 1961, industrial activities ceased and the yard became an administrative center. The Navy Museum is housed there.

Sources:

U.S. Naval Gun Factory. *Ordnance Production.* Washington, DC.: U.S. Naval Gun Factory, 1951 (copy located in National Defense University Library, Fort Leslie J. McNair, Washington, DC).

"The Naval Gun Factory," *Ordnance,* 33 (Jan.–Feb. 1949): 261–264.

F.E. Farnham, comp., *History and Descriptive Guide of the U.S. Navy Yard, Washington, DC.* Washington, DC: Gibson Bros., Printers and Bookbinders, 1894.

Henry B. Hibbon, *Navy-Yard, Washington. History from Organization, 1799 to present date,* Washington, DC: GPO, 1890.

Historic American Building Survey No. DC-442, Prints and Photographs Division, Library of Congress, Washington, DC.

United States Department of the Interior, National Register of Historic Places—Nomination Form, n.d. (Copy located in Legacy/HARP Program files, Naval Facilities Engineering Command, Planning and Engineering Division, Code 150, Alexandria, VA).

George R. Adams and Ralph Christian, "Washington Navy Yard, Washington, DC." MSS, National Register of Historic Places, National Park Service, 1975.

Notter Finegold and Alexander, Inc., EDAW, Inc., Hammer Siler George and Associates, and Daniel Mann Johnson and Mendenhall. "Washington Navy Yard Master Plan." MSS, Washington Navy Yard, 1990.

Crane and Gorwic Associates, Inc. *Washington Navy Yard, Washington, DC.* Detroit, MI: The Associates and Robert L. Plavnick, 1967.

Crane and Gorwic Associates, Inc., *Development Plan—Washington Navy Yard, U.S. Naval Station, Washington, DC*. Detroit, MI: The Associates and Robert L. Plavnick, 1966.

U.S. Naval Gun Factory, Washington, DC, *Building 213: History and Analysis*. Washington, DC., U.S. Naval Gun Factory, 1952 (copy found at Naval Historical Center Library, Washington, DC).

U.S. Naval Gun Factory, Washington, DC. *Report*. Washington, n.p, n.d. (copy found at Naval Historical Center Library, Washington, DC).

FLORIDA

Pensacola Naval Complex

Pensacola, FL

Located 5 miles from downtown Pensacola, Pensacola Naval Complex is comprised of the naval yard, the air station, a hospital, and the formerly Army-owned Fort Barrancas.

Pensacola was originally opened for the manufacture and repair of ships. In 1914, it also became the naval aviation center for flight and ground training and the study of advanced aeronautical engineering. It became the Navy's first permanent air station and the first naval pilot training center. It is the oldest of the Navy's six aviation depots, and its largest industrial employer. Among its activities are: depot level maintenance, a complete range of rework operations on designated aircraft and associated accessories and equipment; manufacture of aircraft parts and assemblies; engineering services in support of assigned aircraft and components, and technical services on aircraft maintenance and logistics problems.

Sources:

Historic Property Associates, "Architectural and Historical Survey of the Naval Air Station, Pensacola." MSS, Naval Complex Pensacola, 1985.

"Pensacola Naval Air Station Historic District," MSS, National Register of Historic Places, National Park Service, 1976.

Navy Public Works Center, Building and Structure Directory, Pensacola Naval Complex. Pensacola, FL: Naval Complex Pensacola.

Pensacola Naval Air Station, FL. "Historical and Archaeological Resources Protection Plan." MSS, Naval Complex Pensacola, September 1991.

GEORGIA

Air Force Plant 6
Marietta, GA

The plant is northwest of Atlanta, GA, near Dobbins AFB and Lockheed-Georgia. The site covers 926 acres (of which the government owns 82%) and includes nearly 7.5 million square feet of industrial floor space (of which the government owns 78%). AFP 6 is operated by Lockheed-Georgia (now Lockheed Martin). The site includes high bay facilities used for the fabrication and assembly of large aircraft. It does not have the capability to service large aircraft once assembled and must use the nearby Lockheed-Georgia facilities for this. The plant has flyaway capabilities from the Dobbins AFB runways.

Air Force Plant 6 was established in 1941 on the Cobb County Airport site and began operation in 1943. From 1943–1945, Bell Aircraft Corporation manufactured B-29 bombers. Production ceased in 1945 and for 6 years the plant was used for machine and tool storage. In 1951, the plant was reactivated and used by Lockheed Aircraft Corp. to modify the B-29. Since then, Lockheed has operated the plant to manufacture, modify, and maintain the B-47, C-130, C-141, C-140, and C-5. From 1951 to 1955 the plant experienced a surge in production, with employment rising to 20,000 employees. By 1960 production declined and employment levels dropped to about half the 1955 total. During the 1960s, with the Cuban Missile Crisis and the Vietnam buildup, the workforce grew again to 33,000. In the late 1980s, the plant supported the C-5B and C-130 production programs and supplied spare parts and kits for the C-130 and C-141.

Sources:

Aeronautical Systems Division, Facilities Management Division, "USAF Industrial Plant Ownership Responsibilities," Wright-Patterson AFB, OH: Air Force Systems Command, [1986?], 19–22.

Histories, Air Force Plant Representatives Office/Air Force Contract Management Division, 1964–1969, K243.0707-4, Air Force Historical Research Agency, Maxwell AFB, AL.

Oral History Interview with A.G. Atkins (on C-141b aircraft), K239.0512-1262 C.1 12 September 1980, Air Force Historical Research Agency, Maxwell AFB, AL.

Warner-Robins Air Logistic Center
Robins AFB, GA

Warner-Robins ALC is 15 miles southeast of Macon, adjacent to Warner Robins, GA.

The site was established in 1941 to serve as a logistics depot and training facility and was originally called Wellston Air Depot. It was renamed Robins Field; then Robins AFB.

During World War II it performed essential modification work on aircraft in addition to supporting the maintenance and repair requirements of the Army Air Forces. Activities declined in first few years after World War II, but, in 1953, construction began for supporting Strategic Air Command (SAC) bombers and refueling air wings, which included new hangars, runways, warehouses, and housing. Additional facilities added in the late 1970s included a protective coating facility, a corrosion control facility, a maintenance hangar and hydraulic system facility, and an altered avionics shop and weapons engineering facility.

Sources:

William P. Head, *Through the Camera's Eye: A Photographic Survey of the Origins of Robins Field, 1941–1943*. Robins AFB, GA: Office of History, Warner Robins Air Logistics Center, 1988.

Robins Air Force Base Heritage Committee, *A Pictorial History of Robins Air Force Base, Georgia*. n.p.: Air Force Logistics Command, 1982.

Warner-Robins Air Materiel Area, History, July 1963–June 1964: Types of Aircraft Produced by WRAMA over Past Five Years," pt. 3, p. 8. Air Force Historical Research Agency, k205.14–33.

HAWAII

Pearl Harbor Naval Complex
Pearl Harbor, HI

Pearl Harbor Naval Shipyard is 9 miles from downtown Honolulu. The naval facility has four dry docks, a marine railway, three repair basins, and a number of shops and storage facilities. There are also auxiliary enterprises such as the Navy Public Works Center, Naval Facilities Engineering Command, Naval Shore Electronics Engineering Activity, and Naval Western Oceanography Center.

The Pearl Harbor Naval Complex was established in 1908. The activities on the base were reduced after World War II but increased again for the Korean War. Today, the facility is the Navy's most important base in the Pacific, with 50 homeported fleet units and 116 tenant commands.

Sources:

Historic American Building Survey No. HI-60, Prints and Photographs Division, Library of Congress, Washington, DC.

Historic American Engineering Record No. HI-6, Prints and Photographs Division, Library of Congress, Washington, DC.

Record Group 181, Records of Naval Districts and Shore Establishments in the Regional Archives, miscellaneous records of Pearl Harbor Naval Shipyard (mostly early 20th c. or World War II). National Archives—Pacific Southwest Region, Laguna Niguel, CA.

ILLINOIS

Rock Island Arsenal
Rock Island, IL

Rock Island Arsenal includes 203 buildings on 946 acres providing 6.5 million square feet of floor space. It was designated a National Historic Landmark in 1969 and is listed in the National Register of Historic Places.

The title to the land was acquired by the government from an 1804 treaty with the Sac and Fox Indians. A fort was later built on the site. The arsenal was established by an act approved 11 July 1862. It is now the largest weapons manufacturing arsenal in the western world. The Arsenal recently completed an extensive modernization program, including state-of-the-art computerized machining centers. Its current production includes gun mounts, recoil mechanisms, carriages and loaders for various artillery pieces, spare parts, and prototypes. The logistics mission includes fabrication of shop sets, tool sets, kits and outfits, and basic issue items. These items, consisting of tools, parts, and accessories, are used in the field to maintain and repair vehicles and weapons. Rock Island also packages and ships these items to their destinations and maintains a depot operation to store and distribute supplies. Arsenal Island also serves as headquarters for the Industrial Operations Command (IOC) and is the location of several other tenant agencies.

Sources:

Internet: http://www-ioc.army.mil/elements/rockisland.html

Ira O. Nothstein and Clifford W. Stephens, *A History of Rock Island Arsenal from Earliest Times to 1954*. 3 vols. Rock Island, IL: U.S. Army, Rock Island Arsenal, 1965.

U.S. Arsenal, Rock Island, *Rock Island Arsenal, 1862–1966*. Rock Island, IL, 1967.

Arsenal Publishing Company of the Tri-Cities, *War's Greatest Workshop, Rock Island Arsenal: Historical, Topographical and Illustrative*. Rock Island, IL: The Arsenal Publishing Company of the Tri-Cities, 1922.

Oliver Morell Babcock, comp., *Rock Island: Her Present and Future. Manufacturing Facilities, Commercial Advantages, and Central Position in the Upper Mississippi*

Valley. *The Future Geographical and Political Center of our Country. To Which is Appended a Description of the Great National Armory, Now in Process of Construction on the Island of Rock Island.* Rock Island, IL: Argus Premium Steam Book and Job Printing Establishment, 1872.

Harry E. Bawden, *The Achievement of Rock Island Arsenal, World War II*, Davenport, IA: Bawden Bros., 1948.

Descriptive Sketch of the Three Cities, Davenport, Rock Island, and Moline, and the Rock Island Arsenal. Davenport, IA: Huebinger's Photo Art Gallery, 1891.

Daniel Webster Flagler, *A History of Rock Island Arsenal from Its Establishment in 1863 to December 1876; and of the Island of Rock Island, the site of the Arsenal, from 1804 to 1863,* Washington, DC: GPO, 1877.

Benjamin Franklin Tillinghast, *Rock Island Arsenal in Peace and War,* Chicago: The H.O. Shepard Company, 1898.

Clifford W. Stephens, *A Synopsis of Events on Rock Island from 1954 Through 1965.* Rock Island Arsenal, 1965. RIA Historical Office.

Thomas J. Slattery, *An Illustrated History of the Rock Island Arsenal and Arsenal Island, Parts 1 and 2.* Rock Island, IL: Historical Office, U.S. Army Armament, Munitions, and Chemical Command, 1990.

Vicki M. Stapes, "The Howitzer Maker." *Ordnance* (Aug. 1991): 22–23.

Vicki M. Stapes, "Rock Island Arsenal Forges Tomorrow's Firepower." *Ordnance* (August 1991): 20–21.

U.S. General Accounting Office. *Army Plans to Modernize the Rock Island Arsenal May Be Inappropriate.* Report LCD-79-418. Washington, DC: GAO, 1979.

Building Technologies, Inc. and MacDonald and Mack Partnership, "Historic Properties Report for Rock Island Arsenal, Rock Island, Illinois." MSS, Rock Island Arsenal, 1985.

Historic American Building Survey No. ILL-20, Prints and Photographs Division, Library of Congress, Washington, DC.

Rock Island Arsenal, annual histories (1965–1969, 1975–1977, 1981–1989), U.S. Army Military History Institute Library, Carlisle Barracks, PA.

Record Group 156, Records of the Office of the Chief of Ordnance, entry 1046, Records of the Rock Island Arsenal, 1940–1950, National Archives—Great Lakes Region, Chicago, IL.

Record Group 338, Records of U.S. Army Commands, Records of Posts, Camps, and Stations: Rock Island Arsenal, 1940–1950. National Archives—Great Lakes Region, Chicago, IL.

INDIANA

Crane Army Ammunition Activity
Crane Division, Naval Surface Warfare Center, IN

Crane AAA is 35 miles southwest of Bloomington, IN. It includes 3,000 buildings, 400 miles of roads and trails, 170 miles of railroad, and an 800-acre lake.

Crane AAA was established as a Naval Ammunition Depot in 1941 to provide a storage and loading site away from the coast. Originally called Naval Ammunition Depot, Burns City, it was renamed in 1943 for Commodore William Montgomery Crane, first Chief of the Bureau of Ordnance. After World War II, it became a major storage site for chemical munitions. Activity increased during the Korean and Vietnam conflicts. In 1975, NAD Crane was renamed the Naval Weapons Support Center (NWSC Crane). In 1977, the Army assumed control of ordnance production and transportation. Thus, Crane Army Ammunition Activity is a tenant of the naval facility. The Navy has maintained its RDT&E and logistic functions. It is now Crane Division, Naval Surface Warfare Center, which is a consolidation of the previous Crane and Naval Ordnance Station Louisville. The sites were combined in 1992.

Sources:

Internet: http://www.nosl.sea06.navy.mil/pr.html

Robert L. Reid and Thomas E. Rodgers, *A Good Neighbor: The First Fifty Years at Crane, 1941–1991.* Evansville, IN: Historic Southern Indiana Project, University of Southern Indiana, 1991.

U.S. Dept. of Defense, Chesapeake Division, Naval Facilities Engineering Command, "Naval Weapons Support Center, Crane, Indiana: Master Plan/Capital Improvements Plan, 1979."

"Historic and Archeological Resources Protection (HARP) Plan for Naval Weapons Support Center, Crane, Indiana," August 1991 (copy located at Naval Facilities Engineering Command, Planning and Engineering Division, Code 150, Alexandria, VA).

Crane Army Ammunition Activity, annual histories (1978–1980, 1983–1988, 1994), U.S. Army Military History Institute Library, Carlisle Barracks, PA.

Legacy/HARP Program files, Naval Facilities Engineering Command, Planning and Engineering Division, Code 150, Alexandria, VA.

Indiana Army Ammunition Plant/Facility One
Charlestown, IN

Indiana AAP is just east of Charlestown, IN, and 15 miles north of Louisville, KY. One of the largest ammunition plants in the Industrial Operations Command, it has 9,790 acres and 1,401 buildings.

The facility was constructed in 1940–1941 with additions throughout World War II. During the war, it had three distinct production facilities: a smokeless powder plant, a rocket-propellant plant, and a bag-manufacturing-and-loading facility for artillery, cannon, and mortar ammuniton. The rocket-propellant plant was never completed and its one line was only in production for 1 month. In the fall of 1945, the whole facility was placed on standby. The government partially reactivated Indiana AAP in 1948, but the plant did not return to large-scale military production until 1952, during the Korean War. Goodyear and duPont, the contractor-operators during World War II, were once again contractors during the Korean War. No new construction for manufacturing purposes was done during the early 1950s, but a number of new storage and maintenance facilities were built. Goodyear and duPont remained as caretakers from 1957–1959 while the plant was again placed in standby status. The whole facility was then taken over by Liberty Powder Defense Corporation, a subsidiary of Olin Mathieson Chemical Corporation. In 1961, the plant again began to produce munitions. In the same year, Olin took direct charge of the plant. During the Vietnam War, it produced cloth bags of 105-mm artillery charges and also produced smokeless powder. ICI America, Inc., a subsidiary of Imperial Chemical Industries PLC, took over the plant in 1972. During the 1970s, the plant was modernized, primarily in order to better manufacture black powder and to make the assembly lines more automated. Production ceased in 1992, and the plant is inactive and in modified caretaker status. It is maintained by ICI America, Inc. The plant was renamed "Facility One" on 9 May 1995. More than 30 tenant companies are located here.

Sources:

Internet: http://www.openterprise.com/fon159.htm
http://www-ioc.army.mil/elements/indiana.htm
http://www-ioc.army.mil/iocfact/INAAP.HTM

Historic American Engineering Record No. IN-55, Prints and Photographs Division, Library of Congress, Washington, DC.

Steve Gaither and Kimberly L. Kane, *The World War II Ordnance Department's Government-Owned Contractor-Operated (GOCO) Industrial Facilities: Indiana Army Ammunition Plant Historic Investigation,* U.S. Army Materiel Command Historic Context Series, Report of Investigations Number 3A, Plano, TX: Geo-Marine, Inc., Dec. 1995, on contract to U.S. Army Corps of Engineers, Fort Worth District.

K. Diane Kimbrell, Kathleen E. Hiatt, and Steve Gaither, *Indiana Army Ammunition Plant: Supplemental Photographic Documentation of Archetypal Buildings, Structures, and Equipment for U.S. Army Materiel Command National Historic Context for*

Forging the Sword: Defense Production During the Cold War

World War II Ordnance Facilities, U.S. Army Materiel Command Historic Context Series, Report of Investigations Number 3B, Plano, TX: Geo-Marine, Inc., Dec. 1994, on contract to U.S. Army Corps of Engineers, Fort Worth District.

"Black Powder Manufacturing Facility, Indiana Army Ammunition Plant." Brochure prepared by ICI Americas, Inc., 1981. ICI Americas, Inc. Archives, INAAP.

R.J. Hammond, "Profile on Munitions, 1950–1977." n.d. Microfiche, Industrial Operations Command, Historical Office Archives, Rock Island, IL. (Contains a brief section on reactivation of INAAP for Korean and Vietnam Wars.)

Indiana Army Ammunition Plant, annual histories (1976–1988), U.S. Army Military History Institute Library, Carlisle Barracks, PA.

Record Group 156, Records of the Office of the Chief of Ordnance, entry 646, Executive Division, Historical Branch, Histories (World War II), boxes 88–90, National Archives II, College Park, MD.

Record Group 156, Records of the Office of the Chief of Ordnance, entry 1043, records of the Indiana Arsenal, 1951–1952, National Archives—Great Lakes Region, Chicago, IL.

Record Group 338, Records of U.S. Army Commands, Records of Posts, Camps, and Stations: Indiana Arsenal, 1951–1952. National Archives—Great Lakes Region, Chicago, IL.

IOWA

Iowa Army Ammunition Plant
Middletown, IA

Iowa AAP is 8 miles west of Burlington, IA, and includes 19,300 acres and 1,148 buildings.

The plant was constructed in 1941 to load, assemble, and pack (LAP) ammunition items for World War II. It was placed in standby condition after the war but reactivated for the Korean War. During the 1940s and 1950s, it also operated an atomic-bomb production complex for the Atomic Energy Commission. This facility ceased operation in 1975. Iowa AAP continued to LAP munitions, including 120-mm tank, 155-mm projectiles, and missile warheads. The contractor is Mason & Hangar-Silas Mason Co., Inc.

Sources:

Internet: http:///www.openterprise.com/iowahome.htm
http://www-ioc.army.mil/elements/iowa.html

Historic American Engineering Record No. IA-13, Prints and Photographs Division, Library of Congress, Washington, DC.

Gordon E. Davis, "Historical Summary of the Iowa Ordnance Plant, 2 September 1945 to 1 July 1951." Unpublished report, 1952. Microfiche, IOC Historical Office, Rock Island, IL.

"Historical Report, Iowa Army Ammunition Plant, 1940–1963." Unpublished report, c. 1964. Microfiche, IOC Historical Office, Rock Island, IL.

"Modernization of Plant Equipment, Iowa Army Ammunition Plant, 1964–1970." Unpublished report, c. 1970. Microfiche, IOC Historical Office, Rock Island, IL.

Iowa Army Ammunition Plant, annual histories (1970, 1973, 1975–1982, 1984–1988), U.S. Army Military History Institute Library, Carlisle Barracks, PA.

Record Group 156, Records of the Office of the Chief of Ordnance, entry 646, Executive Division, Historical Branch, Histories (World War II), boxes 90–96, National Archives II, College Park, MD.

Record Group 156, Records of the Office of the Chief of Ordnance, entry 1078, Records of the Iowa Ordnance Plant, 1940–1951. National Archives—Central Plains Region, Kansas City, MO.

Record Group 338, Records of U.S. Army Commands, Records of Posts, Camps, and Stations: Iowa Ordnance Plant, 1940–1951. National Archives—Central Plains Region, Kansas City, MO.

KANSAS

Kansas Army Ammunition Plant

Parsons, KS

Kansas AAP is 3 miles east of Parson, KS, 115 miles north of Tulsa, OK. The facility has 13,727 acres and 681 buildings.

The construction of the Kansas Ordnance Plant began in 1941 and was completed during World War II. It was one of the 77 government-owned, contractor-operated facilities producing munitions and armaments for the war effort. It was operated by J-M Service Corporation and produced artillery ammunition. In September 1945, it was placed on standby and operated by the government. For the next 5 years, the plant primarily received, stored, and issued ammunition and maintained tools and machinery. A number of acres were leased to private concerns, and the plant, in fact, was declared surplus and put up for sale. However, the war in Korea changed that status, and the plant was par-

Forging the Sword: Defense Production During the Cold War

tially reactivated in 1950. National Gypsum Company became the operating contractor in 1951; by 1954, the plant was fully reactivated, and all production lines were in use. The plant made bombs, artillery ammunition, and component parts, and it reworked 105-mm cartridge cases. After the Korean War, the plant was again placed on standby from 1957 through December 1966, when it was reactivated for the Vietnam War. Day and Zimmerman, Inc. began operating the facility in 1970. During the 1970s, the plant was modernized and became more automated. In the 1980s and early 1990s, the plant produced 155-mm ICMs, detonators, Antiarmor Cluster Munitions (ACM) bombs, and other munitions. Currently, the facility is classified as inactive; all but a small area of the plant is closed, and the government plans to sell the facility. Day and Zimmerman, Inc. is the contractor-operator.

Sources:

Internet: http://www.openterprise.com/kanshome.htm
http://www-ioc.army.mil/elements/kansas.htm
http://www-ioc.army.mil/iocfact/KSAAP.HTM

Steve Gaither, *The World War II Ordnance Department's Government-Owned Contractor-Operated (GOCO) Industrial Facilities: Kansas Army Ammunition Plant Historic Investigation,* U.S. Army Materiel Command Historic Context Series, Report of Investigations Number 5A, Plano, TX: Geo-Marine, Inc., Feb. 1996, on contract to U.S. Army Corps of Engineers, Fort Worth District.

K. Diane Kimbrell and Kathleen E. Hiatt, *Kansas Army Ammunition Plant: Supplemental Photographic Documentation of Archetypal Buildings, Structures, and Equipment for U.S. Army Materiel Command National Historic Context for World War II Ordnance Facilities,* U.S. Army Materiel Command Historic Context Series, Report of Investigations Number 5B, Plano, TX: Geo-Marine, Inc., March 1995, on contract to U.S. Army Corps of Engineers, Fort Worth District.

Kansas Army Ammunition Plant, annual histories (1976–1988), U.S. Army Military History Institute Library, Carlisle Barracks, PA.

Record Group 156, Records of the Office of the Chief of Ordnance, entry 646, Executive Division, Historical Branch, Histories (World War II), boxes 100–106, National Archives II, College Park, MD.

Record Group 156, Records of the Office of the Chief of Ordnance, entry 1079, records of the Kansas Ordnance Plant, 1946–1950. National Archives—Central Plains Region, Kansas City, MO.

Record Group 338, Records of U.S. Army Commands, Records of Posts, Camps, and Stations: Kansas Ordnance Plant, 1946–1950. National Archives—Central Plains Region, Kansas City, MO.

Industrial Facilities Owned by DoD, 1996

Sunflower Army Ammunition Plant
DeSoto, KS

Sunflower AAP is 25 miles southwest of Kansas City, MO, and includes 1,156 buildings on 9,500 acres.

Sunflower was established in 1941 and became operational in 1942, when it was the world's largest powder plant. In June 1946, the plant was placed on partial standby, then on complete standby in 1948. It was reactivated in 1951 for the Korean War, but was placed on standby again in 1960. It was again reactivated for the Vietnam War. In 1984, it began production of nitroguanidine. Presently, Sunflower is an inactive plant. The contractor is Hercules Aerospace Company. Current tenants include Burns & McDowell and the Lenexa Police Department.

Sources:

Historic American Engineering Record No. KS-3, Prints and Photographs Division, Library of Congress, Washington, DC.

Internet: http://www.openterprise.com/snflhome.htm
http://www-ioc.army.mil/elements/sunflowe.htm
http://www-ioc.army.mil/iocfact/SFAAP.HTM

Darryl W. Levings, and Joe Lastelic, "Plant Readied for Wars That May Never Be." *The Kansas City Star,* 28 December 1975.

"Basic Unit History of Sunflower Army Ammunition Plant." Report prepared by Hercules, Inc., 1967. Contractor files, SFAAP (and Supplements); also in Installation File, U.S. Army Military History Institute Library, Carlisle Barracks, PA.

Record Group 156, Records of the Office of the Chief of Ordnance, entry 646, Executive Division, Historical Branch, Histories (World War II), boxes 162–167, National Archives II, College Park, MD.

KENTUCKY

Louisville Naval Ordnance Depot
Louisville, KY

Louisville NOD is 7 miles S of downtown Louisville.

It was commissioned in 1941 as Naval Ordnance Plant Louisville and was a GOCO operated by Westinghouse until after World War II, producing gun systems and munitions. In 1946, it became a GOGO owned and operated by the Navy. In 1950, it was reactivated for the Korean War. In 1966, it was renamed Naval Ordnance Station Louisville. In 1986, it was designated the overhaul and repair facility for Phalanx Close-In Weapons Systems. In 1992, it merged with the Naval Surface Weapons Center, Crane, IN. Today, it is the only GOGO working to overhaul and maintain naval gun systems, missile launchers, and gun control radars and computers, and is operated under Naval Sea Systems Command, Washington, DC.

Sources:

Internet: http://www.nosl.sea06.navy.mil/pr.html

History of the United States Naval Ordnance Plant Louisville, Kentucky, 1959, with supplements, 1960–1973. Operational Archives, Naval Historical Center, Washington Navy Yard, Washington, DC.

LOUISIANA

Louisiana Army Ammunition Plant
Near Shreveport, LA

Located 12 miles east of Shreveport, Louisiana AAP includes 400 buildings on almost 15,000 acres.

The plant opened during World War II and produced 65 different ammunition items during the war. In 1945, the plant was placed on standby status but was reopened in 1951 during the Korean conflict. Remington Rand operated the plant from 1951 to 1958, when the plant was put on layaway status. The plant was reactivated in September 1961 with Sperry Rand as the contractor. It produced mines, shaped charges, fuzes, boosters, bombs, demolition blocks, projectiles, etc. The peak employment of this period was 1969, also the year that marked the height of the Vietnam Era. Thiokol Corporation assumed operation of the plant in 1975 (now Morton Thiokol, Inc.). Production assignments have varied in the last few years but included 155-mm metal parts and LAP operations on M692, 4.2 inch mortar, M107 LAP Composition B, M73 Grenade Assembly, and some 2.75 inch warheads. It is on inactive status.

Sources:

Internet: http://openterprise.com/louihome.htm
http://www-ioc.army.mil/iocfact/LAAAP.HTM

Historic American Engineering Record No. LA-3, Prints and Photographs Division, Library of Congress, Washington, DC.

"Annual History Review, Louisiana Army Ammunition Plant, October 1, 1980 to September 30, 1981." Prepared by Thiokol Corp., 1981. Thiokol Corp. files, LAAP.

"DARCOM Installation and Activity Brochure." June 30, 1980. Thiokol Corp. files, LAAP.

"History, Louisiana Ordnance Plant, Shreveport, Louisiana—September, 1945 through June 30, 1951." Prepared by Remington Rand, Inc., 1951. Thiokol Corp. files, LAAP.

Louisiana Army Ammunition Plant, annual histories (1976–1988), U.S. Army Military History Institute Library, Carlisle Barracks, PA.

Record Group 156, Records of the Office of the Chief of Ordnance, entry 646, Executive Division, Historical Branch, Histories (World War II), boxes 119–120, National Archives II, College Park, MD.

MARYLAND

Edgewood Arsenal

Aberdeen, MD

Edgewood Arsenal was established in 1918 as the primary arsenal for the Chemical Warfare Service. It produced chemical munitions and gas masks during World War II. In 1946, Edgewood Arsenal was renamed the Army Chemical Center. It is no longer a manufacturing facility, and focuses primarily on research and development. Edgewood Arsenal merged with Aberdeen Proving Ground in 1971, and is now known as the Edgewood Area of the Aberdeen Proving Ground.

Sources:

Historic American Building Survey No. MD-1071, Prints and Photographs Division, Library of Congress, Washington, DC.

Historic American Engineering Record No. MD-47, Prints and Photographs Division, Library of Congress, Washington, DC.

Katherine Grandine, Irene Jacson Henry, and William R. Henry, Jr., "DARCOM Historic Building Inventory: Aberdeen Proving Ground, Maryland." MSS, Aberdeen Proving Ground, 1982.

Edgewood Arsenal, annual history (1976), U.S. Army Military History Institute Library, Carlisle Barracks, PA.

Record Group 156, Records of the Office of the Chief of Ordnance, entry 646, Executive Division, Historical Branch, Histories (World War II), boxes 59–60. National Archives II, College Park, MD.

Record Group 156, Records of the Office of the Chief of Ordnance, entry 1022, Records of the Edgewood Ordnance Plant, 1941–1945, National Archives—Mid-Atlantic Region, Philadelphia, PA.

Record Group 338, Records of U.S. Army Commands, Records of Posts, Camps, and Stations: Army Chemical Center, Edgewood Arsenal, 1919–1951. National Archives II, College Park, MD.

Record Group 338, Records of U.S. Army Commands, Records of Posts, Camps, and Stations: Edgewood Ordnance Plant, 1941–1945. National Archives—Mid-Atlantic Region, Philadelphia, PA.

Naval Surface Warfare Center
Indian Head, MD

Located on the peninsula bordered by the Potomac River and Mattawoman Creek, the Naval Surface Warfare Center has 3,500 acres and 1,600 buildings. Three other tenant commands are at this site: Naval School Explosive Ordnance Disposal, the Explosive Ordnance Disposal Technology Division, and the Naval Ordnance Center.

The Indian Head Division, Naval Surface Warfare Center, was established in 1890. The site has undergone many name changes. It was originally called the Naval Proving Ground. In 1932, it was renamed the Naval Powder Factory; in 1958, the Naval Propellant Plant; in 1966, the Naval Ordnance Station. It received its present name in 1992. Today, it primarily researches and develops production techniques for energetic material. For example, it does research on warheads, explosives, propellants, and various chemicals. It then devises a manufacturing scheme on a small scale that could be transferred easily to a large scale plant for mass production. It also develops and tests propulsion systems for rockets and missiles, not only for the Navy, but for the Army and Air Force.

Sources:

Internet: http://www.nsvc.navy.mil/~www/IHD/

Rodney Carlysle, *Powder and Propellants: Energetic Materials at Indian Head, Maryland, 1890–1990.* Indian Head, MD: Naval Ordnance Station, [1993].

Andrea Hammer, ed., *Praising the Bridge That Brought Me Over: One Hundred Years at Indian Head.* La Plata, MD: Charles County Community College, 1990.

U.S. Naval Surface Warfare Center, Indian Head Division, *Ordnance Development and Production.* Indian Head, MD: Indian Head Division, NSWC, [1993?].

Joseph Strauss, *The Manufacture of Smokeless Powder for the United States Navy at the Naval Proving Ground, Indian Head, Md.* Department of the Navy, 1902.

U.S. Congress. House Committee on Armed Services. Subcommittee for Special Investigations. *Utilization of Naval Powder Factory, Indian Head, MD*. Hearings and Report, 85th Cong., 2nd Sess., Washington, DC: GPO, 1958.

U.S. Naval Powder Factory, Indian Head, MD: Historical Background. n.p., 195–? (copy located at Naval Historical Center Library, Washington, DC).

J. Sanderson Stevens, Laura J. Galke, and Elizabeth Barthold, *Phase I Archaeological and Phase II Historic Architectural Investigations of Naval Surface Warfare Center, Indian Head, Charles County, Maryland.* 2 vols. Alexandria, VA: John Milner Associates, June 1994 (copy located at Naval Facilities Engineering Command, Planning and Engineering Division, Code 150, Alexandria, VA).

Legacy/HARP Program files, "NOS Indian Head, Md.," Naval Facilities Engineering Command, Planning and Engineering Division, Code 150, Alexandria, VA.

Record Group 181, Records of Naval Districts and Shore Establishments in the Regional Archives, miscellaneous records of Naval Ordnace Station, Indian Head (incl. Central Subject Files, 1907–1925). National Archives—Mid-Atlantic Region, Philadelphia, PA.

MASSACHUSETTS

Boston Navy Yard

Boston, MA

Boston Navy Yard is on the Mystic River in Charlestown, just northeast of downtown Boston. In 1960 the yard included a marine railway, four graving docks, two shipways, 161 buildings, and 21 miles of railroad track leading to 24 piers.

The site was originally called Charlestown Navy Yard, renamed the Boston Navy Yard, and finally the Boston Naval Shipyard (1945). It was one of America's first naval shipbuilding facilities. Work fell off dramatically after World War II, with only a few new ships and submarines completed. However, much maintenance work was accomplished. At the South Boston Naval Annex, 19 escort carriers were demobilized and stored. In 1950, the yard began converting destroyers and destroyer escorts for radar picket duty. During the 1960s, it performed the Fleet Rehabilitation and Modernization (FRAM) program to extend the lifespan of World War II-era destroyers. By the early 1970s, the Navy considered the yard too small and too expensive to operate. It was officially disestablished 1 July 1974 and transferred to the National Park Service. A portion of the yard remains open to support the USS Constitution.

Sources:

Frederick R. Black, *Charlestown Navy Yard, 1890–1973.* 2 vols. (Boston: Boston National Historical Park, National Park Service, U.S. Dept. of the Interior, 1988).

Edwin C. Bearss, *Charlestown Navy Yard, 1880–1942*. 2 vols. (n.p. National Park Service, 1984).

Command Histories, overview 1800–1958; yearly 1959–1964, 1966–1973. Operational Archives, Naval Historical Center, Washington Navy Yard, Washington, DC.

Legacy/HARP Program files, Naval Facilities Engineering Command, Planning and Engineering Division, Code 150, Alexandria, VA.

Record Group 181, Records of Naval Districts and Shore Establishments in the Regional Archives, miscellaneous records of Boston Naval Shipyard (mostly 19th and early 20th c.). National Archives—New England Region, Waltham, MA.

MICHIGAN

Detroit Arsenal
Center Line, MI

Detroit Arsenal is in Center Line, MI, 12 miles north of downtown Detroit, and 3 miles north of the city limits. It has 340 acres and 81 buildings.

The Detroit Arsenal was established in 1940 for the production of tanks. The government contracted with the Chrysler Corporation for the erection and operation of the arsenal in August 1940, and the first tank was completed in April 1941. The facility was first known as the Detroit Ordnance Plant but in 1941 was changed to "Detroit Tank Arsenal." The Tank-Automotive Center was set up in 1942 and renamed Office, Chief of Ordnance-Detroit (OCO-D) in 1943. In 1945, the operation was taken over by the Ordnance Department. In 1950, it was redesignated Ordnance Tank-Automotive Center, but a year later the Detroit Arsenal and the Ordnance Tank-Automotive Center were made separate installations. In 1960, the arsenal began production of the M60 tank and, in 1981, began production of the M1 Abrams tank. Detroit Arsenal is unusual in that it is both a GOCO and a GOGO: The tank manufacturing plant is contractor operated while the research and development, testing, and administrative facility is government operated. The contractor operator is General Dynamics.

Sources:

Historic American Engineering Record No. MI-12, Prints and Photographs Division, Library of Congress, Washington, DC.

Michael Boudreau, Louis G. Sabo, and Paul Gorishik, "Detroit Arsenal Tank Plant," *Ordnance*, 2 (Fall 1984): 2–5.

Kevin Thornton, *Tanks and Industry: The Detroit Arsenal, 1940–1954*. Warren, MI: History Office, U.S. Army Tank-automotive and Armaments Command, 1995.

Frederick R. Hengy, "Real Property Utilization Survey: Detroit Arsenal," March 1991. Document in History Office, Headquarters, U.S. Army Tank-automotive and Armaments Command, Warren, MI.

Record Group 156, Records of the Office of the Chief of Ordnance, entry 646, Executive Division, Historical Branch, Histories (World War II), boxes 266–331, National Archives II, College Park, MD.

Record Group 338, Records of U.S. Army Commands, Records of Posts, Camps, and Stations: Detroit Ordnance District, 1926–1952 (1950–1952 classified). National Archives—Great Lakes Region, Chicago, IL.

MINNESOTA

Twin Cities Army Ammunition Plant
New Brighton, MN

The site has 2,383 acres and 255 buildings.

Construction on Twin Cities AAP began in August 1941, and production started in February 1942. During the war, the plant produced more than 4 billion rounds of ammunition. After World War II, it engaged in repacking ammunition and demilitarizing unusable ammunition. The repack program was completed in 1947; the demilitarization program was completed in 1951. The plant began producing ammunition again in 1950. From 1950 to 1957, 3.5 billion rounds of small arms ammunition, 3.2 million 195-mm artillery shell metal parts, and 715,000 155-mm shell metal parts were produced. The plant was placed on standby status from August 1958 to December 1965, when it was announced that the plant would be reactivated. By September 1966, the plant was again producing ammunition. It produced more than 10 billion rounds of various types of ammunition for the Vietnam War. An enclosed range was built on the site in the late 1960s to proof test cartridges, and other aspects of the facility were modernized in the late 1960s. The plant was placed on layaway status in several stages from 1971 to 1974. It is now inactive. The contractor-operator is the Federal Cartridge Corp. and Donovan Construction Co.

Sources:

Historic American Engineering Record No.-4, Prints and Photographs Division, Library of Congress, Washington, DC.

Robert C. Vogel and Deborah L. Crown, *The World War II Ordnance Department's Government-Owned Contractor-Operated (GOCO) Industrial Facilities: Twin Cities Ordnance Plant Historic Investigation,* U.S. Army Materiel Command Historic Context Series, Report of Investigations Number 8A, Plano, TX: Geo-Marine, Inc., Dec. 1995, on contract to U.S. Army Corps of Engineers, Fort Worth District.

K. Diane Kimbrell, Matthew Snellgrove, Robert C. Vogel, and Deborah L. Crown, *Twin Cities Army Ammunition Plant: Supplemental Photographic Documentation of Archetypal Buildings, Structures, and Equipment for U.S. Army Materiel Command National Historic Context for World War II Ordnance Facilities,* U.S. Army Materiel Command Historic Context Series, Report of Investigations Number 8B, Plano, TX: Geo-Marine, Inc., May 1995, on contract to U.S. Army Corps of Engineers, Fort Worth District.

Minneapolis Star, May 5, 1952. Article discusses remodeling of the Twin Cities Ammunition Plant during Korean War reactivation.

St. Paul Pioneer Press, June 6, 1952. Article describes repair work and new construction at TCAAP during Korean War reactivation.

"Basic Unit History, Twin Cities Army Ammunition Plant, 1941–1967." Report on microfiche, n.d., U.S. Army Industrial Operations Command Historical Office Archives, Rock Island Arsenal.

"Annual Report of Major Activities, Twin Cities Army Ammunition Plant, U.S. Army Armament Command, 1 July 1973–30 June 1974, MSS [1974], Installations File, U.S. Army Military History Institute Library, Carlisle Barracks, PA.

"Twin Cities Army Ammunition Plant Information Brochure." Prepared by Twin Cities Army Ammunition Plant, n.d., U.S. Army Industrial Operations Command Historical Office, Rock Island Arsenal.

Twin Cities Army Ammunition Plant, annual histories (1969, 1974, 1976–1985, 1987–1988), U.S. Army Military History Institute Library, Carlisle Barracks, PA.

Record Group 156, Records of the Office of the Chief of Ordnance, entry 646, Executive Division, Historical Branch, Histories (World War II), boxes 211–223, National Archives II, College Park, MD.

Record Group 156, Records of the Office of the Chief of Ordnance, entry 1065, Records of the Twin Cities Ordnance Plant, 1941–1945. National Archives—Great Lakes Region, Chicago, IL.

Record Group 156, Records of the Office of the Chief of Ordnance, entry 1047, Records of the Twin Cities Arsenal, 1946–1951. National Archives—Great Lakes Region, Chicago, IL.

Record Group 338, Records of U.S. Army Commands, Records of Posts, Camps, and Stations: Twin Cities Arsenal, 1946–1951. National Archives—Great Lakes Region, Chicago, IL.

Record Group 338, Records of U.S. Army Commands, Records of Posts, Camps, and Stations: Twin Cities Ordnance Plant, 1941–1945. National Archives—Great Lakes Region, Chicago, IL.

Record Group 338, Records of U.S. Army Commands, Records of Posts, Camps, and Stations: Twin Cities Ordnance Plant, 1973 (classified). National Archives II, College Park, MD.

MISSISSIPPI

Mississippi Army Ammunition Plant
Picayune, MS

Mississippi AAP is on the northern portion of Stennis Space Center, NASA's National Space Technology Laboratories facility. There are three separate manufacturing complexes: the Projectile Metal Parts area, the Cargo Metal Parts area, and the Load, Assemble and Pack area, plus support and administrative facilities. The site has 4,337 acres and 15 buildings.

Mississippi AAP was the first and only ammunition plant to be built by the Army after the Korean War. It is capable of producing 120,000 packaged rounds per month of the 15-mm M483A1 projectile, an improved conventional munition (ICM). In 1990, production ceased on the M483A1 projectile, and the plant is now inactive. The facility is operated by Mason Technologies, Inc., a subsidiary of Mason and Hanger-Silas Co., Inc. Current tenants include: Planning Systems Inc., Power Dynamics Inc., Sverdrup Technical Services Division, Versa Tech Company, National Computer Services, Coastal Precision Machine, Inc., U.S. Naval Oceanographic Office, Western Trading Manufacturing Inc., and Global Environmental Services, L.L.C.

Sources:

Internet: http://www.openterprise.com/misshome.htm
http://www-ioc.army.mil.elements/mississi.htm
http://www-ioc.army.mil/iocfact/MSAAP.HTM

Historic American Engineering Record No. MS-4, Prints and Photographs Division, Library of Congress, Washington, DC.

Mississippi Army Ammunition Plant, annual histories (1978–1983), U.S. Army Military History Institute Library, Carlisle Barracks, PA.

"Welcome to the Mississippi Army Ammunition Plant." n.p., 1983. MSAAP Administrative Archives.

"Mississippi Army Ammunition Plant," *National Defense* (March–April 1978): 479, 499.

MISSOURI

Lake City Army Ammunition Plant
Independence, MO

Lake City AAP is within the city limits of Independence, MO, on the eastern edge of the Greater Kansas City metropolitan area. It encompasses 458 buildings on 3,935 acres.

Lake City AAP manufactures and proof-tests small arms ammunition. The plant was opened in 1941 and operated by Remington Arms Company, Inc. from 1941 through 1985 (except for the nonproduction years). From September 1941 to August 1945 the plant produced more than 5.7 billion cartridges. It was placed in standby status in December 1945 but was reactivated in 1950, again to produce small caliber arms ammunition. It stayed in operation after the Korean War and again expanded during the Vietnam War, producing 14.4 billion cartridges between 1965 and 1973. In the 1970s, the facilities and production systems were upgraded. In 1985, Olin Corporation won a bid to operate the plant and is its present contractor. Lake City is currently the only active small-caliber ammunition manufacturing facility within the Department of Defense.

Sources:

Internet: http://www.openterprise.com/lkcthome.htm
http://www-ioc.army.mil/elements/lakecity.html

Historic American Engineering Record No. MO-22, Prints and Photographs Division, Library of Congress, Washington, DC.

William David White, Jr., and Kellie A. Krapf, *Lake City Army Ammunition Plant: Supplemental Photographic Documentation of Archetypal Buildings, Structures, and Equipment for U.S. Army Materiel Command National Historic Context for World War II Ordnance Facilities,* U.S. Army Materiel Command Historic Context Series, Report of Investigations Number 10B, Plano, TX: Geo-Marine, Inc., Nov. 1995, on contract to U.S. Army Corps of Engineers, Fort Worth District.

16 Years of Progress. Independence, MO: Remington Arms Company, Inc., 1967.

"Lake City Arsenal Historical Summary, 1 July 1946 to 30 June 1951." LCAAP Administrative Archives.

"Unit History, Lake City Army Ammunition Plant, Independence, Missouri, 30 December 1940–31 December 1967," LCAAP Administrative Archives.

Lake City Army Ammunition Plant, annual histories (1972, 1976–1988), U.S. Army Military History Institute Library, Carlisle Barracks, PA.

Record Group 156, Records of the Office of the Chief of Ordnance, entry 646, Executive Division, Historical Branch, Histories (World War II), boxes 199–201. National Archives II, College Park, MD.

Record Group 156, Records of the Office of the Chief of Ordnance, entry 1071, Records of the Lake City Arsenal, 1940–1950. National Archives—Central Plains Region, Kansas City, MO.

Record Group 156, Records of the Office of the Chief of Ordnance, entry 1129, Formerly Classified Records of the Lake City Arsenal. National Archives—Central Plains Region, Kansas City, MO.

Record Group 338, Records of U.S. Army Commands, Records of Posts, Camps, and Stations: Lake City Arsenal, 1943–1950. National Archives—Central Plains Region, Kansas City, MO.

NEVADA

Hawthorne Ammunition Depot
Hawthorne, NV

Hawthorne AD is 135 miles southeast of Reno, NV.

Ground was broken for Hawthorne on 24 July 1928, and construction took place 1929–1931. Ninety percent of the buildings date from this original construction period. Constructed by the U.S. Navy, Hawthorne AD served in World War II as a high explosive ammunition depot supporting the Pacific Fleet. During World War II, 1,751 magazines and 200 warehouses were erected, and it grew into the world's largest ammunition depot of the war, employing more than 5,000 workers. There was some construction during the Korean War, primarily 73 inert and explosive storage structures. Manufacturing activities expanded to include loading, assembling, and packing warheads. In 1977, the entire facility was turned over to the Army. In that year the depot began production of hydraulically powered, wire-rope pulling equipment. In 1980, the plant was converted into a GOCO facility. Activities included storage, production, testing, and demilitarization of ammunition. The Western Area Demilitarization Facility at Hawthorne is the premier resource recovery and recycling center of conventional ammunition. Hawthorne has an ammunition surveillance program and is a Tier II cadre ammunition storage site that maintains additional war reserve stocks. Nearly 2,000 bunkers were constructed for storage purposes. As of 1980, Day and Zimmerman/Basil Corporation served as operator.

Sources:

U.S. General Accounting Office, *Ammunition: Analysis of Selected Activities at the Army's Hawthorne Plant.* Briefing to Congressional Requesters. Report No. GAO/NSIAD-88-33BR. Washington, DC: GAO, October 1987.

Historic American Building Survey No. NV-23, Prints and Photographs Division, Library of Congress, Washington, DC.

Historic American Engineering Record No. NV-5, Prints and Photographs Division, Library of Congress, Washington, DC.

"Hawthorne's Centennial, 1881–1981," *Mineral County Independent and Hawthorne News,* 8 April 1981. (Includes a history of the Hawthorne facility.)

"Naval Ammunition Depot, Hawthorne," 19 February 1976. Government files, HWAAP.

Gary A. Baratta, "Assignment: Army Ammunition Plant," *Ordnance* (August 1991): 24–26.

Hawthorne Army Ammunition Plant, annual histories (1978, 1981–1987), U.S. Army Military History Institute Library, Carlisle Barracks, PA.

Record Group 181, Records of Naval Districts and Shore Establishments in the Regional Archives, miscellaneous records of Naval Ammunition Depot—Hawthorne (incl. War Diaries, 1942–1946 [classified], General Correspondence, 1948–1950). National Archives—Pacific Southwest Region, Laguna Niguel, CA.

NEW HAMPSHIRE

Portsmouth Naval Shipyard
Portsmouth, NH

Portsmouth NSY is on the border of New Hampshire and Maine, 50 miles north of Boston, MA.

The shipyard was established in 1800 by the Federal government. The first warship built in North America was constructed at Portsmouth. In 1917, it built the first submarine constructed at a government-owned facility. After World War II, the yard finished work on six submarines started during the war and upgraded several others. The Albacore was built in 1953. In 1956, the yard started work on its first nuclear-powered submarine. Several SSNs and SSBNs* were launched here. The last submarine was commissioned in 1971. Since then, work has reverted to overhaul and repair, particularly of nuclear-powered submarines.

Sources:

Portsmouth Naval Shipyard, Portsmouth, New Hampshire: Cradle of American Shipbuilding (Portsmouth Naval Shipyard, 1976?).

Frank A. Beard and Robert L. Bradley, "Portsmouth Naval Shipyard Historic District," MSS, National Register of Historic Places, National Park Service, 1977.

---

*SSN = submarine (nuclear-powered); SSBN = fleet ballistic missile submarine (nuclear-powered).

James Dolph, *Portsmouth Naval Shipyard, Historical Guide*. San Diego, CA: Blake Publishing Company, 1990.

Naval Facilities Engineering Command. "Portsmouth Naval Shipyard, Master Plan." MSS, Naval Facilities Engineering Command, Philadelphia, 1984.

Legacy/HARP Program files, Naval Facilities Engineering Command, Planning and Engineering Division, Code 150, Alexandria, VA.

Record Group 181, Records of Naval Districts and Shore Establishments in the Regional Archives, miscellaneous records of Portsmouth Naval Shipyard (mostly 19th and early 20th c.; includes central subject files, 1951–1955). National Archives—New England Region, Waltham, MA.

NEW JERSEY

Picatinny Arsenal
Dover, NJ

Located in Rockaway Township in northern New Jersey, Picatinny Arsenal occupies 6,500 acres.

Originally named the Dover Powder Depot, the name was changed to Picatinny in 1907. It was the War Department's first smokeless powder factory. The entire facility was damaged or destroyed in 1926 by explosions from the nearby Lake Denmark Naval Depot. Rebuilding included a new smokeless powder plant and new loading lines for artillery ammunition. Picatinny played a very important role in World War II because of its personnel's knowledge of military explosives and ammunition, and it was able to advise and train civilian companies in their manufacture. Today it is primarily a research center, responsible for the transition of newly developed munitions into mass production. To perform this function, Picatinny still has some production capacity, called semi-plant production methods. They produce, assemble, load, and pack ammunition, and then are able to make recommendations for the production of munitions at large-scale facilities.

Sources:

Eric DeLony et al., "Historic Properties Report, Picatinny Arsenal, Dover, New Jersey." MSS, Picatinny Arsenal, 1985.

Historic American Building Survey No. NJ-36, Prints and Photographs Division, Library of Congress, Washington, DC.

Joel I. Klein et al., "An Archeological Overview and Management Plan for Picatinny Arsenal." MSS, Lyndhurst, Picatinny Arsenal, 1986.

The Picatinny Magazine, Dover, NJ: Picatinny Arsenal, 1919–(series located at the Library of Congress, Washington, DC).

Record Group 156, Records of the Office of the Chief of Ordnance, Histories of Ordnance Field Installations and Activities, 1940–1945, boxes 49–75. National Archives II, College Park, MD.

Record Group 156, Records of the Office of the Chief of Ordnance, entries 1323–1326, miscellaneous records of Picatinny Arsenal, 1918–1939. National Archives—Northeast Region, Bayonne, NJ.

Record Group 338, Records of U.S. Army Commands, Records of Posts, Camps, and Stations: Picatinny Arsenal, 1906–1950 (some boxes classified). National Archives II, College Park, MD.

NEW YORK

Air Force Plant 38
Buffalo, NY

Air Force Plant 38 consists of approximately 562 acres and 33 buildings with 76,000 square feet of floor space. It is operated by Bell Aerospace.

AFP 38 was constructed in 1941. It was renamed Lake Ontario Ordnance Depot in 1953. It was last used for Minuteman construction support (until 1981) and laser research (until 1983). In 1980 the facility was released to GSA, and as of 1996 it is scheduled to be sold.

Source:

Aeronautical Systems Division, Facilities Management Division, "USAF Industrial Plant Ownership Responsibilities," Wright-Patterson AFB: Air Force Systems Command, [1986?], 30.

Air Force Plant 59
Binghamton, NY

AFP 59 is west of Binghamton, NY, and is operated by The Aerospace Control Systems Department of the General Electric Company. It covers 30 acres and includes over 600,000 square feet of floor space, all government-owned. It is one of the largest wooden structures in the United States.

The plant was built to produce aircraft propellers during World War II. Although shut down after the war, it was refurbished and reactivated by GE in 1948 to produce aircraft flight and fire control components for the F-105. The plant had only a limited work force for the next 3 years, but was fully operational by 1951. From 1951 to 1958, the plant made the transition to the F-4 program; in 1961 the transition to the F-111 began and, in 1970, to the F-15. As of the mid-1980s, the plant produced highly sophisticated avionic and electronic controls in support of the A-10, F-18, F-4, F-5, F-15, F-111, C-5, B-1, and V-22 programs. These systems included fire/flight control systems, displays and simulators, propulsion controls and condition monitors, and spacecraft controls. Most production was on subcontract to McDonnell Douglas, Lockheed, and Rockwell. In 1986, the plant was recommended for disposal.

Source:

Aeronautical Systems Division, Facilities Management Division, "USAF Industrial Plant Ownership Responsibilities," Wright-Patterson AFB, OH: Air Force Systems Command, [1986?], 39–41.

Watervliet Arsenal

Watervliet, NY

Watervliet Arsenal is 7 miles north of Albany. It sits on 150 acres and has 72 buildings.

The U.S. government bought land for the arsenal on 14 July 1813, and construction began the same year. It is the country's oldest continuously active arsenal. The name is of Dutch origin meaning "rolling water" or "flood tide." Located near the confluence of the Mohawk and Hudson rivers, the area became known as Watervliet. Watervliet Arsenal was one of the premier facilities for the production of cannon in the United States. During the late 1880s, the Army's new big gun factory was located here. At the beginning of World War II, all of the Army's cannon were supplied by Watervliet until other facilities could gear up for production. After the war, most of the reduced workload was for the conversion of guns and some work on the recoilless rifle. Production rose during the Korean War, then fell off again afterward. In 1955, modernization of buildings began. Today the arsenal is equipped to produce cannon with bore diameters from 40-mm up to 16-inch guns. It also manufactures base plates and mounts for mortars and the breech mechanisms and tube assemblies for large weapons. Orders are filled for all branches of the Armed Forces and U.S. allies.

Sources:

Historic American Engineering Record No. NY-1, Prints and Photographs Division, Library of Congress, Washington, DC.

A History of Watervliet Arsenal, 1813–1968. Watervliet, NY: U.S. Army, Watervliet Arsenal, n.d.

James W. Murray and John Swantek, III (editors and compilers), *The Watervliet Arsenal: A Chronology of the Nation's Oldest Arsenal* (Watervliet Arsenal Public Affairs Office, 1993).

John E. Swantek, III, "Watervliet: America's Oldest and Newest Arsenal." *The Ordnance Magazine,* 3 (Fall 1985): 18–21.

"Watervliet Arsenal, Albany, N.Y.," *Ordnance* (November 1990): 36.

Gregory F. Potts, *Watervliet Arsenal: Snapshot of Industrial Base Future.* Report ICAF 94-F12. Washington, DC: Industrial College of the Armed Forces, 1994. (Copy located at National Defense University Library, Fort Leslie J. McNair, Washington, DC.)

Robert W. Craig and Lauren Archibald. "Watervliet Arsenal Historic Landmark, National Historic Landmark Nomination." MSS, National Park Service, 1985.

Watervliet Arsenal, annual histories (1976–1988, 1991, 1993), U.S. Army Military History Institute Library, Carlisle Barracks, PA.

Record Group 156, Records of the Office of the Chief of Ordnance, Histories of Ordnance Field Installations and Activities, boxes 90–92, National Archives II, College Park, MD.

Record Group 156, Records of the Office of the Chief of Ordnance, entry 1006, Records of the Watervliet Arsenal, 1921–1950, National Archives—Northeast Region, Bayonne, NJ.

Record Group 156, Records of the Office of the Chief of Ordnance, entry 1114, Formerly Classified Records of the Watervliet Arsenal. National Archives—Northeast Region, Bayonne, NJ.

Record Group 156, Records of the Office of the Chief of Ordnance, entry 1116, 1424–1425, 1436–1438, miscellaneous records of the Watervliet Arsenal. National Archives—Northeast Region, Bayonne, NJ.

Record Group 338, Records of U.S. Army Commands, Records of Posts, Camps, and Stations: Watervliet Arsenal, 1921–1950. National Archives—Northeast Region, Bayonne, NJ.

OHIO

Air Force Plant 36
Evendale, OH

Air Force Plant 36 is on the west side of Evendale, OH. It is operated by General Electric Aircraft Engine Business Group. The plant is only a small part of the total industrial complex. It covers 66 acres, which represents 17% of the whole complex, and the government owns only 20% of the industrial floor space. The two properties are interdependent. The government owns the water treatment plant, fuel farm, and jet engine test cells, while the contractor owns the bulk of the facilities, including the major manufacturing assembly area.

The plant was built by the government in 1942 for the manufacture of aircraft reciprocating engines by Curtiss Wright Corp. After World War II, the government retained a portion of the facility, selling the rest to the Autolite Company. In 1958, General Electric Co., which had established a jet engine manufacturing plant in Evendale in 1949, bought the Autolite property and one major government-owned building. The government attempted to sell the rest of the property to GE in the early 1970s, and GE expressed an interest, but negotiations broke down in 1983. At that time, the facility was used to assemble and test the family of large jet engines manufactured by GE, and it manufactured components for all GE jet engines. The facility supported the B-1B, C-5B, F-14, F-15, and F-16 programs through the production and test of the F101, TF39, and F110 engines. As of 1996, the plant was scheduled to be sold.

Sources:

Aeronautical Systems Division, Facilities Management Division, "USAF Industrial Plant Ownership Responsibilities," Wright-Patterson AFB, OH: Air Force Systems Command, [1986?], 26–28.

Chambers Group, Inc., "Request For Determination of Eligibility Report, Environmental Assessment of In-Service Engineering Staging Facility and Engineering Lab at Hangar 19, San Diego, California," Irvine, CA: Chambers Group, Inc., June 1994 (located at Naval Facilities Engineering Command, Southwest Division, San Diego, CA).

Air Force Plant 85

Columbus, OH

Air Force Plant 85 is operated by North American Aviation Operations, Rockwell International Corporation. It covers 518 acres and 3.4 million square feet, all government owned. The plant has a high bay fabrication and assembly area, part of which is used as a machine shop, and flyaway capability from the Port of Columbus Airport.

AFP 85 was constructed in 1941 under the sponsorship of the Defense Plant Corporation (DPC). During World War II, the plant employed over 24,000 people and produced over 3,500 naval aircraft under contracts with Curtiss-Wright Corp. Production declined after the war, and Curtiss-Wright ceased operations in 1950. The Navy acquired the title for the plant from the DPC in 1950 and transferred the operation to North American Aviation, Inc. (NAA) as the Naval Industrial Reserve Aircraft Plant (NIRAP). Several new facilities and buildings were built from 1953 to 1964. Rockwell International acquired NAA in 1967. NIRAP Columbus was transferred from the Navy to the Air

Force in 1982 and redesignated AFP 85. During the 1970s, the plant was virtually idle, with only 2,000 employees in 1979.

The plant produced the F-100 Supersaber, RF-6 Vigilante, T-2 Buckeye, T-28 Trojan, and OV-10 Bronco. As of 1986, it was the main subassembly point for the B-1B Nacelle, Wing Carry Through, and Forward Intermediate Fuselage assembly. The plant is also the assembly plant for the OV-10 and MX Peacekeeper guidance section structure, as well as the shuttle AFT bodyflap, crew module components, and windshield canopy assembly.

Source:

Aeronautical Systems Division, Facilities Management Division, "USAF Industrial Plant Ownership Responsibilities," Wright-Patterson AFB, OH: Air Force Systems Command, [1986?], 48.

Lima Army Tank Plant
Lima, OH

Lima Army Tank Plant is 5 miles from downtown Lima. It originally encompassed 170 acres, then was expanded to 458 acres by June 1951. Some of the land was later sold, and the site is now 369.2 acres. Construction began in 1942.

In World War II, the plant served as a tank depot for modifying and processing new combat vehicles. Between World War II and the Korean War, it served as long-term storage for military vehicles. During the Korean War it briefly operated the Ordnance New Vehicle Maintenance School and reinitiated the work of modifying and preparing tanks. There was very little activity after the Korean War and during the Vietnam War, but in 1976 Lima was chosen to build the new M-1 Abrams tank. Chrysler operated the Lima Plant and the Detroit Arsenal Tank Plant to build the M-1s. Later the plant became a subsidiary of Chrysler Defense and then was sold to General Dynamics in 1982.

Sources:

Historic American Engineering Record No. OH-31, Prints and Photographs Division, Library of Congress, Washington, DC.

Robert P. Klaver and Fred E. Evans, "Lima Army Tank Plant," *Ordnance*, 2 (Fall 1984): 6–9.

Malcolm W. Browne, "American's Mightiest Tank," *Discover*, June 1982.

U.S. Army TACOM, *Historical Overview—Lima Army Tank Center*, 3 March 1980.

Historical Office, U.S. Army Tank-Automotive Command. "U.S. Army Tank-Automotive Command Historical Overview: Lima Army Tank Plant, Lima, Ohio." Unpublished paper, Warren, MI, 1984; copy located in History Office, Heaquarters, Tank-automotive and Armaments Command, Warren, MI.

"Lima Selected for XM-1 Tanks," *U.S. Army Tank-Automotive News,* August 25, 1976.

"A Million-Dollar Supertank for Army," *U.S. News and World Report,* March 10, 1980.

Record Group 156, Records of the Office of the Chief of Ordnance, entry 1051, Records of the Lima Ordnance Depot, 1945–1951. National Archives—Great Lakes Region, Chicago, IL.

"History of the Lima Army Tank Plant, Lima, Ohio," unpublished paper, 9 January 1986; copy located in History Office, Headquarters, Tank-automotive and Armaments Command, Warren, MI.

Ravenna Army Ammunition Plant
Ravenna, OH

Ravenna AAP incorporates 1,371 buildings on 21,418 acres near Ravenna, OH. Ravenna AAP actually consists of two original sites: the Ravenna Ordnance Plant and the adjacent Portage Ordnance Depot. In 1945, the two combined to form the present-day facility.

Though the official start date was 23 March 1942, Atlas Powder Company was already loading shells and bombs at Ravenna Ordnance Plant by the end of 1941. During World War II, it also produced Amatol and nitrate of ammonia, and it stored ammunition for the government. The plant was noted for its innovative success in improving the manufacturing process for TNT. The plant was placed on standby status in August 1945 and returned to government control in November, but continued limited operations. It stored ammunition and produced fertilizer. Ravenna Arsenal, Inc., a subsidiary of Firestone, operated the plant from 1951 to 1957. It loaded shell and antitank mines during the Korean conflict. Loading operations were again shut down in 1957, but the runway was used by the National Advisory Committee for Aeronautics for airplane experiments. The plant began production again for the Vietnam War. It was returned to standby status in 1971 but continued to demilitarize ammunition until 1984. Firestone sold its operation to Physics International Company in 1983; in 1993, Mason & Hangar-Silas Mason Company, Inc. was given the Modified Caretaker Contract.

Sources:

Internet: http://www-ioc.army.mil/elements/ravenna.htm
http://www-ioc.army.mil/iocfact/RVAAP.HTM

Historic American Engineering Record No. OH-30, Prints and Photographs Division, Library of Congress, Washington, DC.

Rita Walsh, *The World War II Ordnance Department's Government-Owned Contractor-Operated (GOCO) Industrial Facilities: Ravenna Ordnance Plant Historic Investigation,* U.S. Army Materiel Command Historic Context Series, Report of Investigations Number 7A, Plano, TX: Geo-Marine, Inc., Dec. 1995, on contract to U.S. Army Corps of Engineers, Fort Worth District.

K. Diane Kimbrell, Matthew Snellgrove, and Rita Walsh, *Ravenna Army Ammunition Plant: Supplemental Photographic Documentation of Archetypal Buildings, Structures, and Equipment for U.S. Army Materiel Command National Historic Context for World War II Ordnance Facilities,* U.S. Army Materiel Command Historic Context Series, Report of Investigations Number 7B, Plano, TX: Geo-Marine, Inc., April 1995, on contract to U.S. Army Corps of Engineers, Fort Worth District.

"Historical Summary of Ravenna Arsenal for the Period 2 September 1945 to 1 July 1951," Government files, Ravenna AAP.

Record Group 156, Records of the Office of the Chief of Ordnance, entry 646, Executive Division, Historical Branch, Histories (World War II), boxes 150–157, National Archives II, College Park, MD.

Record Group 156, Records of the Office of the Chief of Ordnance, entry 1045, Records of the Ravenna Arsenal, 1945–1950, National Archives—Great Lakes Region, Chicago, IL.

Record Group 338, Records of U.S. Army Commands, Records of Posts, Camps, and Stations: Ravenna Arsenal, 1945–1950. National Archives—Great Lakes Region, Chicago, IL.

OKLAHOMA

Air Force Plant 3
Tulsa, OK

Air Force Plant 3 is adjacent to Tulsa International Airport, northeast of Tulsa. The site covers 642 acres (of which the government owns 52%) and includes 3.8 million square feet of floor space (of which the government owns 73%). The plant is shared by McDonnell Douglas Corporation and North American Aviation Operations (Rockwell International).

From 1941 to 1945, the plant was run by the Douglas Aircraft Co. and used to manufacture, assemble, and modify bombers and other airplanes for the Army Air Corps. Production was suspended in 1945, and the plant was used by Tinker AFB for storage. The plant was reactivated in 1950 to manufacture B-47 Stratojets and has remained active to the present time. In 1953, manufacture of the twin-jet Douglas Bomber (B-66) was begun. In the early 1960s McDonnell Douglas began to use the plant to perform maintenance on private aircraft, including the B-52, KC-135, and the F-4. In 1962, Rockwell International moved in to share the plant with McDonnell Douglas. During the 1980s, McDonnell Douglas's facilities manufactured components for the F-15 (aft fuselage, pylons, launchers, and external fuel tank), F-18 (pylons, launchers, and external tank), and AV-8 (external tanks). Rockwell's facilities produced components for the B-1B (overwing fairings, wing flaps, and doors) and the space shuttle. As of 1996, the facility was scheduled to be sold.

Source:

Aeronautical Systems Division, Facilities Management Division, "USAF Industrial Plant Ownership Responsibilities," Wright-Patterson AFB, OH: Air Force Systems Command, [1986?], 12–15.

McAlester Army Ammunition Plant
McAlester, OK

McAlester AAP includes 2,425 magazines and igloos, 503 buildings, 397 miles of roadway, and 194 miles of railroad tracks, located on 454,964 acres.

McAlester AAP was established during World War II as an inland production and storage facility that could serve both coasts equally. Originally a Navy facility, the Army assumed control in 1977. It produces, renovates, stores, and demilitarizes conventional ammunition and related components. It is also an LAP plant for bombs, 20-mm and 40-mm cartridges, and propellant charges. Most of the plant's activity during the Korean conflict involved the renovation and shipment of the huge supply of munitions stored in its magazines after the end of World War II. During the Vietnam War, the facility produced over 13 million 2.75-in. rockets, 556,000 AUNI rockets, nearly 3.5 million low-drag bombs, 34.5 million rounds of 20-mm ammunition, and large quantities of many other types of munitions. Today, it is the second largest facility of its kind in the Department of Defense.

Sources:

Historic American Engineering Record No. OK-1, Prints and Photographs Division, Library of Congress, Washington, DC.

Francis Thetford, "The Navy's Unsinkable Arsenal." *Oklahoma's Orbit* (December 1, 1963): 10–11.

"Command History, U.S. Naval Ammunition Depot, McAlester, Oklahoma, 1 January 1960–31 December 1960." Prepared by Administrative Services Office, McAlester Naval Ammunition Depot, 1961. In files of Administrative Services Office, McAlester AAP. Includes transcripts of historical materials compiled between 1941 and c. 1955.

McAlester Army Ammunition Plant, annual histories (1978–1988), U.S. Army Military History Institute Library, Carlisle Barracks, PA.

"DARCOM Installation and Activity Brochure." June 30, 1980. Administrative Services Office, McAlester AAP.

Oklahoma City Air Logistics Center
Tinker AFB, OK

Oklahoma ALC includes 4800 acres. The Center was established in 1942.

In 1943, Douglas Aircraft began production of cargo planes east of the base. During World War II, Tinker AFB workers repaired B-17 and B-24 bombers and outfitted B-29 bombers for combat. After World War II, the site was expanded to include the Douglas facility and named Oklahoma City Air Materiel Area (OCAMA). It gave materiel support during the Korean War. In the 1960s, it supported the Berlin Crisis, Cuban Missile Crisis, and provided logistics support for B-52 bombers in Vietnam. In 1967, it was designated the inland aerial port of embarkation for Southeast Asia. In 1974, it was renamed Oklahoma City Air Logistics Center (OC-ALC). In the 1980s, the B-1 bomber was added to its management responsibilities.

PENNSYLVANIA

Philadelphia Naval Base and Shipyard
Philadelphia, PA

Philadelphia NSY is on League Island in the Delaware River in Philadelphia.

The original naval yard was established in 1801. The yard underwent numerous upgrades, primarily in the early part of the 20th century. In 1917, the Naval Aircraft Factory was established on the island. After World War I, the factory focused on the development and manufacture of experimental aircraft and aircraft accessories. During World War II, the shipyard constructed 53 ships and repaired 574. The workforce was greatly reduced after World War II, from 40,000 to 12,000. The Naval Aircraft Factory was redesignated the Naval Air Material Center in 1943, and became the Naval Air Engineering Center in 1963. In 1974, the Naval Air Engineering Center was relocated to Lakehurst, NJ. The last ship completely built at the yard was finished in 1970. In 1987, fleet carriers underwent service life extension at the yard. The yard is scheduled for closure in the 1990s.

Sources:

Greenhorne and O'Mara, Inc., "Historic and Archeological Resources Protection (HARP) Plan for the Naval Complex, Philadelphia, Pennsylvania." Draft MSS, Philadelphia Naval Base, 1991.

Naval Facilities Engineering Command-Northern Division, "Master Plan: Naval Complex, Philadelphia, PA, 1989."

S.E. Zubrow, "The History of the Philadelphia Navy Yard: An Official History of the Navy Yard from 1790 to 1945 with particular emphasis on the Navy Yard's role in World War II." Vol. 3, *U.S. Naval Administration of World War II,* Washington, DC: Naval History Center, 1946.

James Laurence Kauffman, *Philadelphia's Navy Yards, 1801–1948.* New York: Newcomen Society of England, American Branch, 1948.

William F. Trimble, *High Frontier: A History of Aeronautics in Pennsylvania.* Pittsburgh, PA: University of Pittsburgh Press, c1982.

William F. Trimble, *Wings for the Navy: A History of the Naval Aircraft Factory, 1917–1956.* Annapolis, MD: Naval Institute Press, 1990.

Record Group 181, Records of Naval Districts and Shore Establishments in the Regional Archives, miscellaneous records of Philadelphia Naval Shipyard, 1794–1957 (incl. Central Subject Files). National Archives—Mid-Atlantic Region, Philadelphia, PA.

Scranton Army Ammunition Plant
Scranton, PA

Scranton AAP is located near the center of Scranton. The site consists of 15.3 acres and 14 buildings.

The site originally was a railroad maintenance facility; the Army bought the property in 1951 and converted it to a production plant for the metal parts for large caliber artillery projectiles for the Korean War. The contractor was the U.S. Hoffman Machinery Company and production began in 1953. In 1963, Chamberlain Manufacturing Corporation became the contractor and has operated the plant ever since. In 1967, a plan for modernizing the facilities and equipment was implemented. Today, they make 5-inch shells for the Navy, 120-mm mortar rounds for the Army and several 155-mm developmental rounds (M898, M795 and XM982) in conjunction with Picatinny Arsenal, although Scranton is officially an inactive plant.

Sources:

Internet: http://www.openterprise.com/scrahome.htm
http://www-ioc.army.mil/elements/scranton.htm
http://www-ioc.army.mil/iocfact/SCAAP.HTM

Historic American Engineering Record No. PA-76, Prints and Photographs Division, Library of Congress, Washington, DC.

Tom Casey, "Size of Shell Plant Fires Imagination," *The Scrantonian*, 31 January 1965.

"Army Ammunition Plant Profile: Scranton AAP, 1st Quarter, F.Y. '83." Scranton Army Ammunition Plant.

Scranton Army Ammunition Plant, "Scranton Army Ammunition Plant Unit History." MSS, [c. 1968], Installations File, U.S. Army Military History Institute Library, Carlisle Barracks, PA.

Scranton AAP, "DARCOM Installation and Activity Brochure," Scranton Army Ammunition Plant, June 30, 1980.

Scranton Army Ammunition Plant, annual histories (1976–1982, 1984–1988), U.S. Army Military History Institute Library, Carlisle Barracks, PA.

SOUTH CAROLINA

Charleston Naval Shipyard
Charleston, SC

Charleston Naval Shipyard is on the Cooper River in the city of North Charleston.

Established in 1901, this yard hosted significant shipbuilding activities during World War II. An ammunition depot was located upriver. In 1945, the Navy Department reorganized the various activities at Charleston by creating Naval Base, Charleston. The navy yard became a component of the base. Much effort was spent in the early postwar years disposing of surplus materials. The base became a major decommissioning and storage location for returning ships. The ammunition depot was placed in maintenance status. However, Charleston remained active as an overhaul facility. In 1948, it was designated as a submarine repair and overhaul yard. The shipyard also activated numerous mothballed vessels for use during the Korean conflict. By 1951, the number of workers employed by the shipyard nearly doubled to over 8,000. In the late 1950s, new facilities for a Naval Mine Craft Base, Mine Warfare School, and Fleet Training Center were located on the site of a former Naval Air Station just south of the main base. Also in the late 1950s, the Navy decided to move two destroyer squadrons to Charleston. The ammunition depot also became home to a Polaris missile submarine weapons facility. During the 1970s, the yard was cited for low productivity. Management efforts picked up the pace. The impact of the end of the Vietnam War was reduced as Charleston picked up work from the closed Boston Navy Yard. The yard was scheduled to close in 1996.

Sources:

U.S. Army Corps of Engineers, Mobile District. "Historic and Archeological Resources Protection Plan for Naval Base, Charleston, Charleston, South Carolina." MSS, Mobile, AL, draft 1991.

University of South Carolina Legacy Project, "The Cold War in South Carolina, 1945–1991: An Inventory of Department of Defense Cold War Era Cultural and Historical Resources in the State of South Carolina; Final Report," 5 vols. Aberdeen Proving Ground, MD: Legacy Resource Management Program, U.S. Department of Defense, 1995.

Capt. P.B. Smith, USN, "Sixty Years at Charleston Naval Shipyard," *Bureau of Ships Journal,* 11 (March 1962). 16–19.

Frederick R. Black, *Charleston Navy Yard, 1890–1973*. 2 vols. Boston: Boston National Historical Park, National Park Service, 1988.

Jim McNeil, *Charleston's Navy Yard: A Picture History*. Charleston, SC: Naval Civilian Administrator's Association, 1985.

"The Industrial History of the Charleston Navy Yard, 1939–1945," typescript MSS, General Collections, Naval Historical Center Library, Washington, DC.

Legacy/HARP Program files, Naval Facilities Engineering Command, Planning and Engineering Division, Code 150, Alexandria, VA.

National Archives, Record Group 80, Records of the General Board.

"Historical Narrative for Charleston Naval Shipyard, 1 September 1945 to 1 October 1946," 216 pp typescript; "Narrative of the Charleston Naval Shipyard, third quarter, 1947," typescript; "Charleston Naval Shipyard History 1901–1958," booklet; Annual Historical Supplements, 1959–1973. Operational Archives, Naval Historical Center, Washington Navy Yard, Washington, DC.

Record Group 181, Records of Naval Districts and Shore Establishments in the Regional Archives, miscellaneous records of Charleston Naval Shipyard (mostly early 20th century; incl. Central Subject Files, 1925–1960, and Station Logbooks, 1903–1952). National Archives—Southeast Region, Atlanta, GA.

TENNESSEE

Holston Army Ammunition Plant

Kingsport, TN

Holston AAP is on two sites. Plant A is in Kingsport, TN; Plant B is about 4 miles away in a less developed part of Hawkins County. The two plants are connected by rail. Plant A has 120 acres. Plant B has 5,900 acres. The site as a whole includes 465 buildings.

The plant was constructed 1942–1944 for use by the government contractor, Tennessee Eastman Corporation, a subsidiary of Eastman Kodak. During World War II, it manufactured Composition B, a very powerful explosive mixture of RDX (cyclonite) and TNT. The facility was placed in standby status after World War II, producing only fertilizer, until it was reactivated in 1949 under the Holston Defense Corporation, a new subsidiary of Eastman Kodak. During the Korean War, the plant continued to manufacture Composition B as well as rework its stockpiled Composition B. New production lines were built during 1951–1954 in order to produce for the war. However, after the Korean War it was reduced to a one-line operation. It did not resume large-scale production until the mid-1960s, when it was again modernized to produce large amounts of Composition B for the Vietnam War. After 1973, production was again reduced to a much smaller amount, but the plant also began producing "special-order" explosives and propellants for the Armed Services, including the Navy's Trident Program. It also handles and stores material for the national defense stockpile.

Sources:

Historic American Engineering Record No. TN-10, Prints and Photographs Division, Library of Congress, Washington, DC.

Internet: http:www-ioc.army.mil/elements/holston.html

William David White, Jr., and Kellie A. Krapf, *Holston Army Ammunition Plant: Supplemental Photographic Documentation of Archetypal Buildings, Structures, and Equipment for U.S. Army Materiel Command National Historic Context for World War II Ordnance Facilities,* U.S. Army Materiel Command Historic Context Series, Report of Investigations Number 9B, Plano, TX: Geo-Marine, Inc., Nov. 1995, on contract to U.S. Army Corps of Engineers, Fort Worth District.

"Holston Army Ammunition Plant, Historical Monograph Covering the Period 1 July 1942 Through 30 June 1963." Report prepared by Holston Defense Corporation, 1963. Holston Defense Corporation Archives, HSAAP. See also various Annual Historical Reviews, also at HSAAP Archives.

Holston Army Ammunition Plant, annual histories (1976–1988), U.S. Army Military History Institute Library, Carlisle Barracks, PA.

Record Group 156, Records of the Office of the Chief of Ordnance, entry 646, Executive Division, Historical Branch, Histories (World War II), boxes 77–81, National Archives II, College Park, MD.

Record Group 156, Records of the Office of the Chief of Ordnance, entry 1040, Records of the Holston Ordnance Works, 1941–1950, National Archives—Southeast Region, Atlanta, GA.

Record Group 338, Records of U.S. Army Commands, Records of Posts, Camps, and Stations: Holston Ordnance Works, 1941–1950. National Archives—Southeast Region, Atlanta, GA.

Industrial Facilities Owned by DoD, 1996

Milan Army Ammunition Plant
Milan, TN

Milan AAP is 100 miles east/northeast of Memphis in the central section of west Tennessee, east of Milan. It has 22,536 acres, 1,461 buildings, and 6 active production lines.

Milan AAP was established in 1941. The plant was placed on standby after World War II but reopened for the Korean War. Currently, this plant does LAP for fuzes and other ammunition items such as demolition charges, mortar rounds, and 155-mm projectiles. It also stores and tests ammunition. Contractor: Lockheed Martin Ordnance Systems, Inc.

Sources:

Historic American Engineering Record No. TN-9, Prints and Photographs Division, Library of Congress, Washington, DC.

Internet: http://www.operterprise.com/milanhome.htm
http://www-ioc.army.mil/elements/milan.html

"Milan Army Ammunition Plant, Basic Unit History Covering the Period from Establishment (1941) through 31 December 1967." Unpublished report, n.d. MAAP Administrative Archives.

Milan Army Ammunition Plant, annual histories (1976–1988), U.S. Army Military History Institute Library, Carlisle Barracks, PA.

Record Group 156, Records of the Office of the Chief of Ordnance, entry 1029, Records of the Milan Arsenal, 1941–1950, National Archives—Southeast Region, Atlanta, GA.

Record Group 156, Records of the Office of the Chief of Ordnance, entry 1121, Formerly Classified Records of the Milan Arsenal. National Archives—Southeast Region, Atlanta, GA.

Record Group 338, Records of U.S. Army Commands, Records of Posts, Camps, and Stations: Milan Arsenal, 1940–1948. National Archives—Southeast Region, Atlanta, GA.

Record Group 338, Records of U.S. Army Commands, Records of Posts, Camps, and Stations: Milan Army Ammunition Plant, 1970–1973 (classified). National Archives II, College Park, MD.

Volunteer Army Ammunition Plant
Chattanooga, TN

Volunteer AAP is 12 miles from downtown Chattanooga, and includes 6,681 acres and 405 buildings.

Volunteer AAP was built between 1941 and 1942 to manufacture explosives for World War II. The plant was shut down after the war but reopened during the Korean War. It was again placed into standby status in 1957. In 1965, Volunteer was directed to activate four TNT lines, and during the peak of operations (1967–1969) it produced 30 million pounds of TNT per month. It has been in standby status since the end of the Vietnam War. It is now under ICI Americas, Inc., and plans are for tenant companies to operate within the facility.

Sources:

Internet: http://www.openterprise.com/voinhome.htm
http://www-ioc.army.mil/elements/voluntee.htm
http://www-ioc.army.mil/iocfact/VOAAP.HTM

Historic American Engineering Record No. TN-8, Prints and Photographs Division, Library of Congress, Washington, DC.

Chattanooga Times, December 10, 1952. News article on the reactivation of VAAP

Chattanooga Times, May 5, 1962. News article about the status of VAAP.

"DARCOM Installation and Activity Brochure. Unpublished document, 1980. Administration Building, VAAP.

Volunteer Army Ammunition Plant, annual history (1976), U.S. Army Military History Institute Library, Carlisle Barracks, PA.

Record Group 156, Records of the Office of the Chief of Ordnance, entry 646, Executive Division, Historical Branch, Histories (World War II), boxes 168–170, National Archives II, College Park, MD.

Record Group 156, Records of the Office of the Chief of Ordnance, entry 1042, Records of the Volunteer Ordnance Works, 1942–1950, National Archives—Southeast Region, Atlanta, GA.

Record Group 338, Records of U.S. Army Commands, Records of Posts, Camps, and Stations: Volunteer Ordnance Works, 1942–1950. National Archives—Southeast Region, Atlanta, GA.

TEXAS

Air Force Plant 4
Fort Worth, TX

The plant covers 604 acres owned by the government and includes 8 million square feet of industrial floor space (the government owns 84%). It is operated by General Dynamics. It is a self-sufficient and self-contained fabrication and assembly operation. Facilities include a high bay structure and flyaway capability (from adjacent Carswell AFB). Support functions (logistics, engineering office space) are conducted from onsite trailers and leased offsite space.

Air Force Plant 4 was opened in 1941. It was operated by the Fort Worth Division of Consolidated Aircraft Company (later Convair) for assembly of the B-24 bomber. Over 3,000 B-24s were constructed in the first 2 years of operation. Later, the plant produced 124 B-32s, the successor to the B-24. Between 1947 and 1954, 383 B-36s were built, and afterwards the mach-2-capable B-58. By 1966, the plant had expanded to 4.7 million square feet, and by 1968 it had expanded further to 6.5 million square feet, to accommodate production of the F-111. Many innovative aircraft were produced at AFP 4, including the first intercontinental bomber (B-36), the first supersonic bomber (B-58), and the first swing-wing aircraft (F-111). As of the end of the Cold War, the plant was fabricating, assembling, and testing the F-16 fighter for the USAF and 10 allied nations.

Source:

Aeronautical Systems Division, Facilities Management Division, "USAF Industrial Plant Ownership Responsibilities," Wright-Patterson AFB, OH: Air Force Systems Command, [1986?], 16–18.

Lone Star Army Ammunition Plant
Texarkana, TX

Located 11 miles from Texarkana, TX, Lone Star AAP includes 882 buildings on more than 15,000 acres.

The construction on Lone Star AAP began in August 1941. The Lone Star Defense Corporation, a subsidiary of the B.F. Goodrich Company, was the prime contractor for this construction. The Red River Ordnance Depot, adjacent to Lone Star, was constructed at the same time. In 1945, the two installations were combined and renamed Red River Arsenal. From 1945 to 1950, the Lone Star Unit demilitarized ammunition. In 1951, the two facilities were separated. Day & Zimmerman, Inc., became the contractor-operator. The plant began production once more, this time in support of the Korean War. Activity was reduced after the war, but it increased again between 1961 and 1968 for the Vietnam War. The plant underwent modernization in the 1960s and some construction and modernization in the 1970s and 1980s. The plant loads, assembles, and packs primers, fuzes, grenades, boosters, bursters, detonators, and tracers, as well as ammunition items ranging from mortars to 155-mm projectiles. The contractor is Day & Zimmerman, Inc. Other tenants of the facility include Arkansas Hardwood and American Dehydrated Foods.

Sources:

Historic American Engineering Record No. TX-5, Prints and Photographs Division, Library of Congress, Washington, DC.

Internet: http://www.openterprise.com/lonshome.htm
http://www-ioc.army.mil/elements/lonestar.html

"[Lone Star Army Ammunition Plant] Annual Historical Review, 1 October 1980 through 30 September 1981 [FY 81]." Report prepared by Day & Zimmerman, Inc., 1981.

"[Lone Star Army Ammunition Plant] Annual Historical Review, Fiscal Year 1982." Report prepared by Day & Zimmerman, Inc., 1982.

William W. Cooper, "History: Lone Star Ordnance Plant, May 1, 1951–December 31, 1951. Report prepared for Day & Zimmerman, Inc., May 6, 1952.

Lone Star Army Ammunition Plant, annual histories (1976–1988), U.S. Army Military History Institute Library, Carlisle Barracks, PA.

Record Group 156, Records of the Office of the Chief of Ordnance, entry 646, Executive Division, Historical Branch, Histories (World War II), boxes 116–117, National Archives II, College Park, MD.

Record Group 156, Records of the Office of the Chief of Ordnance, entry 1083, Records of the Red River Arsenal, 1941–1950. National Archives—Rocky Mountain Region, Denver, CO.

Longhorn Army Ammunition Plant
Karnack, TX

Longhorn AAP is 3.5 miles west of the Louisiana/Texas border in Karnack, 12 miles from Marshall, TX. It includes 451 buildings on 8,493 acres of land.

Longhorn AAP was established to support mobilization requirements for World War II. From 1945 to 1952, it was on standby and GOGO status. The plant was reactivated in 1952 and operated by Universal Match Corporation. In 1955, Plant 3, which was operated by Thiokol Corporation (later Morton Thiokol, Inc.), was designated to produce solid propellant rocket motors. During the Vietnam War, Longhorn AAP produced illuminating and pyrotechnic ammunition. In 1977, the plant was designated a CORE* facility for the production of solid propellant rocket motors and pyrotechnic-type ammunition. The facilities were modernized in the late 1970s and early 1980s. Its current workload includes loading, assembly, and pack-out of illuminating munitions, infrared flares, signals and simulators, but it is currently listed on inactive status. Thiokol Corporation remains the contractor.

Sources:

Historic American Engineering Record No. TX-123, Prints and Photographs Division, Library of Congress, Washington, DC.

Historic American Building Survey No. TEX, 102-MARSH, 4-.

Internet: http://www.openterprise.com/lnhrhome.htm
http://www-ioc.army.mil/elements/longhorn.htm
http://www-ioc.army.mil/iocfact/LHAAP.HTM

Longhorn Army Ammunition Plant, annual histories (1968–1969, 1976–1988), U.S. Army Military History Institute Library, Carlisle Barracks, PA.

Record Group 156, Records of the Office of the Chief of Ordnance, entry 1093, Records of the Longhorn Ordnance Works, 1946–1950. National Archives—Rocky Mountain Region, Denver, CO.

Record Group 338, Records of U.S. Army Commands, Records of Posts, Camps, and Stations: Longhorn Ordnance Works, 1946–1950. National Archives—Rocky Mountain Region, Denver, CO.

UTAH

Air Force Plant 78

Brigham City, UT

Air Force Plant 78 is north of Salt Lake City, UT. Operated by Morton Thiokol, it covers 20,000 acres (8% government owned) and 2.5 million square feet of floor space (22% government owned). The government-owned facility is highly integrated with that of the contractor.

---

*CORE = Contingency Response Program.

Forging the Sword: Defense Production During the Cold War

AFP 78 was completed in 1962 on land deeded to the government by the contractor. The facility was designed for the manufacture of Minuteman first stage rocket motors. The combined production of AFP 78 and the adjacent Thiokol plant reached a peak manufacturing rate in 1963. In 1965, because of reduced production requirements, AFP 78 was approved as part of a single-plant concept with the Thiokol R&D plant, which promotes using the best processing facilities from both plants. At the end of the Minuteman project, the USAF attempted to sell the plant to Morton Thiokol, but the two sides could not agree on a price. As of 1986, the facilities supported the MX Peacekeeper, the Trident II and standard missile programs.

Source:

Aeronautical Systems Division, Facilities Management Division, "USAF Industrial Plant Ownership Responsibilities," Wright-Patterson AFB, OH: Air Force Systems Command, [1986?], 44–47.

Ogden Air Logistics Center
Hill AFB, UT

Ogden ALC is 5 miles south of Ogden, UT, and 30 miles north of Salt Lake City.

The Center was established in 1940 as an aircraft repair depot. After World War II, the base served as a surplus aircraft storage site for B-29, C-45, and C-82 aircraft. The main runway was extended in 1951. In 1954, the acquisition of neighboring Ogden Arsenal from the Army doubled the size of the base and allowed the base to become a center for Air Force munitions. Numerous repair and maintenance, test and evaluation, and production facilities were constructed during this period. The AF Marquardt Jet Laboratory at Little Mountain was dedicated in 1959. Air Force Plant 77 started production of Minuteman missiles nearby in 1962. A Minuteman testing facility was completed in 1966. Additional maintenance, testing, and repair facilities were built during the 1970s. An F-16 training facility was completed in 1978 with an F-16 flight simulator building added 2 years later. In 1974, Ogden Air Materiel Area became Ogden Air Logistics Center.

Sources:

Helen Rice, *History of Ogden Air Materiel Area, Hill Air Force Base, Utah, 1934–1960.* 2 vols. Hill AFB, UT: Air Force Logistics Command, 1963.

History Office, Ogden Air Logistics Center, *History of Hill Air Force Base.* n.p.: Air Force Logistics Command, n.d.

Industrial Facilities Owned by DoD, 1996

VIRGINIA

Norfolk Naval Shipyard
Portsmouth, VA

In 1964, the yard occupied 811 acres and had 30 miles of paved roads, 424 buildings, 350 cranes and derricks, 2 shipways, and 7 dry docks.

Norfolk Naval Shipyard was originally established as a private shipyard in 1767 and named Gosport. It was later owned by the Commonwealth of Virginia. The shipyard was sold to the U.S. Government in 1801. The yard played a key role in producing warships during World War II. There were many layoffs after the war, but activity and employment increased during the Korean War, primarily in ship repair. It also overhauled numerous ships built during World War II. In the 1960s, new facilities were built and others improved to handle emerging electronic and nuclear technologies.

Sources:

Marshall W. Butt, *Norfolk Naval Shipyard, Portsmouth, Virginia: A Brief History*. (Portsmouth, VA: Public Information Office, 1951, rev. ed. 1965).

"Tidewater Navy: The Norfolk Naval Complex: Combat Camera Group Atlantic Fleet," *U.S. Naval Institute Proceedings*, 98 (Aug. 1972): 203–10.

Legacy/HARP Program files, Naval Facilities Engineering Command, Planning and Engineering Division, Code 150, Alexandria, VA.

Record Group 181, Records of Naval Districts and Shore Establishments in the Regional Archives, miscellaneous records of Norfolk Navy Yard (incl. Central Subject Files, 1922–1960). National Archives—Mid-Atlantic Region, Philadelphia, PA.

Radford Army Ammunition Plant
Radford, VA

Radford AAP is in southwestern Virginia, 40 miles west of Roanoke. The facility consists of two units: the 4,111-acre Radford Unit near the city of Radford and the 2,840-acre New River Unit near the town of Dublin. Originally, they were designated separate units but were combined after World War II. (Much of the New River Unit has since been sold.) There are 6,901 acres at the site and 1,038 buildings.

Radford AAP was established during World War II and produced approximately 600 million pounds of powder during the war years. It was placed in standby status after World War II but was reactivated to full operating capacity during the Korean and Vietnam Wars. It manufactures a wide variety of propellants. The propellants are both solvent (single- and multiple-base) and solventless. The facility underwent extensive renovation during the Korean War and further expansion during the 1960s. The present contractor is Alliant Techsystems, Inc. Current tenants include Carilion Wellness Center, a fireworks manufacturer, Virginia Tech, and Energy Conservation Training Firm.

Sources:

Internet: http://www.openterprise.com/radfhome.htm
http://www-ioc.army.mil/elements/radford.html

Robert F. Jackubi and William P. Mulokey, "Army's Automated Propellant Plant." *The Military Engineer,* 67 (May–June 1975): 148–150.

Historic American Engineering Record No. VA-37, Prints and Photographs Division, Library of Congress, Washington, DC.

Ashley M. Neville and Debra A. McClane, *The World War II Ordnance Department's Government-Owned Contractor-Operated (GOCO) Industrial Facilities: Radford Ordnance Works Historic Investigation,* U.S. Army Materiel Command Historic Context Series, Report of Investigations Number 6A, Plano, TX: Geo-Marine, Inc., Feb. 1996, on contract to U.S. Army Corps of Engineers, Fort Worth District.

K. Diane Kimbrell and Kathleen E. Hiatt, *Radford Army Ammunition Plant: Supplemental Photographic Documentation of Archetypal Buildings, Structures, and Equipment for U.S. Army Materiel Command National Historic Context for World War II Ordnance Facilities,* U.S. Army Materiel Command Historic Context Series, Report of Investigations Number 6B, Plano, TX: Geo-Marine, Inc., April 1995, on contract to U.S. Army Corps of Engineers, Fort Worth District.

"Historical Report of Radford Arsenal, Radford, Virginia, 2 September 1945 through 30 June 1951. Feb. 18, 1954. RAAP Administrative Archives, unpublished report.

Basic Unit History, Radford Army Ammunition Plant. September 9, 1968. RAAP Administrative Archives, unpublished report.

Radford Army Ammunition Plant, annual histories (1968, 1972, 1976–1988), U.S. Army Military History Institute Library, Carlisle Barracks, PA.

Record Group 156, Records of the Office of the Chief of Ordnance, entry 646, Executive Division, Historical Branch, Histories (World War II), boxes 131–132, 145–149, National Archives II, College Park, MD.

Record Group 156, Records of the Office of the Chief of Ordnance, entry 1013, Records of the Radford Arsenal, 1946–1950, National Archives—Mid-Atlantic Region, Philadelphia, PA.

Industrial Facilities Owned by DoD, 1996

Record Group 338, Records of U.S. Army Commands, Records of Posts, Camps, and Stations: Radford Arsenal, 1946–1950. National Archives—Mid-Atlantic Region, Philadelphia, PA.

Yorktown Naval Weapons Station
Yorktown, VA

Yorktown Naval Weapons Station is about 3 miles from Yorktown, 35 miles from Norfolk, VA.

The site was established in 1917 as an oil, coal, and mine depot. During World War II, it developed mines, depth charges, and new ordnance devices. After World War II, activities at the Navy Mine Depot were reduced. In 1953, Skiffes Creek Annex was commissioned with Guided Missile Service Unit No. 211. In 1958, the base was redesignated as a Naval Weapons Station. In the 1970s, additional support facilities were constructed to support missile rework.

Source:

Paolo E. Coletta, "Naval Mine Warfare (Pictorial)," *U.S. Naval Institute Proceedings*, 85 (November 1959): 82–96.

WASHINGTON

Puget Sound Naval Shipyard
Seattle, WA

Puget Sound NSY is 15 minutes from Seattle on Lake Washington.

The site originally opened as a repair facility, then expanded in World War I to accommodate shipbuilding. Many mothballed ships were stored here after World War II. The Korean War caused reactivation of many of these ships, and several carriers received alterations. During the war, the workforce doubled to over 15,000. Ships completed at the yard included AOEs, LPDs, and FFs.* In 1979, ship construction ended at the yard and overhaul work was performed on carriers and submarines.

Sources:

Charles E. Talmadge, "The Growth of the Puget Sound Naval Shipyard and Its Influence on the City of Bremerton." Masters Thesis, University of Washington, 1983.

---

*AOE = fast combat support ship; LPD = landing platform, dock; FF = fast frigate.

Edwin C. Bearss, "Navy Yard Puget Sound Historic District." MSS, National Register of Historic Places, National Park Service, 1990

Caroline Gallacci and August Gene Grulich, "Puget Sound Naval Shipyard Shore Facility Properties in Bremerton, Washington." MSS, National Register of Historic Places, National Park Service, 1986.

Grulich Architecture and Planning Services, "Historic Survey, Puget Sound Naval Shipyard, Bremerton, Washington." MSS, Puget Sound Naval Shipyard, 1985.

Historic American Engineering Record No. WA-116, Prints and Photographs Division, Library of Congress, Washington, DC.

Legacy/HARP Program files, Naval Facilities Engineering Command, Planning and Engineering Division, Code 150, Alexandria, VA.

Record Group 181, Records of Naval Districts and Shore Establishments in the Regional Archives, miscellaneous records of Puget Sound Naval Shipyard (incl. Central Subject Files, 1924–1961; and Directives Case Files, 1954–1958). National Archives—Pacific Northwest Region, Seattle, WA.

WISCONSIN

Badger Army Ammunition Plant
Baraboo, WI

Badger AAP is in Sauk County, south central Wisconsin, 35 miles northwest of Madison. The site has 7,354 acres with 1,438 buildings.

Originally called the Badger Ordnance Works, the plant was established in 1941, and production began in January 1943. It produced propellant during World War II, and was placed on standby status after the war. Badger was reactivated for the Korean War under the management of Liberty Powder Defense Corporation (subsidiary of present-day Olin Corp.). New facilities were completed in 1954–55. During this phase, the plant produced about 286 million pounds of propellant, including the new "Ball Powder." It was again placed in standby status in 1958. In 1963, it was redesignated Badger Army Ammunition Plant. It was reactivated in January 1966 in support of the Vietnam War. More than 445 million pounds of propellant were produced between 1966 and 1975. All production ceased in 1975, and the plant is designated as inactive. It is presently under the management of Olin Co. Other tenants of the site are Flambeau Plastic, CENEX, Dairy Forage Research Center, Orbitex, and others.

Sources:

Internet: http://www.openterprise.com/bdgrhome.htm.
http://www-ioc.army.mil/elements/badger.htm.
http://www-ioc.army.mil/iocfact/BAAAP.HTM

Historic American Engineering Record No. WI-8, Prints and Photographs Division, Library of Congress, Washington, DC.

Scott C. Shaffer and Deborah L. Crown, *The World War II Ordnance Department's Government-Owned Contractor-Operated (GOCO) Industrial Facilities: Badger Ordnance Works Historic Investigation,* U.S. Army Materiel Command Historic Context Series, Report of Investigations Number 2A, Plano, TX: Geo-Marine, Inc., February 1996, on contract to U.S. Army Corps of Engineers, Fort Worth District.

K. Diane Kimbrell and Kathleen E. Hiatt, *Badger Army Ammunition Plant: Supplemental Photographic Documentation of Archetypal Buildings, Structures, and Equipment for U.S. Army Materiel Command National Historic Context for World War II Ordnance Facilities,* U.S. Army Materiel Command Historic Context Series, Report of Investigations Number 2B, Plano, TX: Geo-Marine, Inc., April 1995, on contract to U.S. Army Corps of Engineers, Fort Worth District.

Badger Army Ammunition Plant. "Historical Summary: 1942–1967." Unpublished document on file at the Administration Building, BAAP.

Badger Army Ammunition Plant, annual histories, 1969–1970, 1976–1984, U.S. Army Military History Institute Library, Carlisle Barracks, PA.

Record Group 156, Records of the Office of the Chief of Ordnance, entry 646, Executive Division, Historical Branch, Histories (World War II), boxes 42–46. National Archives II, College Park, MD.

Record Group 338, Records of U.S. Army Commands, Records of Posts, Camps, and Stations: Badger Army Ammunition Plant, 1970–1978 (classified). National Archives II, College Park, MD.

Record Group 338, Records of U.S. Army Commands, Records of Posts, Camps, and Stations: Badger Ordnance Works, 1949–1950. National Archives—Great Lakes Region, Chicago, IL.

Index

A

Aerojet General Strategic Propulsion Co., 114
Aircraft industry, expansion of, 8–10
Aircraft plants, 15–16
Air Force Air Logistics Centers, 1
Air Force Historical Research Agency, 90
Air Force History Office, 90–91
Air Force Material Command, 118
Air Force Plant 3 (Tulsa), 152–53
Air Force Plant 4 (Fort Worth), 161
Air Force Plant 6 (Marietta, GA), 124
Air Force Plant 16 (Downey, CA), 58
Air Force Plant 19 (San Diego), 58, 113
Air Force Plant 36 (Evendale, OH), 148–49
Air Force Plant 38 (Buffalo, NY), 146
Air Force Plant 42 (Palmdale, CA), 112–13
Air Force Plant 44 (Tucson, AZ), 110
Air Force Plant 59 (Binghamton, NY), 146–47
Air Force Plant 65 (Neosho, MO), 60
Air Force Plant 70 (Sacramento, CA), 114
Air Force Plant 78 (Brigham City, UT), 163–64
Air Force Plant 85 (Columbus, OH), 149–50
Air Force Plant PJKS (Denver), 118–19
Air Force production and facilities in the missile era, 54–61
Airframe plants, 15–16, 40
Air Materiel Areas (AMA), 73
Air-to-air missiles, 62
Alabama, Defense Department owned industrial facilities in, 109–10
Albacore, 62
Allegheny Ballistic Laboratory, 63
Amatol, 24
American Locomotive and Fisher Body, 49
American Safety Products, 117
Ammunition plants, 2, 16–25, 47
  demobilization of, 40
Arkansas, Defense Department owned industrial facilities in, 111–12
Armament Development Center, 72
Armament Materiel Readiness Command, 71
Army Air Corps, 4, 10
Army Air Forces, 10
Army and Navy Munitions Board, 10–11, 44, 45
Army Center of Military History, 89
Army History Offices, 89–90
Army Materiel Command (AMC), 69
Army Military History Institute, 89–90
Army Missile Command, 109
Army Munitions Command (MUCOM), 69, 78
Army Ordnance Department, 11, 15
Army production and facilities in the missile era, 64–66
Arsenal system, 3–5
Asroc missiles, 62
Atlas missiles, 57–58, 60
Automated machine tools, 57
Avco Corporation, 47–48

B

B-17 bombers, 10
B-24 bombers, 9, 10
B-25 bombers, 10
B-47 bombers, 56

Badger Army Ammunition Plant
 (Baraboo, WI), 21, 168–69
Balanced Force concept, 55
Barbel, 62
Barstow (CA) Marine Logistics Center,
 114–15
Base Realignment and Closure
 Commission, 85
Basil Corporation, 143
Bechtel Corp., 117
Blackout design, 16
Blue-Bonnet powder plant, 58
Boeing, 54
Boston Naval Shipyard, 4, 70, 83, 137–38
Braun, Wernher von, 109
Bristol (VA) Naval Ammunition Depot, 25
Burster Line 1, 25

C

California, Defense Department owned
 industrial facilities in, 112–18
Canton (OH) Naval Ordnance Plant, 29
Carbine production, 11
Cats and dogs facilities, 40
Center Line (MI), 29
Chamberlain Manufacturing
 Corporation, 155
Chance-Vought Aircraft, 16, 47, 121
Charles, Robert H., 73
Charleston (SC) Naval Shipyard, 4,
 156–57
Charlotte (NC) Naval Ammunition
 Depot, 25
Chemical Corps, 69
Chemical plants, 17
Chemical Warfare Arsenal, 111
Chemical Warfare Service, 4, 20, 21,
 119
 cutbacks at, 41
Chester (PA) Tank Depot, 31
Chillicothe (OH) Naval Ammunition
 Depot, 25
Chrysler, 6, 9, 30, 70
Cleveland Army Tank Plant, 49
Coca Cola, 10

Cohasset Naval Magazine, 25
Cold War
 bibliography of defense production
  during, 87–108
 end of, 77–85
Colorado, Defense Department owned
 industrial facilities in, 118–20
Command histories, 99–100
Congressional hearings and reports,
 91–93
Connecticut, Defense Department owned
 industrial facilities in, 120–21
Continuous Automated Single-Base Line,
 78
Convair, 56
Corps of Engineers, 20
Cradle-to-grave approach to technology
 management, 55
Crane, William Montgomery, 128
Crane Army Ammunition Activity
 (Bloomington, IN), 81, 128

D

Day and Zimmerman, 132, 143, 162
Defense Department, industrial facilities
 owned by, 109–69
Defense Plant Corporation (DOC)
 contracts, 7, 15, 39
Defense Product Act, 47
Defense production, bibliography of,
 during cold war, 87–108
Defense production facility, 1
Delaware Tank Plant, 49
Demobilization, 39–43
Departmental Industrial Reserve, 73
Detroit Arsenal, 6, 11, 30, 41–42, 69,
 138–39
Dewey, 61
Dickson Gun Plant, 26
District of Columbia, Defense
 Department owned industrial
 facilities in, 121–23
Donovan Construction Co., 139
Doolittle, James, 10n
Douglas Aircraft, 58

Dover Powder Depot, 145
duPont, 5

E

Eastman Kodak, 157–58
Edgewood Arsenal (Aberdeen, MD), 4, 24, 69, 135–36
Eisenhower, Dwight D., 53, 55
Electronics manufacturing facilities, 1
Electronic systems, 61
Elkton (MD) Naval Ammunition Depot, 25
Elwood (IL) Ordnance Plant, 42
Emergency Period (1940-41), 6, 8–9
Emergency Plant Facilities (EPF) contracts, 7
Engine plants, 16
Explosives works, 20
Extension gun plants, 29

F

F-86 Sabrejet, 43
F-102 contrct, 56
F-86 Sabrejet, 43
F4U-1 Consair, 16
Fairfield (OH) Air Depot, 10
Federal Cartridge Corp., 139
Five-Year Defense Plan, 82
Fleet ballistic missiles, 61
Florida, Defense Department owned industrial facilities in, 123
Ford Motor, 9
Forest Park (IL) Naval Ordnance Plant, 29
Frankford Arsenal (Philadelphia), 4, 23, 25, 26, 69, 71–72, 79

G

Gadsden (AL) Ordnance Plant, 20
Gansler, Jacques, 84
Garand rifles, 3, 11

General Dynamics, 113, 138, 150
General Electric, 146, 148
General Motors, 9
General Services Administration, 44
Georgia, Defense Department owned industrial facilities in, 124–25
Goodyear Tire and Rubber, 9
Government-owned, contractor-operated (GOCO) plants, 1, 7, 15, 20–21, 26, 29, 41, 43, 46, 65, 74, 78
Government-owned, goverment-operated (GOGO) installations, 3, 15, 20–21, 41, 65
Greenslade Board Report, 31
Grumman Corporation, 8, 40
Gun plants, 2, 25–30

H

Hanover (MA) Naval Ammunition Depot, 25
Harding, Warren G., 5
Hawaii, Defense Department owned industrial facilities in, 125–26
Hawthorne (NV) Ammunition Depot, 5, 25, 81, 143–44
Hercules Aerospace Company, 133
High-explosive shells, 75
Hingham (MA) Naval Ammunition Depot, 25
Holston Army Ammunition Plant (Kingsport, TN), 157–59
Hoosier Ordnance Plant, 42
Howitzers, 24
Hughes Aircraft, 110
Huntsville (AR) Arsenal, 24, 41

I

ICI America, Inc., 129, 160
Illinois, Defense Department owned industrial facilities in, 126–28
Illinois Ordnance Plant, 17
Indiana, Defense Department owned industrial facilities in, 128–30

Indiana Army Ammunition Plant/Facility One (Charlestown, IN), 42, 129–30
Indianapolis (IN) Naval Ordnance Plant, 29
Indian Head (MD) Naval Powder Factory, 21, 62
Industrial base, 15
   decline of, 80–83
Industrial facilities, 1
   owned by the Defense Department, 109–69
Industrial Mobilization Plans, 11
Industrial Operations Command, 129
Industrial Plant Reserve, 45, 53
Intercontinental ballistic missiles (ICBMS), 61, 65
Iowa, Defense Department owned industrial facilities in, 130–31
Iowa Army Ammunition Plant (Middletown, IA), 130–31

J

Joliet (IL) Arsenal, 42
Jupiter missiles, 64

K

Kankakee (IL) Ordnance Works, 42
Kansas, Defense Department owned industrial facilities in, 131–33
Kansas Army Ammunition Plant (Parsons, KS), 23, 131–32
Kentucky, Defense Department owned industrial facilities in, 133–34
Korean War, 45–50, 53
   ceasefire in, 53

L

Lake City (MO) Army Ammunition Plant, 79
   small arms ammunition production at, 74

Lake Denmark disaster, 5
Lehman, John, 84
Lend-Lease Act (1940), 6
Licensing method, 9
Lima (OH) Army Tank Plant, 31, 150–51
LMC-West, 117
Load, Assemble, and Pack (LAP) plants, 17, 20, 23, 25
Loading plants, 20
Lockheed Martin, 112, 124, 159
Long Beach Naval Shipyard (Los Angeles), 115
Longhorn Army Ammunition Plant (Karnack, TN), 64, 162–63
Long Star Army Ammunition Plant (Texarkana, TX), 161–62
Long Tom gun tubes, 27
Louisiana, Defense Department owned industrial facilities in, 134–35
Louisiana Army Ammunition Plant (Shreveport), 134–35
Louisville (KY) Naval Ordnance Depot, 2, 29, 62–63, 133–34

M

M-14 rifle, 71
Machine tools, 43–44, 46
   automated, 57
Macon (GA) Naval Ordnance Plant, 29
Mare Island Naval Activities (Vallejo, CA), 25, 116–17
Maritime Commission, 31
Martin, Glenn L., Company, 8, 54
Martin Marietta Aerospace, 118
Maryland, Defense Department owned industrial facilities in, 135–37
Mason & Hangar-Silas Mason Co., 130, 151
Mason Technologies, Inc., 141
Massachusetts, Defense Department owned industrial facilities in, 137–38
Massive retaliation strategy, 53
Mayfield (KY) Naval Ammunition Depot, 25

McAlester (OK) Army Ammunition Plant, 80, 81, 153–54
McDonnell Douglas Corporation, 152–53
McNamara, Robert S., 69–73
Merchant Marine Act (1970), 82
Metal parts, 46
Michigan, Defense Department owned industrial facilities in, 138–39
Middletown (PA) Air Materiel Area, 73
Milan (TN) Army Ammunition Plant, 159–60
Military procurement, 5
Minnesota, Defense Department owned industrial facilities in, 139–41
Missile Command (MICOM), 69
Missile era, 53–66
    Air Force production and facilities in, 54–61
    Army production and facilities in, 64–66
    Navy production and facilities in, 61–64
Mississippi, 61
Mississippi, Defense Department owned industrial facilities in, 141–42
Mississippi Army Ammunition Plant (Picayune), 79, 141–42
Mobile Air Materiel Area, 73
Mobility Command (MOCOM), 69
Mobilization for total war, 5–8
Morton Thiokol, 134, 163–64
Munitions Production Base Modernization Agency (MPBMA), 78

N

National Archives, 87–89
National Association of Government Employees, 72
National Center for Toxicological Research, 111
National Industrial Plant Reserve, 44, 45, 53, 69
National Security Act, 44
National Security Clause, 44
National Security Council Directive 162/2, 55
National Security Resources Board (NASB), 44, 45, 47
Nautilus, 61
Naval Aircraft Factory, 4, 43
Naval Air Systems (NAVAIR), 69
Naval Ammunition Depots, 5, 25
Naval Facilities Engineering (NAVFAC), 69
Naval Gun Factory, 2, 4–5, 27, 62, 70, 122
Naval Industrial Reserve Aircraft Plant, 149
Naval Industrial Reserve Ordnance Plants (NIROP), 63–64
Naval Ordnance Plants, 15, 29–30
Naval Ordnance Systems (NAVORD), 69
Naval Ordnance Test Station, 63
Naval Powder Factory, 5, 41, 62
Naval Sea Systems (NAVSEA) Command, 69, 134
Naval shipyards, 4, 31–37
    attempt to dispose of surplus, 39–40
    impact of new technology on, 61–62
    need for, 70
Naval Submarine Support Activity, 120
Naval Surface Warfare Center (Indiana Head, MD), 5, 134, 136–37
Naval Torpedo Factory, 25
Navy Bureau of Aeronautics, 15
Navy Bureau of Ordnance, 15
Navy Bureau of Ships, 40–41, 43
Navy Historical Center, 91
Navy Museum, 122
Navy production and facilities in the missile era, 61–64
Nero, 112
Nevada, Defense Department owned industrial facilities in, 143–44
New Hampshire, Defense Department owned industrial facilities in, 144–45
New Jersey, Defense Department owned industrial facilities in, 145–46
New London (CT) Naval Submarine Base, 120
Newport News Shipbuilding and Drydock Company, 83

New York (state), Defense Department owned industrial facilities in, 146–48
New York (NY) Navy Yard, 4, 70
New York Shipbuilding Coporation, 83
Nike Ajax missiles, 64
Nike Zeus missiles, 64
Nimitz-class aircraft carriers, 83
Nitrocellulose, 21
Nitroglycerin, 21
Nixon, Richard, 75
   and banning of biological weapons, 111
Norfolk (VA) Naval Shipyard, 4, 165
Norris Industries, 117
Northrop, 112
Nuclear propulsion, 61

O

Office of Defense Mobilization, 45
Ogden (UT) Air Logistics Center, 164
Ohio, Defense Department owned industrial facilities in, 148–52
Oklahoma, Defense Department owned industrial facilities in, 152–54
Oklahoma City (OK) Air Logistics Center, 10, 154
Olin Co., 168
Ordnance Corps, 69

P

Pearl Harbor (HI) Naval Complex, 4, 125–26
Pennsylvania, Defense Department owned industrial facilities in, 154–56
Pensacola (FL) Naval Complex, 123
Peru (IN) Naval Ammunition Depot, 25
Pharmaceutical manufacturers, contracting by, to make powder, 10
Philadelphia Naval Base and Shipyard, 4, 154–55
Picatinny Arsenal (Dover, NJ), 4, 5, 21, 23, 69, 79, 145–46
Pine Bluff (AZ) Arsenal, 24, 41, 69, 111–12

Pocatello (ID) Naval Ordnance Plant, 29, 30
Polaris missiles, 61, 62, 82
Portsmouth (NH) Naval Shipyard, 4, 62, 80, 144–45
Poseidon missiles, 82
Powder works, 20
Preparedness planning, 43–45
Production base in 1945, 15–37
Project REARM, 78
Puget Sound Naval Shipyard (Seattle), 4, 31–37, 167–68
   drydocks at, 31–32
   specialized industrial shops at, 32–37

Q

Quaker Oats, 10
Quartermaster Corps, 20, 69

R

Radford (VA) Army Ammunition Plant, 21, 42, 64, 165–67
Rat missiles, 62
Ravenna (OH) Army Ammunition Plant, 42, 151–52
Reagan, Ronald, 77, 83–84
Reconstruction Finance Corporation, 7
Records repositories, 87–91
Red River (TX) Arsenal, 42
Redstone Arsenal (Huntsville, AL), 24–25, 41, 43, 69, 70, 109–10
Redstone missiles, 64
Redstone Rocket Test Stand, 109
Regional archives, 89
Remington Rand, 134
Renovation of Armament Manufacturing (Project REARM), 78
Republic Aviation Corporation, 57
Richmond (CA) Tank Depot, 31
Riverbank (CA) Army Ammunition Plant, 117
Riverside (CA) facility, 46

Rock Island (IL) Arsenal, 4, 5, 25, 41, 42, 126–28
Rockwell International, 112, 152–53
Rocky Mountain Arsenal (Commerce City, CO), 24, 41, 69, 119–20
Roosevelt, Franklin D., 6, 10–11

S

Sacramento Air Logistics Center, 118
Safety features, 20
St. Juliens Creek Naval Ammunition Plant, 25
St. Louis Naval Ordnance Plant, 29
San Antonio (TX) Air Depot, 10
San Bernardino (CA) Air Materiel Area, 10, 73
Saturn missiles, 57
Scrambled facilities, 40
Scranton (PA) Army Ammunition Plant, 46, 155–56
Seacoast Gun Shop, 26
Shipyard Modernization Program, 80
Shumaker Naval Ordnance Plant, 25
Sidewinder missiles, 62
Sikorsky Aero Engineering Corporation, 121
Small arms ammunition plants, 24
Small Caliber Ammunition Program (SWAMP), 78–79
Smokeless powder propellant, 17, 21
South Carolina, Defense Department owned industrial facilities in, 156–57
South Charleston (WV) Naval Ordnance Plant, 6, 30, 44
Sparrow missiles, 62
Springfield (MA) Arsenal, 3, 4, 25, 69, 71
Springfield rifles, 4
Sputnik, 65
Stratford (CT) Army Engine Plant, 120–21
Submarine-launched ballistic missiles (SLBMs), 61

Surface-to-air missiles, 62
Surface-to-subsurface missiles, 62
Surplus Property Administration, 39
Swordfish, 62

T

Talos missiles, 62
Tang, 62
Tank plants, 30–31
Tarheel Army Missile Plant, 64
Tartar missiles, 62
Technology management, cradle-to-grave approach to, 55
Tennessee, Defense Department owned industrial facilities in, 157–61
Terrier missiles, 62
Texas, Defense Department owned industrial facilities in, 161–63
Titan missiles, 54
TNT, 24
Toledo (OH) Tank Depot, 31
Total war, legacy of, 3–11
Trident missiles, 61
Truman, Harry, 44, 46, 47
Twin Cities Army Ammunition Plant (New Brighton, MN), 20, 24, 42, 77, 139–41

U

Utah, Defense Department owned industrial facilities in, 163–64

V

Vanguard missiles, 54
Vietnam era (1961-1973), 69–75
Vinson-Trammel Act (1934), 43
Virginia, Defense Department owned industrial facilities in, 165–67
Volunteer Army Ammunition Plant (Chattanooga, TN), 160–61

W

Warner-Robins (GA) Air Logistic Center, 10, 124–25
War Production Board, 11, 44
Wartime production record, 10–11
Washington (state), Defense Department owned industrial facilities in, 167–68
Washington National Record Center, 87, 89
Washington Naval Treaty (1922), 5
Washington Navy Yard, 4–5, 121–23
Watertown (PA) Arsenal, 4, 25, 42, 69, 70, 71
Watervliet (NY) Arsenal, 4, 25, 26, 27, 29, 41, 42, 69, 74, 78, 147–48

Weapons Command (WECOM), 69
Weapon System Program Office, 56
Western Electric, 64
Westinghouse Electric Corporation, 44–45
Willow Run (MI) plant, 9, 39
Wisconsin, Defense Department owned industrial facilities in, 168–69
World War II, legacy of, 3–11

Y

Yorktown (VA) Naval Weapons Station, 167

www.ingramcontent.com/pod-product-compliance
Lightning Source LLC
Chambersburg PA
CBHW080322020526
44117CB00035B/2602